THE ABUSING FAMILY

Blair Justice and

Rita Justice

HUMAN SCIENCES PRESS
Formerly *BEHAVIORAL PUBLICATIONS INC.*
72 FIFTH AVENUE, NEW YORK, N.Y. 10011 ● (212) 243-6000

Library of Congress Catalog Number 76-6478

ISBN: 0-87705-294-8

Copyright © 1976 by Human Sciences Press
72 Fifth Avenue, New York, New York 10011

Printed in the United States of America
6789   987654321

Library of Congress Cataloging in Publication Data

Justice, Blair.
    The abusing family.

    Bibliography: p.
    Includes index.
    1. Child abuse.   2. Family psychotherapy.
I. Justice, Rita, joint author.   II. Title.
HV713.J87   362.8'2   76-6478
ISBN 0-87705-294-8

CONTENTS

ACKNOWLEDGEMENTS

This book is an outgrowth of our earlier studies and writings devoted to violent behavior. When we began doing therapy together, it seemed natural to focus on child abuse. In the course of our work in this field, we have grown close not only to the abusing parents in our therapy groups but also to a number of child welfare workers. We have trained 14 of them to do group therapy so that help will be available to more parents who abuse their children. We are grateful for the associations we have had with these parents and our trainees.

We also appreciate the stimulation we have received from the many seminars we have attended or participated in at the Texas Research Institute of Mental Sciences, where we conduct the groups for abusing parents. We acknowledge too the support and cooperation of students and faculty at the School of Public Health, University of Texas Health Science Center at Houston, where much of *The Abusing Family* was written.

Production of the actual book would have been impossible without the helpful efforts of David Duncan, a teaching and research assistant at the University of Texas School of Public Health. We also thank Doris Krakower for typing much of the manuscript and Sydney Foorman for helping us with the footnotes.

Blair Justice
Rita Justice

INTRODUCTION

Child abuse is increasingly being described as reaching epidemic proportions.[1] It is a serious problem not only in North America but in Europe, Asia, Africa, and Australia.[2]

By 1975 a mobilization of national concern and resources had begun in the United States that exceeded all previous efforts to alleviate child abuse—a problem that has its roots in ancient history but did not receive widespread public recognition until 1962, when a description of "The Battered Child Syndrome" made headlines.[3] By 1975 there was convincing evidence that a turning point had been reached—evidence that violence inflicted on children was beginning to be viewed as a public health problem which affected the entire society, not merely a medical and legal problem which affected individual parents and children. The Child Abuse Prevention and Treatment Act had been signed into law, the National Center on Child Abuse and Neglect was in operation, and, on the voluntary front, the National Committee for Prevention of Child Abuse had been established.

For the first time, the federal government made long-term grants of millions of dollars available to programs designed to prevent child abuse, identify cases, and alleviate the consequences to parents, children, and the community. Many states launched public education campaigns to encourage the reporting of suspected cases of abuse and promote early case finding. All these steps represented "the first effort in the United States to provide a nationally coordinated system for trying to deal with the problem of child abuse."[4]

Although these developments seem more promising than any previous efforts, so much remains to be done that a dent has barely been made in the child abuse problem. Primary prevention programs, designed to keep abuse from occurring in the first place, are virtually nonexistent. Secondary prevention programs, which focus on the treatment of parents to prevent repetition of abuse, are widely scattered and largely unevaluated.

Much of this failure to combat the problem is related to the defeatist attitude that all that can be done is to punish the parents and place their children in foster homes. Pessimism concerning the rehabilitation of parents who abuse their children has prevailed for far too long; professionals and laymen alike have viewed abusing parents as beyond help.[5] Individual psychotherapy has been described as unsuccessful, and professional therapeutic efforts have remained limited.[6] Reports of group therapy for abusive parents have been conspicuously lacking.[7]

One purpose of this book is to present a detailed description of what can be accomplished through group therapy of parents involved in abuse, based on our work with couples since 1973. In addition to a discussion of innovative interventions and techniques, we will provide a conceptual framework for therapy with abusing parents that stems from our own model concerning the causes of abuse.

Another purpose is to emphasize the systems nature of child abuse so that causes and "cures" can be properly understood and interventions appropriately designed. Child abuse requires a systems approach for several reasons: (1) The entire family is involved, not just a mother, father, or some other caretaker who deliberately injures a child. The father, mother, child—and the environment—all play a part. The interlocking symbiosis that develops between spouses and between spouses and child can be understood and broken up only through a systems approach. (2) On the community level, any effort at primary prevention will succeed only if the different parts that make up the system of host, agent, environment, and vector are properly identified. No family exists in a vacuum. Environmental stresses as well as the community's support networks must be considered. (3) On the societal level, attempts to prevent and alleviate child abuse by concentrating on individual families or their environments is doomed to failure unless it is recognized that family, environment, and society are all part of a single system and that what affects one will affect another. As long as our cultural "scripts" lead parents to believe that all babies are cute and cuddly at all times and that mothers must maintain the serenity of the Madonna, the danger that anger, resentment, and frustration will spill over into violent behavior is bound to increase.[8] As long as violence is a major motif of society, some authorities contend that violence will inevitably occur in the home.

Violence throughout the world is influencing the lives of individual families as never before. Instant communication has not only made people inhabitants of a worldwide McLuhan village, it has also spotlighted the way individuals are bound into a network of a single system—one part affecting all others.[9] But instant communication is just one example of the rapid technological change in which all of us are all swept up. A kind of "future shock" society is upon us, and the epidemic proportion of child abuse is one striking manifestation.

A third purpose of this book is to demonstrate how too much change coming too fast plagues the lives of families in which child abuse occurs. Although we recognize that stress is a factor in child abuse, we will suggest that a more important problem is that the abusing family lives in a relentless "life crisis," based on continuous readjustment to constant change. We will present preliminary research findings on the excessive number or magnitude of changes that mark the lives of families 12 months prior to the act of child abuse. Just as excessive change precedes the onset of illness, accidents, or injury, our evidence suggests that it also is a predisposing factor in child abuse. This evidence comes from a survey we did of 35 abusing parents, compared with the same number of nonabusers.

Still another purpose of *The Abusing Family* is to address the question of when it is safe for a child in custody to return home and how the effect of intervention strategies in child abuse can be measured. Few effective evaluations of outcomes exist concerning the delivery of human services. The results of psychotherapy are in desperate need of evaluation.[10] Therapists and other professionals who deal with child abuse need specific measures for determining whether a home is safe for return of a child. The critical question of how much abusive parents change as a result of the interventions offered must be answered if further abuse is to be prevented and the lives of family members are to be enhanced. One quantitative tool for measuring outcome that is applicable to both therapy and delivery of broader services will be presented in this book. The need for evaluation will grow as more public funds are channeled into child-abuse programs and as the lives and well-being of more families are affected.

Although national attention and resources are now being focused on child abuse, the question is how long will it all last?[11] The public is fickle in terms of its interest in unpleasant problems, regardless of the fact that the welfare of so many children is at stake. There is good reason to believe that people would rather pretend that child abuse is none of their business, and they almost have to be forced to face the fact that it not only exists but is a major public health problem. Why this attitude prevails is related to the negative feelings that most people have about their own children and how they may treat them.

> Is there any mother or father who has not been "provoked" almost to the breaking point by the crying, wheedling, whining child? How many parents have not had moments of concern and self-recrimination after having, in anger, hit their own child much harder than they had expected they would? How many such incidents makes a "child abuser" out of a normal parent? There may be a tacit agreement among us not to meddle in each other's private matters unless it is simply impossible to ignore the behavior involved.[12]

Despite the inclination to ignore the problem, there have been at least two previous periods of "excitation" about child abuse.[13] One lasted for several years after radiologists began reporting in 1946 that subdura hematoma (brain hemorrhage) and abnormal X-ray findings in the long bones were commonly associated with some trauma in early childhood. A second period of concern and attention, which involved the public this time as well as the medical profession, occurred after the American Academy of Pediatrics conducted a symposium on child abuse in 1961 and C. H. Kempe coined the headline-making term "the battered child."

In the wake of the second wave of excitation, the Children's Bureau of the U.S. Department of Health, Education, and Welfare drafted a model law on child abuse for states to consider. Between 1963 and 1968 all the states enacted legislation that required the reporting and confirming of cases of abuse and the provision of protective services for children.[14] But both waves of attention and concern reached a high pitch and then subsided again to levels of public, if not professional, apathy.[15]

As a result, intervention strategies in child abuse have consisted primarily of temporarily removing the child from the home, severing parental rights in the worst cases, and providing catch-as-catch-can casework counseling for parents who retain their child or will get the child back. This time there is promise of a broader and more lasting commitment. Much is at stake since it is generally agreed that a child does indeed belong with his natural parents, and if they do not receive proper help, abuse is likely to occur again after the child is returned home.

Drawing public attention to child abuse will spotlight other thorny issues that people would prefer to ignore. For example, spanking and discipline are inextricably involved in the problem of abuse. One point of view is that the line between a spanking and a beating is a thin one indeed, that abuse is often a spanking that simply went too far.[16] Thus the matter of corporal punishment and how parents are to discipline their children will invite controversial scrutiny and national debate as the problem of child abuse becomes more of a public issue.

How discipline may be related to abuse holds promise of stirring up intense public feeling. Historically, children have been viewed as the property of their parents, and parents have the right to rear their child as they see fit.[17] As for discipline, "parents have the right to punish their child however they like."[18] By custom, as well as by law, parents' rights are well established. This is not true of children's rights however.

National surveys have shown that a majority of people believe almost anyone could deliberately injure a child in his care.[19] If discipline or punishment is so severe that it amounts to abuse, does a parent forfeit the right to raise his child as he sees fit? The easy answer is yes, but a sampling of national opinion shows that most people believe a child should be removed from the home only as a last resort, not after he has been abused only once.[20]

Alongside the view that children are the property of their parents and that removal from the home should be a last resort—even if there is evidence of abuse—is the sense of outrage the public reserves for anyone who abuses a child. If these two phenomena appear to be contradictory, they simply reflect the society's ambivalence toward the question of whether parents have the right to treat children as they see fit and are entitled to use whatever physical discipline they believe is necessary. This ambivalence can be detected even in the law. Texas, for instance, has a Family Code designed to protect the child against nonaccidental physical injury (child abuse), but another law concerning parent-child relationships, which went into effect in January 1974, says the following:

> The use of force, but not deadly force, against a child younger than 18 years is justified: (1) if the actor is the child's parent or stepparent. . . . (2) when and to the degree the actor reasonably believes the force is necessary to discipline the child. . . .[21]

Under this law, then, a parent can use whatever force he believes is necessary for discipline, short of killing the child. As the role that physical discipline plays in child abuse receives greater attention, society will be confronted head-on by these contradictions and paradoxes.

Public furor is also likely to emerge as we face the hard fact that there is nothing biological or instinctual that equips women to be good mothers. The myth that mothers are born, not made, will conflict with the obvious need for teaching people how to be parents. To prevent child abuse, there must be a major thrust toward instructing more parents on how to be effective mothers and fathers. Some individuals who never learned what it means to be nurtured will find it almost impossible to nurture others unless role models are provided: i.e., parents who were fortunate enough to be endowed with "the mothering imprint" will be needed in growing numbers to enter the homes of potential abusers and provide them with models they were never exposed to in childhood.[22] It also means that potential abusers will need the kind of community support that gives them a place to leave their child in the hands of a good surrogate mother when the going gets rough.

All this may point to the need for "professional parents," women and men who can provide the nurturing that children must have to develop normally. The elevation of mothering or parenting to the status of a profession or occupation deserving good pay and respect will violate some time-honored notions that parenting comes naturally and all parents can do it. They cannot.

> The idea that blood is thicker than water and people must take care of their own is destructive to everyone. Face the reality that mothering will not occur [in some families], parenting will not occur, and the child should have another chance. . . .[23]

But whether our society is ready to provide support systems consisting of surrogate or "professional" mothers who can help children both in and out of the home remains an open question. There are already parent aides who act as surrogates, but this question goes considerably beyond what presently exists. The changing role of church, school, and job must be examined, both in terms of providing support for mothers, children, and families and in terms of relieving sources of stress. "Of particular importance is study of the child-rearing function in our society. Who is to care for the child, attend to his physical needs, socialize him, teach him? Who is to love the child?"[24]

One answer to these questions may be to make professional parents responsible for rearing children whose biological parents are not prepared to do the job. The professional parents would be well-paid for such services and the biological parents could "fill the role presently played by interested godparents, namely that of friendly and helpful outsiders."[25]

Such a proposal may not be welcome in a society where biological parents are still considered to be instinctively equipped for effective child rearing. But to make primary prevention of child abuse a reality, a number of innovations will be necessary. Serious attention must be given to universal parent training and possibly to licensing for parenthood. A national health screening program may be necessary, with "health visitors" or health advocates who go into the home of every newborn to follow his emotional and physical development. If this program is unfeasible, then an acceptable method of identifying high-risk parents and children—those most likely to commit abuse or be subjected to it—must be developed so that effective intervention can be made before violence occurs.

Because child abuse is a public health problem requiring a multidisciplinary effort, community support, and national understanding, several public health approaches will be presented in this book. When appropriate, public health terms will be used. Primary prevention, as we have already indicated, means reducing the incidence of new cases: i.e., keeping child abuse from happening.[26] Secondary prevention applies to keeping parents from repeating abuse through therapy and thus reducing the prevalence of the problem.[27] The terms host, agent, vector, and environment will be defined later.

As for what the term child abuse means, there are multiple definitions.[28] A number include the broad view that child abuse applies to neglect and psychological abuse as well as physical abuse. Some definitions are so broad that they describe child abuse as anything that is not conducive to the child's general welfare.[29] In this book a more restricted definition of child abuse will be used: child abuse is any nonaccidental physical injury inflicted on a child by a parent or other caretaker deliberately or in anger. This definition encompasses the kind of abuse specified in Kempe's "battered child syndrome" but applies only to the physical aspect of Silver's "child abuse syndrome," which includes "social" and emotional abuse as well as physical mistreatment.[30] Our definition is also more restrictive than the one offered in the Child Abuse Prevention and Treatment Act of 1973, which includes mental injury.

As Martin has noted: "Maltreatment of children is a spectrum. Physical assault, neglect and nutritional or emotional deprivation are points on that spectrum and overlap considerably."[31] In this book, we will address the physical-assault point on the spectrum.

Our chief reason for confining the term child abuse to physical mistreatment is as follows: terms such as social, psychological, and emotional abuse or deprivation are so general that they mean different things to different people. We agree with Gelles' observation that "while broken bones can be identified by X-ray, how can we identify a mental injury?"[32] Until such questions are answered and specific definitions can be agreed on and written into law, the characteristics of persons who commit mental as well as physical abuse cannot be accurately determined—nor can the circumstances and conditions under which it occurs. Unless these characteristics, circumstances, and conditions are clearly defined, there is little hope of designing effective primary and secondary prevention programs. We do not mean to minimize the problem of nonphysical abuse of children; we simply believe that physical child abuse, defined as nonaccidental injury, is itself such a complicated problem that an understanding of the causes and what to do about them has only begun.

Child neglect is also a separate problem: child abuse is an act of commission whereas neglect is one of omission, although the two may overlap in terms of some basic personality features characterizing both abusing and neglectful parents.[33] Gil, for example, estimates that one-third of abusing parents also neglect their children.[34] Our experience indicates that the percentage is smaller than this. Furthermore, studies generally indicate that there are usually sharp distinctions between parents who abuse and those who neglect their children—e.g., a person who abuses has much more of an emotional investment in the child.[35] Again, our concern here will be physical abuse: its causes, treatment, and prevention.

Chapter 1 describes how abusing families differ from nonabusing ones in terms of the amount of change that characterizes their lives. We will present findings on the part that multiple "life change events" play as a predisposing factor in abuse as well as how the key concept of symbiosis can be used to explain both the excessive change and the abuse that follows.

Chapter 2 presents current ideas and theories on the causes of child abuse in terms of seven models, ranging from the psychodynamic model to the mental illness model.

Chapter 3 describes an eighth model we developed, which emphasizes the family as a system and child abuse as a product of family interaction, influenced by environmental and cultural forces. Chapter 4 reviews the epidemiological features of child abuse as they relate to the public health triad of host, environment, and agent.

Our group therapy interventions and techniques as well as our goal-setting and evaluation measures are discussed in Chapters 5 and 6. Chapter 7 presents a comprehensive summary of other approaches to secondary prevention.

Chapter 8 outlines proposals for primary prevention programs. These range from far-reaching programs that go beyond the child-abuse problem to those that focus on identifying and helping high-risk parents and children before abuse occurs.

NOTES

1. M. L. Blumberg, "Psychopathology of the abusing parent," *American Journal of Psychotherapy,* 28 (January 1974), pp. 21–30; C. H. Kempe, "The battered child and the hospital," *Hospital Practice,* 4 (October 1969), p. 44; R. I. Bishop, "Children at risk," *Medical Journal of Australia,* 1 (March 1971), pp. 623–628; and J. H. Ryan, "Child abuse among Blacks," *Sepia* 22 (November 1973), pp. 27–30.
2. B. Justice and D. F. Duncan, "Physical abuse of children as a public health problem," *Public Health Reviews,* 4 (May–June 1975), pp. 183–200.
3. C. H. Kempe et al., "The battered-child syndrome," *Journal of the American Medical Association,* 181 (July 1962), pp. 105–112.
4. E. Lord and D. Weisfeld, "The abused child," in A. R. Roberts (ed.), *Childhood deprivation* (Springfield, Ill.: Charles C Thomas, 1974), p. 61.
5. "Neglect in this country." Report to the Joint Commission on Mental Health for Children (February 1968) as quoted in D. G. Gil, *Violence against children,* (Cambridge, Mass.: Harvard University Press, 1970), pp. 43–47, and R. Ten Have, "A preventive approach to problems of child abuse and neglect," *Michigan Medicine,* 64 (September 1965), pp. 645–649.

6. R. J. Gelles, "Child abuse as psychopathology: A sociological critique and reformulation," *American Journal of Orthopsychiatry*, 43 (July 1973), pp. 611–621; M. J. Paulson and P. R. Blake, "The abused, battered and maltreated child: A review," *Trauma*, 9 (December 1967), pp. 1–136; and Ryan, op. cit., p. 30.

7. M. J. Paulson et al., "Parents of the battered child: A multidisciplinary group therapy approach to life-threatening behavior," *Life-Threatening Behavior*, 4 (Spring 1974), p. 19; B. F. Steele, "Working with abusive parents: A psychiatrist's view," *Children Today*, 4 (May–June 1975), p. 5; and A. B. Savino and R. W. Sanders, "Working with abusive parents: Group therapy and home visits," *American Journal of Nursing*, 73 (March 1973), pp. 482–484.

8. C. H. Kempe, "Paediatric implications of the battered baby syndrome," *Archives of Disease in Childhood*, 46 (February 1971), pp. 28–37.

9. M. McLuhan, *Understanding media* (New York: McGraw-Hill, 1965).

10. J. Haley, "Why a mental health clinic should avoid family therapy," *Journal of Marriage and Family Counseling*, 1 (January 1975), pp. 3–12.

11. D. Thursz, "Eiplogue," in A. R. Roberts (ed.), *Childhood deprivation* (Springfield, Ill.: Charles C Thomas, 1974), pp. 199–203.

12. S. Zalba, "Battered children," *Trans-Action*, 8(9–10) (July–August 1971), p. 61.

13. S. Felder, "A lawyer's view of child abuse," *Public Welfare*, 29 (Spring 1971), pp. 181–188.

14. Ibid.

15. S. X. Radbill, "A history of child abuse and infanticide," in R. E. Helfer and C. H. Kempe (eds.), *The battered child* (Chicago: University of Chicago Press, 1968), pp. 15–16.

16. G. V. Laury, "The battered child syndrome," *Bulletin of the New York Academy of Medicine*, 46 (September 1970), p. 678.

17. Radbill, op. cit., p. 6.

18. *Lift a finger: The teacher's role in combating child abuse* (Houston, Tex.: Education Professions Development Consortium C, 1975).

19. See D. G. Gil, *Violence against children* (Cambridge, Mass.: Harvard University Press, 1970), pp. 55–70.

20. Ibid.

21. *Texas penal code* (St. Paul, Minn.: West Publishing, 1974), pp. 22–23.

22. C. H. Kempe and R. E. Helfer (eds.), *Helping the battered child and his family* (Philadelphia, Pa.: Lippincott, 1972), p. xiv.

23. C. H. Kempe, "A practical approach to the protection of the abused child and rehabilitation of the abusing parent," *Pediatrics*, 51 (April 1973), p. 807.

24. M. H. Lystad, "Violence at home: A review of the literature," *American Journal of Orthopsychiatry*, 45 (April 1975), p. 339.

25. A. Toffler, *Future shock* (New York: Random House, 1970), p. 217.

26. G. Caplan and H. Grunebaum, "Perspectives on primary prevention: A review," in H. Gottesfeld (ed.), *The critical issues of community mental health* (New York: Behavioral Publications, 1972), p. 128.

27. Ibid.

28. See, for example, J. D. Delsordo, "A protective casework for abused children," *Children*, 10 (November 1963), pp. 213–218; E. Elmer, "Hazards in determining child abuse," *Child Welfare*, 45 (January 1966), pp. 28–33; J. E. George, "Spare the rod: A survey of the battered-child syndrome," *Forensic Science*, 2 (1973), pp. 129–167; D. G. Gil, "Incidence of child abuse and demographic characteristics of persons involved," in R. E. Helfer and C. H. Kempe (eds.), *The battered child* (Chicago: University of Chicago Press, 1968), pp. 19–39; M. Morris and R. W. Gould, "Role reversal: A concept in dealing with the neglected and battered child syndrome," in *The neglected-battered child syndrome* (New York: Child Welfare League of America, 1963); *Procedures and concepts manual* (Redondo Beach, Calif.: Parents Anonymous, 1973), pp. 37–39; L. B. Silver, "Child abuse syndrome: A review," *Pediatrics*, 96 (August 1968), pp. 803–820; *Texas family code* (Austin: State Department of Public Welfare, 1973), p. 40; Bishop, op. cit.; Gil, *Violence against children*, pp. 4–6 and 33; Kempe, "Paediatric implications of the battered baby syndrome"; Kempe and Helfer, op. cit., and Kempe et al., "The battered-child syndrome."

29. George, op. cit.

30. Kempe, "The battered-child syndrome"; and Silver, op. cit.

31. H. Martin, "The child and his development," in C. H. Kempe and R. E. Helfer (eds.), *Helping the battered child and his family* (Philadelphia, Pa.: Lippincott, 1972), p. 100.

32. R. J. Gelles, "The social construction of child abuse," *American Journal of Orthopsychiatry*, 45 (April 1975), pp. 365.

33. *Lift a finger*, p. 5.

34. Gil, *Violence against children*, p. 128.

35. See, for example, N. A. Polansky, C. De Saix and S. A. Sharlin, *Child neglect: Understanding and reaching the parent* (New York, N.Y.: Child Welfare League of America, 1973), pp. 2–3.

Chapter 1

LIFE CRISIS AS A PRECURSOR TO CHILD ABUSE

What distinguishes the abusing family from the nonabusing one? Parents who abuse their children are not cruel maniacs, nor do they lack love for their child. Furthermore, the vast majority of them are not crazy; in fact, they defy psychiatric classifications. "It is striking how few relationships discriminate between abusing and non-abusing families. . . . This implies that in many ways abusing families are 'just like everyone else.' "[1] So how are abusing parents different from nonabusing parents?

With this question in mind, we set out to study a group of 35 abusing parents and an equal number of nonabusers who were similar in age, education, and income.[2] Although the nonabusive parents also had problems with their children, none had ever been abusive. We asked the parents in each group to fill out a questionnaire containing 39 questions plus a 43-item Social Readjustment Rating Scale. The most striking differences between the groups centered on their responses on the rating scale, which represents 43 different changes that could occur in a year's time in the lives of abusing and nonabusing parents—changes that require readjustment as a means of coping.

It became evident that the abusing parents had undergone too much change too fast. They had either experienced many more changes or had undergone more serious changes than the nonabusers. The number and magnitude of the changes they had to adjust to constituted a "life crisis," which preceded the onset of abuse. The nonabusing parents had not experienced a life crisis and had not been exposed to an excessive number of changes.

As we will see in Chapter 2, one theory about the cause of child abuse is that parents are under too much environmental stress. Those who take this position emphasize economic stress—the stress that results from having too little education to know what to do about problems and too few vocational skills to have hopes for the future—and argue that a disproportionate amount of abuse occurs in poor families.

This argument has largely been refuted by studies which show that child abuse also occurs among the affluent. If economic stress were the overriding factor, no abuse would occur among middle- and upper-income familes, and most, if not all, poor people would abuse their children. This is clearly not the case.

When we compared abusing and nonabusing parents (the poor and affluent were equally represented in both groups) we found that change, not economic or environmental stress, was the distinguishing factor. Change requires constant readjustment. Although it is possible to adapt to chronic stress, excessive change constantly throws a person off balance. It is as though he never has time to catch his breath or mobilize his resources before he is confronted with a new change. Because change requires decision-making and problem-solving, the person must be constantly on the alert, waiting for the new and unexpected to happen. The result is what Toffler described as a kind of numbness caused by sensory overload.[3]

Up to now, it was believed that living in a life crisis led to illnesses, accidents, and injuries: the more excessive the change, measured in terms of life change units, the more serious the illness, accident, or injury.[4] Our study suggests that a large number of life change units in a year is also associated with the onset of abusive behavior.

We do not mean that excessive change—constituting a prolonged life crisis—is the cause of child abuse (causes will be examined in Chapters 2 and 3). However, change is a predisposing factor that heretofore has not been investigated and deserves further research because more and more people in our society will be subjected to greater change as we move into the kind of future that Toffler has described.[5]

A rapid series of changes is more difficult for a person to deal with than is a situational crisis. In a situational crisis, which may involve divorce, loss of job, or sickness, a person's defenses are weak when the stress is most severe, but the individual has time to mobilize new resources to deal with his problem. If he deals with it successfully, he achieves a higher level of functioning—with greater emotional equilibrium—than before.[6]

A life crisis, however, consists of a series of situational events that are compressed together and sometimes accompanied by maturational crises such as marriage, pregnancy, a son or daughter leaving home, or retirement. Table 1–1 presents the situational and maturational events that the abusing and nonabusing groups of parents were asked about. The 43 items constitute the Social Readjustment Rating Scale, which predicts the onset of illness, accident, and injury.[7] Each item is weighted in terms of the amount of readjustment necessary to cope with the event: e.g., death of a spouse requires the most readjustment and is assigned a numerical value of 100, while minor violations

Table 1-1   Social Readjustment Rating Scale

Rank	Life event	Mean value
1	Death of spouse	100
2	Divorce	73
3	Marital separation	65
4	Jail terms	63
5	Death of close family member	63
6	Personal injury or illness	53
7	Marriage	50
8	Fired at work	47
9	Marital reconciliation	45
10	Retirement	45
11	Change in health of family member	44
12	Pregnancy	40
13	Sex difficulties	39
14	Gain of new family member	39
15	Business readjustment	39
16	Change in financial state	38
17	Death of close friend	37
18	Change to different line of work	36
19	Change in number of arguments with spouse	35
20	Mortgage over $10,000	31
21	Foreclosure of mortgage or loan	30
22	Change in responsibilities at work	29
23	Son or daughter leaving home	29
24	Trouble with in-laws	29
25	Outstanding personal achievement	28
26	Wife begin or stop work	26
27	Begin or end school	26
28	Change in living conditions	25
29	Revision of personal habits	24
30	Trouble with boss	23
31	Change in work hours or conditions	20
32	Change in residence	20
33	Change in schools	20
34	Change in recreation	19
35	Change in church activities	19
36	Change in social activities	18
37	Mortgage or loan less than $10,000	17
38	Change in sleeping habits	16
39	Change in number of family get-togethers	15
40	Change in eating habits	15
41	Vacation	13
42	Christmas	12
43	Minor violations of the law	11

Source: T. H. Holmes and R. H. Rahe, "The social readjustment rating scale,"
Journal of Psychosomatic Research, 11 (1967), pp. 213–218.

of the law require the least amount of readjustment and have a value of 11.

The abusing parents had high scores on the Social Readjustment Rating Scale: i.e., they had experienced excessive change during the 12 months prior to the onset of their abusive behavior.[8] As Table 1–2 shows, the life change scores of the abusing parents were significantly higher than those of non-abusing parents. The excessive change of the abusing parents constituted a series of situational and maturational crises that exceeded their ability to adapt. In fact, we postulate that, unlike persons who undergo a single situational or maturational crisis, these individuals had no time to regroup before they were hit by a new crisis. In terms of Selye's three stages of response to stress (shock and countershock, resistance, and exhaustion), they no sooner passed through the first phase of shock and countershock and entered the resistance stage than they were confronted with a new crisis, which plunged them into the third stage, exhaustion.[9] It is in this third stage that their defenses were lowest and their inner controls against acting out were weakest.

We should emphasize that our findings on the part played by life crises in child abuse is far different from what

Table 1-2   Distribution of Life-change Scores for Abusing and Nonabusing Parents[a]

| Parent group | Life-change scores | | | |
	No crisis 0–149	Mild crisis 150–199	Moderate crisis 200–299	Major crisis 300 +
Abusers (N = 35) $\bar{X}$ = 233.63	4	9	14	8
Nonabusers (N = 35) $\bar{X}$ = 123.62	25	5	3	2
[a] x^2 = 25.69, p < .001; t_{ind} = 4.28, p < .001.				

many other investigators have noted about the role of stress and situational crisis. We have no argument with Kempe's and Helfer's contention that a broken washing machine may represent a crisis to a parent with the potential to abuse and can trigger an explosive outburst.[10] Nor do we quarrel with the idea that those who abuse are under pressure. What we do say, however, is this: the reason that a broken washing machine—or some other seemingly minor problem—may assume the proportions of a crisis in the eyes of the potentially abusive parent is that he has been bombarded for a long time with a series of stressful changes. Thus his ability to cope with even minor problems is at a low point and he is unable to exercise his usual control over lashing out at others.

It is the *life crisis*—the prolonged series of changes—that predisposes him to abuse, not the situational disturbance that is simply an appendix to that life crisis. Similarly, it is not day-to-day economic pressure and stress that frame the context in which abuse occurs. It is the unpredictability of all kinds of changes, most of which have nothing to do with the threat of poverty. (Only 4 items on the Social Readjustment Rating Scale relate directly to money or financial change, while 13 concern marriage and family and 5 concern sickness and death. In other words, many of the changes to which a person must adjust are related to interpersonal problems and losses rather than economic factors.) Again, the end state of the life crisis is exhaustion: a decreased ability to adjust and an increased risk of losing control.

An important question is why a person who undergoes a life crisis resorts to abusing a child. If excessive change can lead to illness, accident, or injury, what determines its expression in violence toward a child? We do not know whether child abuse is a substitute for the other outcomes. From our work with abusing parents, we know that a large percentage of them do have serious illnesses and accidents.

For child abuse to be an outcome, other factors must also be present. The results of our study suggested some of the most critical of these factors.

In addition to the striking difference in the number of life change units between abusing and nonabusing parents, we also found a significant difference in their answers to questions related to the crucial issue of symbiosis. Symbiosis, which will be described in detail in Chapter 3, is the attachment that one individual establishes with another in an effort to be taken care of. The symbiotic relationship that exists between mother and child is healthy and necessary, but symbiosis between adults, or when a parent tries to make his child take care of him, is destructive.

The answers of abusing and nonabusing parents to three questions related to symbiosis differed sharply: the abusive parent was more likely to believe that his spouse had a closer relationship with the child than he had,[11] and was more inclined to say that it was difficult to get his spouse to discipline the child.[12] In addition, the abusive parent was five times more likely to have difficulty getting his spouse to make decisions or accept responsibility. These answers are typical of persons who are involved in symbiotic relationships.[13] In abusing families there is constant competition over who will be taken care of.[14] First, the spouses compete with each other; when one "loses" and has to care for the other, he turns to the child in a last-ditch effort to be taken care of himself. When the child fails to deliver, a lifetime of frustration caused by unmet dependency needs is likely to be unleashed in the form of overt aggression toward the child. This is particularly true if the person has experienced a life crisis such as those we have described.

Because the abusing parent chronically feels he is losing in the struggle to be taken care of, it is not surprising that he believes his spouse is closer to the child and is avoiding the responsibility of disciplining the child or making decisions. Again, the abusing parent perceives himself as carrying the greater burden in the family and shouldering responsibilities that others should assume. He views himself as apart from other people and as a loser in the competition for love and comfort from others.

In our work with abusing families, we have found that discipline and decision-making are a frequent source of strife between spouses. Much anger is generated during the struggle to get the other to do the "parenting," to make the decisions and discipline the child. As we will see, discipline in the abusing family is often only one kind: physical punishment. In other words, when the child fails to meet the excessive expectations of his parent, who constantly wants to be cared for himself, the child is beaten.

The struggle to establish symbiosis was also reflected in the way abusing parents responded to items on the Social Readjustment Rating Scale. The most highly significant differences between the abusing and nonabusing parents showed up in "sex difficulties," "change in financial state," "trouble with in-laws," and "change in living conditions."[15] The abusing group experienced many more problems in these four areas than did nonabusers. Our experience with parents who abuse their children confirms these findings.

Sexual difficulties are often present because the spouses are engaged in internecine warfare to make one take care of the other. In sex, neither partner is willing to try to satisfy the other; instead, each demands to be satisfied. The sexual difficulties between spouses also reflect unresolved problems in other areas of daily life. Many abusing parents have never learned to get close to others. They are distrustful. They are not inclined to get the problems they are having with their mates out in the open. They may pout or stew in silence. All these problems can be expressed as problems with sex.

As for "change in financial state," the abusing parent often goes through many financial ups and downs. This does not necessarily mean that he is poor. Usually it reflects the difficulty he has making decisions and assuming responsibility. He tends to put things off, even critical things such as paying bills, and is likely to get into financial trouble by overspending. It is as though he expects someone else to come along and pay the bills for him. He wants to be rescued, to be cared for. He may skip work to the point where he loses money and gets into severe financial straits. He has trouble accepting responsibility for making ends meet and bringing in a steady income. He may change jobs often. As a result, there is the same pattern of ups and downs in terms of living conditions as in financial states.

The struggle with symbiosis is expressed in problems with in-laws as a result of viewing them as additional competitors for attention. The abusing parent is easily threatened by others who may interfere with his quest to be cared for. In-laws may divert the attention of his spouse or his child, refuse to give him the attention and care he wants, or incite jealousy and resentment.

As noted, sexual difficulties, change in financial status, change in living conditions and trouble with in-laws represent the four most highly significant areas of difference between abusing and nonabusing parents in terms of life change events. When all 43 items are taken as a whole, the abusers still differ markedly from the nonabusers. Does this mean that abusing parents are simply unfortunate victims of changes over which they have no control? No. Although they obviously cannot control changes such as death of spouse or a close friend, many of the changes that characterize their lives are self-induced. An analysis of the 43 items shown in Table 1–1 indicates that the changes that plague them fall into several categories related to family, marriage, health, occupation, economics, residence, group and peer relationships, education, religion, and recreation. A majority of the changes represented by these categories are the product of a particular kind of personality interacting with others and the environment. It is our thesis that the abusive parent's personality is such that he brings many changes on himself. As we will discuss later, he is inclined to be an isolated, distrusting, impatient individual with a poor self-image who is in conflict with his spouse. But primarily he is searching for a symbiotic relationship with someone who will make decisions for him, assume responsibility for him, and take care of him—in short, be his parent. (We will discuss why he is this way in considerable detail in later chapters.) As long as he is this way, he is likely to subject himself to a life crisis characterized by excessive change that requires enormous and constant readjustments. The life crisis exhausts him to the point where his defenses are lowered and his control over his behavior is weakened: in other words, it predisposes him to abuse.

We believe the life crisis can be averted by changing the abusing parent. Central to this change is breaking up the symbiotic pattern that is of such critical importance in abusing families. This change is impossible, however, unless the following considerations are addressed as well: (1) both spouses in the abusing family are essentially alike, regardless of which one actually strikes out at the child, (2) the family functions as a system and the child plays a role as well as the spouses, the environment, and the culture, and (3) the causes of child abuse are multidetermined and require an evaluation of social and cultural as well as psychological forces.

NOTES

1. R. J. Light, "Abused and neglected children in America: A study of alternative policies," *Harvard Educational Review*, 43 (November 1973), p. 587.
2. For a description of the two groups, see B. Justice and D. F. Duncan, *Public Health Reports*, 91 (March–April 1976), pp. 110–115.
3. A. Toffler, *Future Shock* (New York: Random House, 1970).
4. H. G. Wolff, S. G. Wolf, Jr., and C. C. Hare, *Life stress and bodily disease* (Baltimore: Williams & Wilkins, 1950); R. H. Rahe, et al., "Social stress and illness onset," *Journal of Psychosomatic Research*, 8 (1964), pp. 35–44; and T. H. Holmes and R. H. Rahe, "The social readjustment rating scale," *Journal of Psychosomatic Research*, 11 (1967), pp. 213–218; and Rahe et al., op. cit.
5. Toffler, op. cit.
6. G. Caplan, *Principles of preventive psychiatry* (New York: Basic Books, 1964), p. 48.
7. Holmes and Rahe, op. cit.
8. The mean score for the abusing parents was 234; for nonabusing parents it was 124. Any score above 150 has been classified by Holmes and Rahe as representing a life crisis. A score of 234 represents more than a mild life crisis but less than a major one (any score above 299) and is classified as moderate. Some abusing

parents scored almost 650. The means for the abusing and control groups are significantly different at the .001 level, as determined by *t*-test. (See Table 1–2 for a distribution of life change scores for the two groups.)

9. H. Selye, *The stress of life* (New York: McGraw-Hill, 1956), pp. 31–33.

10. C. H. Kempe and R. E. Helfer (eds.), *Helping the battered child and his family* (Philadelphia, Pa.: Lippincott, 1972), p. xiv.

11. The difference between the two groups on this item had a chi-square probability of .0117 at 2 degrees of freedom.

12. The difference on this item had a chi-square probability of .0339 at 2 degrees of freedom.

13. A. W. Schiff and J. Schiff, "Passivity," *Transactional Analysis Journal,* 1 (January 1971), p. 1.

14. R. Justice and B. Justice, "TA work with child abuse," *Transactional Analysis Journal,* 5 (January 1975), pp. 38–41.

15. The chi-square probabilities for the differences on these items were .0123, .008, less than .0000, and .0271, respectively, at 1 degree of freedom.

Chapter 2

CAUSAL MODELS OF CHILD ABUSE

When the theories and ideas on the causes of child abuse
are reviewed, the findings can be framed in terms of seven
models: (1) the psychodynamic model, (2) the personality
or character trait model, (3) the social learning model, (4)
the family structure model, (5) the environmental stress
model, (6) the social-psychological model, and (7) the mental illness model.[1] In Chapter 3 we will describe an eighth
model—the psychosocial systems model—which we developed and find most useful to account for the multiple
factors in child abuse and to design strategies for intervention.

With the exception of the eighth model, none is complete in itself—that is, the seven overlap to some degree or
take into account other factors that also play a part in producing child abuse. However, each contains a central core
of determinants that is considered basic to causation.
These determinants are viewed as sufficient to explain why
child abuse occurs.

One basic question involved in causation is whether people abuse children because they are driven by environmental pressures and the provocation of a child or because they are predisposed to abusive behavior by psychological forces at work from within. In the last analysis, dividing the issue of causation in this way is misleading. Both external pressures and internal dynamics play a part and interact in such a way that one cannot be considered without the other. In fact, the question involves more than the environment and the personality. It also extends to structure: that is, how a family arranges itself in terms of who is allied with whom, what coalitions exist, and who is distant and disengaged.

To complicate the picture even further, the kind of cultural cues that continuously bombard parents must also be considered. These cultural messages conjure up images of what parents should be like and how children should behave. When their own and their children's real-life behavior differs from the messages parents have absorbed, all kinds of conflict can result and feed into the process of abuse. Therefore, only a public health model that approaches the problem from a systems point of view, incorporating host, agent, environment, and vector, can properly represent the interplay of multiple forces that result in child abuse. This is not to say, however, that simpler models lack explanatory power. Each one has merit.

PSYCHODYNAMIC MODEL

The model that developed out of the work of the earliest pioneers in identifying and describing the battered child relies on psychodynamic determinants to explain the problem. Kempe et al. see the lack of a "mothering imprint" as the basic dynamic of the potential to abuse.[2] In other words, a person has been reared in a way that precluded the experience of being mothered and nurtured. Thus as an adult he cannot mother and nurture his own child.

Combined with this inability to nurture is an interplay of other dynamics: a lack of trust in others, a tendency toward isolation, a nonsupportive marital relationship, and excessive expectations toward the child. According to Kempe, two other factors must be present before the potential to abuse is activated: a "special" child (the abusing parent views him as retarded, hyperactive, or in some other way different) and a crisis (a major stress or something as minor as a broken washing machine).[3]

Thus, Kempe and his colleagues do not ignore environmental stress in their formulations of what causes child abuse. However, one distinguishing feature of the psychodynamic model is that it assigns a secondary role to everything except the individual internal psychology. Those who subscribe to this model note that child abuse occurs in all socioeconomic classes. Poor people live under more stress than persons with greater income, but if stress alone explained child abuse, then what explains the fact that the vast majority of lower-income individuals do not harm their children?

An important implication of the psychodynamic model is that no matter how much environmental stress there is, the act of abuse will not occur unless the psychological potential is present. As we pointed out in the Introduction, the majority of people believe that almost anyone can injure a child, given enough stress and frustration. Kempe, in effect, says no: if a person does not have the psychological potential, nothing will make him abuse. And, as we have seen, that potential rests largely on whether a person was mothered as a child and thus acquired the ability to mother. One problem with this notion is that there are varying degrees of mothering, and whether a person acquires an early mothering imprint is not likely to be an all-or-none matter. Persons with a less delible imprint may have some potential to abuse and if the stress becomes severe enough, abuse may occur.

Another feature of the psychodynamic model is the recognition it gives to "role reversal"—the parent expects the child to act like an adult and give the parent love and care rather than vice versa.[4] The reason for this behavior can be traced to the parent's own childhood, when his parents did not provide him with sufficient mothering and care and his needs for dependency were therefore unfulfilled. Galdston notes that persons who abuse their children tend to see in the child their own rejecting father or mother.[5] This again is a psychodynamic determinant of child abuse.

Still another root of problems within the person who abuses is the abuse that he himself suffered as a child, either physically or emotionally. This view has been adopted by a number of investigators.[6] More than just being rejected, the adult who abuses demonstrates the kind of behavior he received as a child. If this theory is true, it partially explains why the person who abuses expresses his problems in the form of violence rather than in other kinds of disturbed behavior.

One lingering concern when attempting to account for child abuse is finding specific reasons why violence is expressed instead of other problem behavior. Being rejected as a child, developing no trust or close relationships, learning no love, having little tolerance for stress—all these factors can produce problems that find a wide range of expression. Some people withdraw from life, some become alcoholics, others are suspicious of everything and everyone, still others act out in ways other than attacking their own children. Why then does a disturbed background or, in Helfer's words, "the world of abnormal rearing" express itself specifically in child abuse?[7] Although the question has not been answered fully, one possible explanation is that the person who was physically abused as a child may have learned that this is the only way to relate, as an adult, to his own child.[8]

Personality or Character Trait Model

The personality or character trait model of child abuse is similar to the psychodynamic model. The difference between the two is that the personality or character trait model pays less attention to the factors which underlie the traits of the person who abuses. Also there is more inclination to describe the individual in terms of labels or imply that this is just the way he is. Thus, descriptions such as "parents who abuse their children are immature," "self-centered," or "impulse-ridden" are included in the personality or character trait model.[9] Other authors have termed abusive parents as "chronically aggressive," and "highly frustrated," or "immature, lonely, impulsive, suspicious and untrusting people. . . ."[10]

Merrill divided abusive mothers and fathers into three groups according to their psychological characteristics.[11] Parents in the first group were described as chronically hostile and aggressive, traits that often result in conflict with the world in general. His second group was made up of parents who are rigid, compulsive, and lack warmth and a reasonable approach to things. The parents in the third group demonstrate a high degree of passivity and dependence, and many are depressed and unresponsive as well as immature. Merrill also had a fourth group, marked by extreme frustration. It consists of young fathers who are unemployed and stay at home to take care of the child. Their frustration often vents itself in child abuse.

Identifying the personality or character traits that are typical of an abusing person is likely to end up as a form of branding or labeling unless they are associated with the context in which abuse occurs and the reasons the traits are present. Merrill made this association, but others have not. Merely to describe the personality of an abusive person does not explain why abuse occurs. Many people are immature, impulsive, or self-centered, but they do not act violently toward their children. Thus there are limitations to the personality or character trait model; however, these limitations are reduced when the personality factors are considered in a larger context of environmental influences and the part the child may play in abuse.

Social Learning Model

Equally restrictive is the social learning model, which emphasizes the failure of abusive persons to acquire the skills to function adequately in the home and society. These individuals lack social skills, "gain little satisfaction from their role as parents . . . [and] are frequently ignorant of child development. They expect behavior too advanced for young children."[12] Moreover, they "do not know age-appropriate behavior for young children. They also have mistaken notions of how to rear children, how to encourage and guide them at different ages."[13] They also are inclined to use the only kind of discipline they know—physical discipline, which they received as children.

Although the social learning model is limited in accounting for the behavior of people who abuse, it has considerable power in the formulation of intervention and treatment strategies. The model requires the monitoring of specific behavior, on the part of both parents and child, that ends in abuse. The idea is that if the immediate antecedents of abuse are properly identified, steps can be taken to modify the behavior they represent—and perhaps prevent abuse. Social learning theory is also useful for teaching parents about child rearing and how to modify their expectations concerning what the behavior of children and parents should be.

Nearly all couples we have worked with since 1973 have a distinct lack of knowledge about the stages of child development, what children need at different ages, and how healthy parents respond. Learning theory lends itself to a behavior modification approach in working with parents and teaching them about child management. Other therapists have been successful in teaching parents effective child-rearing practices through programmed learning.[14] The social learning model, then, holds promise in work with parents who abuse. As an explanation of why abuse occurs, it has some usefulness but fails to account for several relevant influences.

FAMILY STRUCTURE MODEL

The formulations that fit the family structure model concern alliances, coalitions, enmeshments, and disengagements among family members. Although family systems concepts and family theory have not focused on the problem of child abuse, they offer considerable promise in terms of explaining the causes of abuse and designing therapeutic interventions. The repeated finding that illegitimate and unwanted children are high risks in terms of child abuse[15] is related to the concept of coalitions. For example, a coalition may involve a parent who sides with one child against the abused child or both spouses who side against the abused child. Other arrangements in family structure may also result in abuse. One mother we worked with was so invested in her child that her husband literally tore the child from her arms on several occasions. The child was injured when her head slammed against a door facing.

Scapegoating is another behavior often cited as result-ing in abuse.[16] Although the term may apply when a parent takes out his frustration on a child, it can also be used to describe the power struggles a child gets caught up in or an alliance that one spouse resents and makes the child pay for through physical injury. Disengagement on the part of a mother or father who declines to play a significant role in the family can also be central to child abuse. We have worked with more than one father who was on the periph-ery of the family and assumed little responsibility for man-aging his child. The wife in these cases often boils with resentment toward both her husband and child. Since it is the child who demands her time and attention and is an easy target for her resentment, he is the one who gets hurt.

ENVIRONMENTAL STRESS MODEL

Gil, the leading exponent of the environmental stress model, sees child abuse as a multidimensional problem and places heavy emphasis on stress as the cause.[17] He indi-cates that if it were not for chance environmental factors, such as poverty, poor education, and occupational stress, there would be no child abuse. He argues that economic stresses on poor people weaken their self-control and lead to violence against their own children. He advocates sweeping programs to cure poverty, educate people, up-grade their skills, and change their style of discipline as the answer for child abuse. But as Spinetta and Rigler point out:

> Eliminating environmental stress factors and bettering the level of society at all stages may reduce a myriad of social ills and may even prove effective, indirectly, in reducing the amount of child abuse. But there still remains the problem, insoluble at the demographic level, of why some parents abuse their children while others under the same stress fac-tors do not.[18]

Gil weakens his case by concluding that child abuse is highly concentrated in the lower socioeconomic classes. He bases this conclusion on a nationwide survey of cases of abuse reported by public agencies such as child welfare departments. Obviously, these sources do not accurately reflect the cases of abuse that occur in higher-income families, which have the resources to conceal abuse and deal only with the private sector of the health delivery system, where child abuse is grossly underreported. But as other investigations have shown, enough cases involving middle- and upper-income families are reported to continue asking the following question: If economic and related stress accounts for the problem of abuse, why does the problem occur in higher income families, and why does it not occur even more often in lower-income families than it does? Obviously, environmental and economic stress alone is not enough to explain child abuse. Even Gil said in 1975: "It should be emphasized . . . that poverty, per se, is not a direct cause of child abuse in the home, but operates through an intervening variable, namely, concrete and psychological stress and frustration. . . ."[19]

Those who subscribe to the environmental and economic stress theory note that as stress increases, so does child abuse. As economic pressures from the deep recession in 1975 mounted, an increase in child abuse cases was reported in a number of areas of the nation.[20] Fontana attributes the increase to "the stresses and strains that our society is suffering today—the frustrations, the poor quality of life, the increase in drug addiction and alcoholism."[21]

Bennie and Sclare also view child abuse as a lower-class phenomenon.[22] Blumberg and Steinmetz and Straus argue that intrafamily violence is more common among the working class and that child abuse is part of the style of physical discipline that poor people use.[23] Again, this theory does not take into account the fact that most poor people, despite stress or style of discipline, do not physically abuse their children.

SOCIAL-PSYCHOLOGICAL MODEL

Gelles has developed a social-psychological model of the cause of child abuse.[24] His model assumes that "frustration and stress are important variables associated with child abuse" and that this stress comes from several sources: marital disputes, too many children, unemployment, social isolation, unwanted children, a "problem child." These stresses combine with other contributing factors such as the influence of social class and community (norms that sanction violence as a way to deal with problems) and the effects of "socialization experiences" in which parents act as role models for violence. Gelles believes that these experiences lead to psychopathic states, personality traits, character traits, poor control, and neurological disorders that contribute to the potential for abuse. The final set of events necessary for actual abuse is described as "immediate precipitating situations": e.g., a child misbehaves. The end product is a single physical assault, repeated assault, or "psychological violence."

The implications Gelles draws from his model are that intervention strategies must go beyond what he calls "the treatment of psychopathic disorders of abusive parents," which tends to have limited effectiveness. He then quotes Kempe as saying that "psychiatrists feel that treatment of the so-called sociopath or psychopath is rarely successful," and that "the only remaining strategy of intervention is to remove the child from the parents."[25]

Gelles' confusing use of terms such as sociopath, psychopath, and psychopathological states and disorders is one of the problems with his model and his implications for intervention. He infers that investigators who follow a psychopathological model of intervention assume that all abusive parents are psychopaths, and everyone knows that efforts to treat them are rarely successful. The fact is that most investigators, including those who follow the so-called psychopathological or medical model, view parents who abuse as Steele and Pollack do.[26] Their experience—as well as ours—is that parents who have abused children would not, in Steele's and Pollack's words, "seem much different than a group of people picked by stopping the first several dozen people one would meet on a downtown street. . . . In other words, they represent a random cross section of the general population."[27] Gelles mistakenly assumes that when investigators such as Kempe, Steele, and Pollack use the term psychopathology, they are referring to psychopaths.[28] They are not. Although they may consider all people who abuse as suffering from psychopathology (i.e., some form of psychic sickness), the number who are diagnosed as psychopaths is only about 5 per cent.[29]

A second shortcoming of Gelles' model is that it fails to recognize the important symbiotic interaction between spouses and between parent and child in abusive families.[30] Although he does mention marital disputes, he does not note the shifting symbiosis that can be found between husband and wife or parent and child. This symbiotic relationship is a miniature system that is part of a larger one which includes the relationship between parent and employer and between parent and the culture at large. Later, we will discuss the shifting nature of the symbiosis and its significance as well as the systems approach.

MENTAL ILLNESS MODEL

One reason we have included the mental illness model is to clarify the way that terms such as psychopathology, psychosis, neurosis, and character defects are used in child abuse. Furthermore, because child abuse seems unthinkable to so many people, there is a tendency to regard the guilty as sick or mentally ill. In reality, the mental illness model applies to only a fraction of abusive parents. The overwhelming majority of them do not suffer from hallucinations or delusional systems, which characterize what we regard as psychosis or mental illness. Other investigators, particularly psychiatrists and other physicians, use these terms more loosely, but Kempe states that in his experience no more than 5 per cent of abusive parents are psychotic.[31] A study in England concluded that "the attacking adult can rarely be fitted into a psychotic or parapsychotic grouping. . . ."[32] Lascari, an American, holds that approximately 2 per cent of abusing parents are psychotic, and Blumberg states that psychosis is rarely a factor in child abuse.[33]

Many psychiatrists include emotional disturbances, character defects, personality problems, and neuroses as well as psychoses under the heading of mental illness. Again, the literature on child abuse does not reflect wide use of the term mentally ill when applied to persons who abuse children. However, there are fairly frequent references to emotional disturbances, psychopathology, character defects, personality disorders, and neuroses. Before Kempe identified child abuse for what it is in 1961, Woolley and Evans studied 12 infants with multiple fractures and discovered that they came from households with what was considered a high incidence of neurotic and psychotic behavior.[34] The suggestion was that only a mentally ill parent willfully inflicts physical abuse on a child.

Since then, mental retardation and organic brain disturbances have also been suggested as the cause of some cases of abuse.[35] Brain research indicates that the limbic system may be disturbed in some people who are excessively aggressive and show tendencies toward violence. Whether this disturbance accounts for some child abuse is still an open question. But the fact remains that everything from neurosis to organic brain dysfunction is included in the psychiatric profession's definition of mental illness. Thus if the American Psychiatric Association's *Diagnostic and Statistical Manual II* is taken literally, neuroses, psychoses, character defects, personality disorders, mental retardation, and organic brain problems are all mental disorders. In this sense, some psychiatrists and other physicians argue that abusive parents are mentally ill. Most authorities, however, do not stick to literal use of the psychiatric manual or to the idea that the problems of most people who abuse are mental disorders. In fact, investigators such as Zalba conclude that abusive parents do not easily fit any psychiatric classification.[36] Friedman notes that "it is difficult to characterize by use of psychiatric diagnoses parents who physically abuse or neglect their children."[37] And Kempe adds that "the concept stressed by us that young parents can attack their small child without being necessarily 'bad' or 'mentally ill' causes a great deal of consternation."[38]

If people who commit child abuse are not "bad" or mentally ill, what are they? We believe strongly that the use of a medical model or psychiatric diagnosis to understand abusing parents and design effective intervention strategies is unnecessary. The psychosystems model described in the next chapter presents our view of people who abuse their children. Branding these people as sick or mentally ill may militate against their psychological development and emotional growth, causing them to flee from help because they feel that no one understands them, or providing them with a crutch or cop-out about the way they are and what they have done.

Investigators who continue to describe some abusive parents as psychotic refer to specific kinds of behavior that can be explained in other ways. For instance, Galdston used the term transference psychosis to describe the parent who transfers the anger and hostility developed during relationships in his own childhood to the child that he abuses.[39] Galdston also emphasized that the parent views the child as an adult and expects him to act accordingly. These behaviors can be explained on the basis that the parent expects mothering and nurturing from the child. When the child fails to deliver, the anger that mounted when the parent was a child and was rejected and disappointed by his own non-nurturing parent occurs all over again. To call this a psychosis is unnecessary and misleading.

When is the term psychotic appropriate? The parent who does cruelly sadistic things to a child or batters the child unmercifully may appropriately be called mentally ill. Parents who torture a child with cigarette burns, who bite the child or administer bizarre punishment may well be behaving in response to hallucinations or crazy delusional systems. As Laury notes: "Some battering parents are mentally sick, and the child may become part of their distorted reality and delusional system. A paranoid parent may thus view his child as part of his persecuting environment and then feel justified in retaliating against him."[40]

Fortunately, the number of abusive parents who hallucinate or cling to elaborate delusional networks is small. One woman we worked with insisted that her behavior was under the control of "vibes." The vibes seemed to be her way of diverting her attention from real problems with her marriage and her children. As she learned effective ways of dealing with the problems, the vibes gradually receded and were no longer important to her.

In addition to constructing models that account for the causes of child abuse, as we have done here, parents can be classified by the types of abuse they commit. Delsordo includes abuse by mentally ill parents in his classifications.[41] Of the 80 cases he studied, four fell into this category; in two of these cases, the abuse involved a "ritual rather than an impulsive approach." A situation was devised either to petrify the child with fear or provoke him into behavior that "justified" punishment.

Other types of abuse that Delsordo identified were overflow abuse, battered child abuse, disciplinary abuse, and misplaced abuse.[42] The types fit the various models that have been presented here. Parents with an "overflow" of frustration, irresponsibility, and lack of belief in themselves or anything else (a mixture of the personality- and character-trait model and environmental stress model) tend to commit overflow abuse. Battered child abuse is regarded as being committed by parents with "severe interpersonal conflict" and marked dependency who view the child as a competitor or burden (psychodynamic model). Disciplinary abuse is seen as occurring in families that require strict compliance with parental expectations or rules (social learning model). Misplaced abuse, regarded as the most common form, includes cases in which the parent projects his conflicts onto the abused child. Forty-three of Delsordo's 80 cases illustrated misplaced parental abuse. The parents involved exhibited varying degrees of marital conflict and viewed the child as different or special because he was illegitimate or retarded, misbehaved repeatedly, or symbolized trouble with a spouse (a mixture of the psychodynamic and family structure models).

Although the psychosocial systems model we will discuss in the next chapter accounts for each of these categories of abuse, it also includes others that Delsordo did not mention. We believe that our model also overcomes the deficiencies and limitations of the models that have been reviewed so far.

NOTES

1. Although there are numerous ideas about the causes of child abuse, explanatory models are virtually nonexistent. Light proposed a "random model" and a "stress model"; neither, however, addressed the cause of abuse, only "the locus in which the cause operates." R. J. Light, "Abused and neglected children in America: A study of alternative policies," *Harvard Educational Review*, 143 (November 1973), pp. 592–593.
2. C. H. Kempe, "Paediatric implications of the battered baby syndrome," *Archives of Disease in Childhood*, 46 (February 1971), pp. 28–37.
3. Ibid.
4. M. G. Morris and R. W. Gould, "Role reversal: A concept in dealing with the neglected/battered child syndrome," in *The neglected battered-child syndrome: Role reversal in parents* (New York: Child Welfare League of America, 1963).
5. R. Galdston, "Observations on children who have been physically abused and their parents," *American Journal of Psychiatry*, 122 (October 1965), pp. 440–443.
6. J. J. Spinetta and D. Rigler, "The child-abusing parent: A psychological review," *Psychological Bulletin*, 77 (April 1972), pp. 296–304.
7. R. E. Helfer, *A self-instructional program on child abuse and neglect* (Committee on Infant and Preschool Child of the American

Academy of Pediatrics, Chicago, Ill., and National Center for the Prevention and Treatment of Child Abuse and Neglect, Denver, Colo., 1974), Unit 1, p. 2.

8. *Lift a finger: The teacher's role in combating child abuse* (Houston, Tex.: Education Professions Development Consortium C, 1975), p. 35.

9. Spinetta and Rigler, op. cit., pp. 299–300.

10. See B. Melnick and J. R. Hurley, "Distinctive personality attributes of child-abusing mothers," *Journal of Consulting and Clinical Psychology*, 33 (1969), pp. 746–749; and R. W. Sanders, "Resistance to dealing with parents of battered children," *Pediatrics*, 50 (December 1972), pp. 853–857.

11. E. J. Merrill, "Physical abuse of children: An agency study," in V. DeFrancis (ed.), *Protecting the battered child* (Denver: American Humane Association, 1962).

12. J. J. Tracy and E. H. Clark, "Treatment for child abusers," *Social Work*, 19 (May 1974), p. 339.

13. M. H. Lystad, "Violence at home: A review of the literature," *American Journal of Orthopsychiatry*, 45 (April 1975), pp. 328–345.

14. R. C. Hughes, "A clinic's parent-performance training program for child abusers," *Hospital and Community Psychiatry*, 25 (1974), pp. 779–782; and A. B. Savino and R. W. Sanders, "Working with abusive parents: Group therapy and home visits," *American Journal of Nursing*, 73 (March 1973), pp. 482–484.

15. M. G. Morris, "Psychological miscarriage: An end to mother love," *Trans-Action*, 3 (January–February 1966), pp. 8–13; F. I. Bishop, "Children at risk," *Medical Journal of Australia*, 1 (March 1971), pp. 623–628; D. Bakan, *Slaughter of the innocents* (San Francisco: Jossey-Bass, 1971); and R. J. Gelles, "Child abuse as psychopathology: A sociological critique and reformulation," *American Journal of Orthopsychiatry*, 43 (July 1973), pp. 611–621.

16. M. L. Blumberg, "Psychopathology of the abusing parent," *American Journal of Psychotherapy*, 28 (January 1974), pp. 21–29; and M. J. Paulson et al., "Parents of the battered child," *Life-Threatening Behavior*, 4 (Spring 1974), pp. 18–31.

17. D. G. Gil, *Violence against children* (Cambridge: Harvard University Press, 1970).

18. Spinetta and Rigler, op. cit., p. 301.

19. D. G. Gil, "Unraveling child abuse," *American Journal of Orthopsychiatry*, 45 (April 1975), p. 352.

20. *Time*, March 17, 1975, p. 88.

21. V. J. Fontana, "The neglect and abuse of children," *New York State Journal of Medicine*, 64 (January 1964), p. 215.

22. E. Bennie and A. Sclare, "The battered child syndrome," *American Journal of Psychiatry*, 125 (January 1969), pp. 975–979.

23. M. L. Blumberg, "When parents hit out," *Twentieth Century,* 173 (Winter 1964), pp. 39–44; and S. Steinmetz and M. Straus, "Some myths about violence in the family." Paper presented before the American Sociological Association, Denver, Colorado, 1971.
24. Gelles, op. cit.
25. Gelles, op. cit., pp. 620–621.
26. B. F. Steele and C. Pollock, "A psychiatric study of parents who abuse infants and small children," in R. E. Helfer and C. H. Kempe (eds.), *The battered child* (Chicago: University of Chicago Press, 1968), pp. 103–147.
27. Ibid., pp. 106–107.
28. Gelles, op. cit., pp. 613–614.
29. Kempe, op. cit., p. 30.
30. See R. Justice and B. Justice, "TA work with child abuse," *Transactional Analysis Journal,* 5 (January 1975), pp. 38–41; and B. Justice and D. F. Duncan, "Physical abuse of children as a public health problem," *Public Health Reviews,* 4 (April–June 1975), pp. 183–200.
31. Kempe, op. cit., p. 29.
32. "Violent parents," *Lancet,* November 6, 1971, pp. 1017–1018.
33. A. Lascari, "The abused child," *Journal of the Iowa Medical Society,* 62 (May 1972), pp. 229–232; and Blumberg, op. cit., p. 22.
34. P. V. Woolley and W. A. Evans, "Significance of skeletal lesions in infants resembling those of traumatic origin," *Journal of the American Medical Association,* 158 (June 1955), pp. 539–543.
35. E. Lord and D. Weisfeld, "The abused child," in A. R. Roberts (ed.), *Childhood deprivation* (Springfield, Ill.: Charles C Thomas, 1974).
36. S. Zalba, "Battered children," *Trans-Action,* 8 (July–August 1971), pp. 58–61.
37. S. B. Friedman, "The need for intensive follow-up of abused children," in C. H. Kempe and R. E. Helfer (eds.) *Helping the battered child* (Philadelphia, Pa.: Lippincott, 1972), p. 81.
38. Kempe, op. cit., p. 28.
39. Galdston, op. cit.
40. G. V. Laury, "The battered-child syndrome: Parental motivation, clinical aspects," *Bulletin of The New York Academy of Medicine,* 46 (September 1970), p. 681.
41. J. D. Delsordo, "Protective casework for abused children," *Children,* 10 (November–December 1965), p. 214.
42. Ibid., pp. 213–218.

Chapter 3

THE ABUSING FAMILY: A PSYCHOSOCIAL SYSTEM AND SHIFTING SYMBIOSIS

As we have seen, the question of child abuse cannot be adequately examined by subscribing to the idea that the abusing parent is mentally ill, focusing on the situational stress he is under, looking at a set of personality or character traits, or concentrating on the psychodynamic potential for abuse. Abuse is the product of all these factors and still more. The "still more" is included in a psychosocial systems model, which takes into account the shifting dynamic forces at work in the family in which abuse occurs and in the environment and culture in which the family lives.

Abuse is the end result of a system of interaction between spouses, parent and child, child and environment, parent and environment, and parent and society. What affects one affects another.

Since the family is the main system in which all the interaction takes place, it is impossible to speak of child abuse without mentioning the abusing family, the forces that operate in the total unit, and the influences that impinge on it. As Helfer points out, "the family must be considered as a total unit. Child abuse is a family affair."[1]

The precursors of abuse will be found not only in the individual parents and child and their life change events, but in the systems and subsystems of which they are a part. As we just noted, the main system to which they belong is the family; hence the idea of "the abusing family."

The notion of the family as a system is not new. Bowen noted that "the relationships between family members constitute a system in the sense that a reaction in one family member is followed by a predictable reaction in another, and that reaction is followed by a predictable reaction in another and then another in a chain-reaction pattern."[2] Thus, when a parent competes with his small son or daughter for the "child position" of being cared for, the other parent—and the child—reacts. The climate for an abusing family can be fostered in just this way.

The psychosocial systems model is primarily concerned with two systems: the family system and the larger system of family, environment, and culture. The larger system is depicted in terms familiar to public health: host, environment, agent, and vector. Figure 3-1 represents this triad of interaction.

In public health, the question of whether a host suffers from a physical, mental, emotional, or social problem is the function of several considerations: his own resistance or vulnerability, the nature of stressful influences in the environment, the presence and potency of a precipitating agent, and a vector that transmits a stimulus to the responding host. When the model is adapted to the problem of child abuse, the host represents the parents, the environment represents physical and social influences and stresses, the agent is the child and the behavior he embodies, and the vector is the stimulus imparted from agent to host that carries the cultural "scripting" which governs interaction between the two.

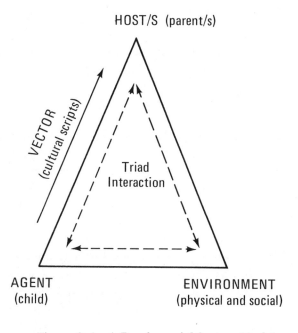

**Figure 3–1   A Psychosocial System Model
of Child Abuse**

Because there is continuing interaction and feedback between any two points on the triangle as well as among all points taken as a whole, there are subsystems within the larger system. Again, any change in one affects the other. Although the system is primarily psychosocial, it also includes a biological element. For example, as Bishop suggests, the host's child-rearing abilities "are determined by her own genetic endowment modified positively or negatively by her own parenting experience; her adaptation to it; her present emotional and physical health; as well as current socio-economic and interpersonal stresses."[3] Thus the variables at any point in the host-environment-agent triad are themselves multiple. Although we do not suggest that they involve only psychological and social variables, it is in the psychological and social arena that the action takes place. But the individual's biological makeup and the physical attributes of the environment also play a part. Examples of characteristics of the environment, host, agent, and vector will be more fully developed in Chapter 4. At this point, we will present a few elements of each to illustrate the psychosocial system and how the triadal model lends itself to intervention.

Our model identifies the parents as the host of the problem of child abuse. It does not focus on the parent who actually beats or injures the child to the exclusion of the one who does not act out. As Isaacs has pointed out: "Both parents are the same. . . . It doesn't matter which one did the actual battering."[4] Other investigators, including Kempe, have reached the same conclusion.[5]

Abusing parents, as we indicated earlier, are commonly described as seeking from the child satisfaction of their own needs for comfort and nurturing. They expect the child to fulfill their needs and make up for the deprivations they suffered in their own childhoods. Furthermore, we have found that both husband and wife often compete to be taken care of in a culturally accepted manner. In public, the husband permits his wife to occupy this position so that he appears to be the strong decision-maker who is unaffected by problems no matter how severe. At home, however, he sits in front of the television set and expects his wife to bring him a beer or a drink. If one of his children asks him for permission to play across the street, for example, he replies "Go ask your mother," because she is in fact the one who is usually the decision-maker at home.

As will be seen, the parents are locked into a shifting symbiotic relationship in which each seeks from the other satisfaction of his need to be cared for or nurtured. As a result, neither parent's needs are met and each may, at different times, turn to the child, no matter how young, to be the nurturer and decision-maker.[6]

In the environment in which abuse occurs, the most marked feature is change. A constant need to readjust is imposed on parent and child. Defenses drop, controls weaken. Support systems are lacking. Isolation is common. The physical environment often adds more stress since the home is frequently overcrowded because of too many children, too little space, or both.

In our model the child and the stressful behavior or conditions he embodies are considered the agent that precipitates abuse. As we emphasized earlier, abuse results from a system of multiple interactions between parent and child, husband and wife, adult and environment, child and environment, and culture and parent. All play a part, but the child is most commonly the immediate source of external stress for the abusing parent. The child's very proximity makes him an easy target for the parent whose frustrations spill over into physical aggression.

An assumption about some babies and children who are abused is that they are particularly difficult, aggravating, and hard to handle (see Chapter 8). According to Flynn, the "obnoxious child" is a natural stimulus for abuse.[7] Parents who seek nurturing and comfort from their child may be provoked to anger and violence if the child responds with crying or agitated behavior. When the child makes unusually great demands or represents an exceptional stress, he is in even greater danger. Chapter 8 describes a number of high-risk children that have been identified: premature babies, illegitimate babies, and children who are congenitally malformed or mentally retarded.[8]

The vector in our psychosocial systems model represents the "cultural scripting" of the parents and carries the stimulus from the agent to the host. By cultural scripts we mean the accepted and expected patterns of interaction between individuals in a society. Cultural scripts are spoken

and unspoken assumptions about human behavior that result from culturally endorsed messages, injunctions, and
myths about how people should act, feel, and think.[9]

It will be seen in Chapter 4 that cultural scripts have
a significant influence on the expectations of parents and
their responses to children. The myth of the Madonna and
child places the mother in the position of expecting herself
to be unfailingly loving. Parents who are imbued with this
idea may be unwilling to admit their anger toward the child,
and their hostility may mount to the point where all that is
needed to bring release is a provocative stimulus. Another
product of cultural scripting is the notion that physical
punishment is a necessary ingredient of child management.
However, the line between physical punishment and child
abuse is frequently a thin one.

One advantage of the triadal systems model is that it
offers an opportunity for preventive interventions at various levels, which is the pattern in public health practice.
Intervention may occur at the level of the host (parents),
the agent (the child), the environment, or the vector (cultural scripts). We will devote more attention to this topic
in our discussion of primary prevention in Chapter 8.

THE ABUSING FAMILY SYSTEM

Now that we have highlighted the features of the larger
system bearing on child abuse, we can address the family
system—the arena of action. Jenkins and Lystad have
pointed out that child abuse often occurs generation after
generation in the same family, as if a cycle of violence is
inherited.[10] What is inherited is not a genetic propensity
for abuse but a particular kind of emotional and relationship system that requires the family to absorb large
amounts of tension. One expression of this tension is violence, and one target of the violence is a child. The term

"emotional and relationship system" is derived from Bowen, who noted that "the term emotional refers to the force that motivates the system, and relationship to the ways it is expressed."[11]

The kind of emotional and relationship system that characterizes the abusing family is one of great intensity, force, and fusion (the "stucktogetherness" that has been found in dysfunctional families).[12] Either the spouses are tightly bound to one another, one parent is fused with the child, or the husband or wife is still intensely tied to his or her family of origin. This fusion is healthy and necessary only when it exists between mother and infant; it is imperative that the infant fuse with his mother or some other adult to survive. But in some families, the emotional and even physical stucktogetherness continues far beyond infancy and sometimes throughout life. These people grow up looking for others with whom they can fuse or form a symbiotic relationship. Together they try to form a common self. Both are "feeling" people: i.e., they orient themselves to the world and to others strictly on the basis of what feels right. They are not "thinking" people in the sense of rationally planning goals and ways to meet them. Since they are not "whole" people, they do not have a defined self. They exist as part of others and are so busy "seeking love and approval, or attacking the other for not providing it, that there is little energy left for self-determined, goal-directed activity."[13]

Bowen calls these people "undifferentiated." They are undifferentiated in the sense of being fused into others who make up the nuclear or extended family; they do not have a separate self. The more undifferentiation there is, the more likely that problems will occur during stress. These problems can be expressed in three areas: marital conflict, dysfunction in a spouse, and transmission of the problem to one or more children.[14] The marital conflict takes the form of fights between the spouses as if to see which one will obtain more of the common self. Dysfunction in one of the spouses usually means that one has given in to the other. The dysfunction may be physical, emotional, or social. Social dysfunction includes acting-out behavior such as violence. When the problem is transmitted to the child, the same kinds of dysfunction may occur.

In child abuse, the dysfunction in a spouse spills over into violent behavior that is directed at the child. The family system must absorb so much undifferentiation that there may not only be violence by father or mother but a problem in all three areas: conflict between spouses, the dysfunction of one, and something wrong with the child. The root of the problem is competition within the family system over which one will be taken care of by the other. The spouses fight over who will give in to whom, who will wait on whom, who will do more for whom. The winner is taken care of, and the loser turns to more extreme behavior to obtain care. Thus he or she will begin acting out to get attention and care. The acting out is directed at a "special" child— the one the parent perceives as being most in need of attention or care and is therefore the most threatening competitor to the parent seeking the same thing. The parent's violent behavior toward the child represents an extreme effort to get somebody to step in and give the parent the attention and care that he seeks.

When there is only one parent in the nuclear family, there is nearly always some fusion between that parent and a relative in the family of origin. If that relative does not provide the parent with the attention and care he desires, he turns to the child, who cannot possibly meet his demands. The attention and care comes only after there has been abuse and the authorities have stepped in. Even then, the care is often not the kind that is likely to promote the parent's rehabilitation and growth.

Undifferentiation, and the immaturity that results, is a multigenerational process: that is, the stucktogetherness or fusion of family members that characterizes a family in one generation is passed on to the next.[15] Members in each generation fail to learn how to individuate, become whole people, meet their own needs, and overcome the need to fuse with others. As a result, child abuse often occurs in one generation after another in the same family.

The family system is the arena in which two fundamental issues must constantly be addressed: how to meet one's need to belong and simultaneously individuate—to become one's own person with a distinct self. Whitaker identified these two issues as basic to all problems of human existence.[16] It is in the family system where these issues are struggled with most intensely. This struggle goes on in all families and in all emotional systems, whether a work, social, or cultural system. Dysfunction sets in only when fusion occurs to such a degree that belongingness becomes stucktogetherness and individuation is obliterated.

Undifferentiation generates tension and latent anger. The tension results from the constant struggle to merge oneself with another, to incorporate the other, to become part of someone else as though in a desperate effort to meet primitive needs to belong and be cared for. The latent anger results from suppressing the opposing drive to be an individual, have a separate self or identity, and be one's own person. Because the process of individuation or separation is painful, undifferentiated people tend to view the process as impossible for them, so they try desperately to fuse with others. It is almost as if they are saying: "I can't stand alone so I can exist only as part of others." But like everyone, they still want to be apart, and the more they merge themselves (or are merged) into an undifferentiated mass representing the family, the more their latent anger mounts. Thus they are caught in the middle; they "long for closeness but . . . are allergic to it."[17]

The "allergy," the tension, the anger—all must be absorbed by the family system. Fights between husband and wife can absorb a certain amount. Sickness on the part of one spouse can absorb some. And physical, emotional, or behavioral problems with a child can absorb a certain quantity. But if the undifferentiation and the accompanying tension and anger are too great, the entire system becomes dysfunctional. This is what occurs in the abusing family. So much tension and anger must be absorbed that conflict and sickness are not enough. Violence too is necessary. Yet violence occurs in some instances in families where there is no evidence of overt conflict or sickness. In these cases, the spouses express pride about how few arguments they have. Thus the tension between them, blocked from being partially expressed through overt conflict, must find other avenues for release. When the tension mounts to the boiling point, it is released through violent channels, sending the family system into dysfunction and partial collapse.

How does this process get started in the first place? It begins with the symbiosis between mother and infant: the intense attachment necessary for the newborn's survival. This is a healthy and constructive relationship. It becomes destructive only when the mother fails to meet the baby's needs or when the symbiotic attachment lasts beyond the time when the child should begin to establish a separate sense of self and individuation. Mothers are not the only ones to establish symbiotic attachments with children. Fathers and even grandparents are sometimes involved.

In cases where the symbiosis is insufficient or inconsistent, the baby receives little nurturing and care and is left with a hunger for dependency. As he grows up, he is likely to seek someone to attach to. Much of his feeling and fantasy system revolves around a fusion with others. In fact, he devotes so much energy to his need to fuse and attach to someone else that he remains undifferentiated and lacks a defined self of his own. When he marries, he usually picks someone with similar needs and the fight for who will care for whom begins. If the husband wins, his wife is likely to resort to physical illness or emotional disturbance to obtain attention and care. Just as fighting is one expression of fusion between two people, sickness is another. When the tension is so great it cannot be absorbed by conflict or illness, it may be expressed in violence. This is what happens in the abusing family: the child who is considered different or special and in need of attention becomes the target of the violent tension that the system is unable to absorb. The spouse who does the actual abuse is losing the battle to be cared for and must therefore eliminate competition that the child represents. Only when the entire system becomes so dysfunctional that outside intervention occurs is the tension dispersed; at that point, everyone gets attention, if only temporarily or partially.

The same outcome results when the original symbiosis is intense and prolonged rather than insufficient. In this case, the child grows up knowing no other way to function or live than to attach himself to someone else. Although he is dependent on the attachment, his suppressed anger over being "smothered" by his mother or other relative increases. He has little differentiation as a person, little sense of self or individuation. When he marries, he chooses someone he can shift his attachment to—a person who seeks fusion and wholeness through being a part of somebody else. The same tension develops from undifferentiation—from the struggle over a common self, over who is to care for whom. And mixed with it is the submerged anger over being dependent and not being a separate individual. The tension and anger are too much for the system to absorb through conflict and sickness, and, again, violence is the outcome: violence directed at the child, to whom the parent turns for continuation of his original symbiotic attachment.

The issue of differentiation versus fusion must be dealt with in all family systems because it touches on the fundamental need to belong, to be part of a group, yet at the same time to individuate, to be apart. Fusion (symbiosis) then is an intensification of a process that goes on in all human relationships, a process of belonging, of merging with others.[18] In an intensified form, the process may result in schizophrenic dysfunction or collapse.[19] In another extreme form, it produces violence in the family. And child abuse, like schizophrenia, may be passed on from one generation to another through the process of fusion.

At the root of the multigenerational transmission process is the merger of two persons of insufficient differentiation. In child abuse, as we have seen, the level of differentiation is so low that marital conflict and sickness—sickness of a parent, a child, or both—are not enough to absorb the tension, anger, and immaturity. This does not mean that both spouses will necessarily appear to function at an extremely low level of differentiation—that is, seem extremely dependent, irresponsible, immature, impulsive, and narcissistic. Either one or both may be poorly differentiated but shift to a higher level of functioning.[20]

We have worked with families in which the father appears to be self-sufficient, competent, and "whole." One father was a computer analyst, another a geologist; both were quiet and showed few feelings. Later we found that each had ways of getting cared for by his wife: one suffered from back pain; the other was waited on at home by his wife and controlled what she did. Although both men avoided closeness, they were fused with their mothers and competed with their wives to be cared for. In these families, the wives had given in and were the ones who abused the children.

These men also had a heavy emotional investment in their work. Work can serve as another area of emotional fusion. Men who are geographically separated from their families of origin but still remain tied to them in fantasy and feeling frequently behave like the two fathers we have just described; they are quiet, professional, distant. The emo-

tional system of work absorbs some of their undifferentiation. At the same time, there is an effect at home: as the
men work harder and longer, their wives are forced to
further extremes to obtain attention and care.

Intervention in this kind of system must focus on helping the spouses gain a sense of differentiation and separateness. This is essential for the child not only to escape abuse
but to gain a sense of self. As long as the same degree of
fusion exists in the family, the emotional stucktogetherness
keeps all members from defining their own boundaries.
There is much narcissism in the family system in terms of
"I want" and "Give me," but little expression of individual-
ity, as evidenced in statements such as "I am," "I believe,"
"I will do," "I will not do."[21] We encourage spouses to
start taking "I positions" and make statements that clearly
mark where they stand and who they are.

One way to accomplish this is to use the kind of "I
messages" taught in Parent Effectiveness Training.[22] We
teach parents to use "I messages" in relations with their
spouses and children. When one family member does
something that causes problems for another, the "I message" is a nonthreatening way of confronting and keeping
communication open. The person with the problem states
how he feels, describes the behavior that bothers him, and
explains why it bothers him. These "I messages" let others
know what his position is, what his feelings are, and why he
feels the way he does.

The self-definition process also involves going back to
the fusion with the family of origin. Although the immediate problem is the tension, anger, or dysfunction that exists
between two spouses in the nuclear family, the roots lie in
emotional ties with their own mothers, fathers, or other
relatives. Although they may be geographically separated
from the family of origin, they still have much fantasy or
feeling invested in it. This is true, as we pointed out earlier,

of some fathers we work with. They seem to be independent, self-contained adults, but they are still tied back home.

In other cases, the ties with the family of origin are more obvious. One couple in our group used all their savings to buy expensive Christmas presents for their mothers and fathers. The wife's mother had a heavy emotional investment in the couple's abused child and was given temporary custody. However, placing a child in the home of the grandparents is usually a bad practice because it is in the families of origin that the mother and father of the child were either abused themselves or were caught up in a mass of undifferentiation. As Martin has observed, "this ... makes the practice of placing battered children with their grandparents a dubious if not patently ridiculous therapeutic regime," and Helfer adds that "relatives are rarely helpful because they created the problem in the first place."[23]

Although not all abusive parents were physically abused as children, the number who were is large enough to cause concern about how violence frequently begets violence. Not only are future offspring at risk in terms of how an abused person may behave toward his children, but the very safety of society is involved. Several studies have shown that violent criminals were abused as children.[24] When a policewoman in the Child Abuse Unit of the Los Angeles Police Department did a follow-up study of children who had been rescued from abusive parents by police 18 years earlier, she discovered that more than half had acquired criminal records as juveniles and even a larger percentage had committed crimes as adults.[25]

Breaking the multigenerational cycle of child abuse, then, is of paramount importance. Accomplishing this often means that children must be kept out of the hands of their grandparents and the abusing parents must be helped to break away from their families of origin.

The intervention approach with parents involves moving them toward separate "I positions," not only in terms of one another but in terms of their own fathers and mothers. This approach promotes differentiation in the nuclear family. As the fusion in the nuclear family begins to break up, the child's opportunity to individuate increases. And as each family member gains a greater sense of separateness and self, the intensity of the emotional system tones down and the climate for abuse decreases.

We will discuss the topic of separating spouses in symbiosis in Chapter 5. Here we will examine the process of shifting symbiosis, which is a basic element of the abusing family's violent behavior.

SHIFTING SYMBIOSIS: A CENTRAL THEORETICAL CONCEPT

> Basic in the abuser's attitude toward infants is the conviction, largely unconscious, that children exist in order to satisfy parental needs. Infants who do not satisfy these needs should be punished . . . to make them behave properly. . . . It is as though the infant were looked to as a need-satisfying parental object to fill the residual, unsatisfied, infantile needs of the parent.[26]

When a child is born, his survival depends on the willingness of a parent or caretaker to meet his needs. In addition to having a willingness to meet the child's needs, the parent must be able to assess what those needs are without a specific request from the infant. In other words, an infant's survival demands a symbiotic relationship.

Symbiosis, as we noted, begins as a life-sustaining relationship between mother and child in the earliest stage of development.[27] An example of normal symbiosis is when a mother awakens at her infant's first whimper and gets up to feed, change, or in some other way attend to his needs. In general, symbiosis is experienced as meeting mutually shared needs: the infant's need to be nurtured and the mother's need to nurture.

If the symbiotic relationship is not terminated when it has served its original purpose of sustaining life, problems in emotional growth develop. A symbiotic relationship that continues between parent and child or is established by any two people keeps each from becoming a whole person, from doing his own feeling, thinking, and acting. At that point, symbiosis becomes "a condition in which a person depends upon others, not for cooperative mutual support and affection but for exploitation and the satisfaction of neurotic needs."[28]

Dysfunctional symbiosis, which occurs later in life, is likely to result from disturbances in the original symbiotic relationship between the child and the mother.[29] As we noted earlier, premature separation or a lack of responsiveness on the parent's part leaves infantile needs sufficiently unmet so that growth beyond a symbiotic relationship tends to be prohibited. Neglect and overprotection can also retard or even prevent the differentiation process. Malfunctional symbiosis can be attributed to "instances where parenting is inadequate to prepare the child to function as an independent person who can solve problems in the world."[30]

When a child, for whatever reason, does not grow beyond symbiosis and into a separate identity, the result is a continual quest for someone to meet his unmet needs symbiotically. This quest is relentless because the person believes, at some level of consciousness, that to survive he *must* find someone else to take care of him. The difference between meeting one's needs through symbiosis and through autonomy is that the autonomous person is aware of his needs and consciously takes steps to meet them. In other words, he is aware of his ability to meet his own needs. In symbiosis, the person manipulates others into meeting his needs without considering whether they are willing or able to do so. In short, symbiosis involves the denial of one's own ability to meet needs directly and the demand that someone else meet them—in essence, these are the dynamics that exist in infancy.

The demand takes the form of passivity. Passivity, in the context of symbiosis, means devoting one's energies to reestablishing a symbiotic relationship—as opposed to taking direct action to meet one's own needs.[31] There are four types of passive behavior: (1) doing nothing, (2) overadaptation, (3) agitation, and (4) incapacitation or violence. The person who does nothing mobilizes all his energy to avoid responding when confronted with a problem. Doing nothing is usually accompanied by not thinking. The person who overadapts tries to solve a problem according to someone else's expectations rather than deciding on his own solution and carrying it out. Again, the element of not thinking is involved. Agitation is non-goal directed activity, such as wiggling one's foot or chain smoking, which may relieve tension to an extent but does nothing to solve the problem. Although violence and incapacitation seem to be opposites, they both serve to discharge the energy built up by passivity and the element of helplessness, or the refusal to assume responsibility. Not thinking, again, is an element in agitation as well as it is in violence and incapacitation.

Since nonthinking is involved in the passive behaviors defined here, one consequence of the resulting symbiotic relationship is that because the passive person is not solving his problem, someone else is left with the task. For example, extreme forms of passive behavior—insanity, violence, physical incapacitation—demand that someone else do something to stop or contain the insanity, violence, or physical incapacitation. Thus mental institutions, prisons, and hospitals exist to ensure that those who do not assume the responsibility to think about their own behavior have someone to do it for them. On a more individual level, the man who batters his child forces his community to respond to him. The community may respond with punishment or therapy, but either way his behavior demands a response.

The thought process underlying passive behavior is discounting—lessening the significance or value of something or considering something as worth less than its actual value.[32] The four forms of discounting observed in passivity are (1) discounting the problem, (2) discounting the significance of the problem, (3) discounting the solvability of the problem, and (4) discounting the person. Discounting the existence of a problem is involved when parents insist that they are adequate parents, although child welfare authorites have taken away their infant after it was hospitalized for multiple fractures, lacerations, bruises, or failure to thrive. "She bruises easily" is a common means of discounting the significance of the problem in abuse cases. Parents who lament that a child will not learn respect unless he is beaten are discounting the solvability of the problem. By saying "That kid's impossible; I couldn't help it," the parent discounts himself as well as the child. Usually, all four forms of discounting underlie passive behavior, and all four involve not using relevant information: in other words they involve not thinking.

Symbiosis in Transactional Analysis Terms

One technique we use when working with abusive parents is transactional analysis (TA), which views individuals in terms of three ego states: Parent, Adult, and Child. As Berne notes, "Parent-Adult-Child are all ego states which are observable realities that can be consciously experienced. . . ."[33] In what way are they observable? As a person operates from one of his three ego states, he uses words, gestures, and other expressions typical of the Parent, Adult, or Child. The three ego states, then, are distinguishable by "skeletal-muscular variables and the content of verbal utterances. Certain gestures, postures, mannerisms, facial expressions and intonations, as well as certain words, are typically associated with one of three ego-states."[34]

The Parent is the judgmental, opinionated, rule-making ego state. It is virtually a "videotape" of the words, feelings, and mannerisms of the individual's own parents. A person in the Parent ego state uses words such as should, ought to, supposed to, have to, gotta, everybody, nobody, never, always. The Parent performs both caretaking (nurturing) and critical (disciplinary) functions. Mannerisms accompanying the Parent ego state are a wagging finger; a stern, critical, or loving facial expression; and an appearance of talking down to the other person.

The Adult ego state acts as the computer of the personality. The Adult asks questions such as how, when and where and answers them. In other words, the Adult represents the objective ego state—it obtains the information necessary to achieve a goal.

Feelings, spontaneous or modified, are in the Child. Creativity, joy, sadness, fear, hate, love, and all the other human emotions find their outlet in the Child, and a person in this ego state reflects the mannerisms of a small child.

Symbiosis involves a relationship between two people in which one uses two of these ego states and the other person uses the remaining ego state. Together they exhibit one complete set of ego states.[35] Figure 3–2 represents the togetherness that occurs in symbiosis.

In the most common form of symbiosis, one person pretends not to have a Parent and Adult and the other pretends not to have a Child. For example, a wife may act as though she is incapable of being judgmental or nurturing like a parent and cannot make decisions like an adult; her husband may behave as though he lacks emotions—the part of him that is like a child. The wife, sobbing uncontrollably, greets her husband at the door with "I've had a horrible day. The kids were so bad I couldn't do anything!" and her husband replies "Don't worry dear. You're just

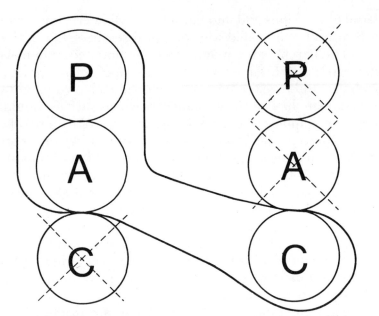

HUSBAND acts as if
he has no C ego state,
no feeling part —
no mad, sad, glad,
excited, scared part.

WIFE acts as if she
has no P and A
ego states — no
"take care of others"/
judgmental part and
no decision-making part.

**Figure 3–2   A Symbiotic Relationship
At One Point In Time**

upset. I'll take care of everything. Now, what did they do?"
In other words, the husband is the Parent and Adult to her
helpless Child. She pretends that she cannot handle discipline problems herself and he pretends he is not upset
about being greeted at the door by a tearful wife.

The pretense is the result of early learning about what
brings positive strokes (positive attention and recognition)
and verbal and nonverbal messages or injunctions their
parents gave them early in life. These messages in effect tell

a child: "Mommy and Daddy will be happy if you do or feel this or that." "This" or "that" may be thinking, expressing feelings, growing up, being successful, or any number of other behaviors or accomplishments. In TA, these messages are called script injunctions.[36]

For example, according to the traditional cultural script, a man will receive positive strokes for being brave and intelligent—for using Parent and Adult. So our hypothetical husband is "brave" in the face of a household crisis and "figures out" what to do. Women, on the other hand, receive positive strokes for looking pretty and being helpless, i.e., for childlike qualities.

Symbiotic relationships may develop around one or many issues and may involve a large or small part of a person's life. Furthermore, a person can shift positions frequently or remain primarily in the "top dog" (Parent and Adult) or "underdog" (Child) position.[37]

Symbiosis in the Abusing Family

We have already mentioned that individuals who enter into and struggle to maintain a symbiotic relationship believe they are incapable of surviving on their own. This fear of independence results from the problems in symbiosis described earlier. Most abusing parents have early developmental histories that often result in an unsatisfying mother-child symbiosis. When questioned, the battering parent often describes a history "of severe emotional deprivation in childhood, . . . that as a child his rights were not respected and he could not satisfy his own parents' emotional demands."[38]

Coexistent with the belief in one's inability to survive alone is the idea that only one person in a relationship can have his needs met. In other words, "Either I get what I want or he gets what he wants. We can't both be satisfied." Since both persons in a symbiotic relationship share this belief, there is a continuous struggle for the Child position. This struggle can occur between husband and wife, parent and child, and at times grandparent and parent. This hunger for dependency has been pointed out by Blumberg, who described one group of abusing parents as "markedly passive, dependent, moody, and immature. They often competed with their own children for the love and attention of spouses. . . . [A] mother may actually want a child with the hope and desire for comfort from the child for herself. . . . She seeks and expects gratification from the child."[39] Further evidence of the shifting symbiosis was provided by Paulsen, who described a case of a three-month-old baby who died of malnutrition and dehydration because his mother fed him only when she and her husband got along well together.[40] In other words, she was a Parent to her infant only when her husband took care of her Child.

What happens in the abusing family, then, is a frantic struggle to be taken care of, with any and all forms of passivity escalated to whatever level is necessary. Thus the parent beats his biological child into "obedience" because his own Child needs to be responded to. Kempe has described one result: "Some children . . . learn to survive by taking care of their parents and, in a curious role reversal, becoming the mothering figure to the battering parent."[41]

Siamese-twinning Scripts

Symbiosis, then, is the result of messages conveyed, both verbally and nonverbally, in infancy and early childhood. Those messages can be viewed as life-script injunctions or parent-conveyed dictums about how to survive. Since these life plans are basically unconscious, they motivate a person's actions and thoughts outside his awareness.[42]

Partners in a symbiotic relationship have interlocking scripts, so that one cannot act without involving the other, just as one Siamese twin cannot move without moving the other.[43] Thus, the partners tacitly agree about the direction in which they will move. This agreement is true even if only one person acts and the other goes along by doing nothing to stop him or change the course of that action. This is the case in the abusing family, where there is usually one actor and one passive observer. The scripts of both members of an abusing couple are usually similar, but usually one person is scripted to do the acting while the other does the observing.

The script matrix (see Figures 3–3 and 3–4) demonstrates how messages that reinforce symbiotic patterns are conveyed from the biological parents or parent-surrogates to the child.[44] The messages conveyed from the parent's Parent to the child's Parent are usually verbal. Those passed from the parent's Child to the child's Child are most often nonverbal and are the major determinants of his later feelings and behavior. The message from the parent's Adult to the child's Adult is conveyed in the form of behavior that demonstrates how the script messages are to be carried out.

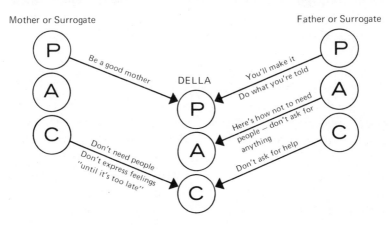

Mother or Surrogate — Father or Surrogate

Be a good mother
DELLA
You'll make it
Do what you're told
Here's how not to need people – don't ask for anything
Don't ask for help
Don't need people
Don't express feelings "until it's too late"

Figure 3–3 "Siamese Twinning" Script Matrix of Child Abuser

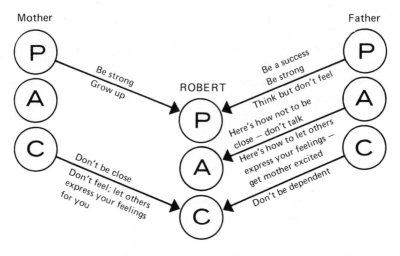

Figure 3–4   "Siamese Twinning" Script Matrix of Child Abuser's Partner

Figures 3–3 and 3–4 illustrate the similarity between the script injunctions (Child-to-Child messages) of spouses in an abusing family. Della is the actor and Robert, the observer. In terms of symbiosis, Della acts out the role of Child, letting tension about her baby's constant, colicky crying build up until, in rage, she fractures the child's arm. Robert, having assumed the roles of Parent and Adult, does nothing ahead of time to alleviate Della's stress, but coolly takes care of things after the child's arm is broken. Both parents have been programmed not to ask others for anything and not to show feelings.

Clyde and Frances, like Della and Robert, have Siamese-twinning, or interlocking scripts. As seen in Figure 3–6, Frances is the Parent and Adult to Clyde's Child (Figure 3–5) in terms of functioning at home: e.g., Clyde plays on the floor with the children while Frances tries to control all of them. Clyde is the one who beats their four-year-old daughter with a belt while Frances stands by, angry but too ineffectual to stop him. Both parents have been pro-

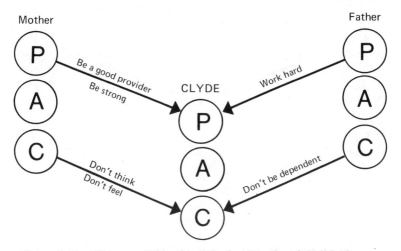

Figure 3–5 "Siamese Twinning" Script Matrix of Child Abuser

grammed not to be dependent and to be inadequate in controlling their feelings. Although each can think and feel, neither can do both at the same time. Neither Frances nor Clyde, and few others in a symbiotic relationship, think about feelings.

A FINAL WORD ABOUT SHIFTING SYMBIOSIS

Symbiosis is commonly found among many couples who never abuse their children. The major difference between these parents and abusing parents seems to be a matter of internal restrictions; these restrictions prevent nonabusive parents from taking the Child role in a symbiotic relationship with their own children. In other words, these parents turn to each other, their own parents, or outsiders to be taken care of symbiotically, and they are usually aware of what ego-states they are turning on and off. They possess some kind of internal brake that keeps them from turning

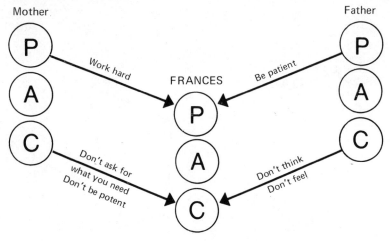

Figure 3–6 "Siamese Twinning" Script Matrix of Child Abuser's Partner

to a child for nurturing. Unfortunately, abusing parents seem to lack that brake, perhaps because their own parents turned to them for nurturing when they were children. Thus when their own child fails them in the symbiosis, the failure seems to be the last straw and frustration turns to overt aggression. According to Dollard's frustration-aggression hypothesis, violence is often the end result of a high level of frustration.[45]

NOTES

1. R. E. Helfer, *Child abuse and neglect self-instructional program* (Committee on Infant and Preschool Child, American Academy of Pediatrics, Chicago, Ill., and National Center for the Prevention and Treatment of Child Abuse and Neglect, Denver, Colo., 1974), Unit 1.

2. M. Bowen, "Family therapy and family group therapy," in H. I. Kaplan and B. J. Sadock (eds.), *Comprehensive group psychotherapy* (Baltimore, Md.: William & Wilkins, 1971), p. 399.

3. F. I. Bishop, "Children at risk," *Medical Journal of Australia,* 1 (March 1971), pp. 623–628.

4. S. Isaacs, "Neglect, cruelty and battering," *British Medical Journal,* 3 (July 1972), pp. 224–226.

5. C. H. Kempe, "Paediatric implications of the battered baby syndrome," *Archives of Disease in Childhood,* 46 (February, 1971), pp. 28–37.

6. B. Justice and D. F. Duncan, "Physical abuse of children as a public health problem," *Public Health Reviews,* 4 (April-June 1975), pp. 183–200.

7. W. R. Flynn, "Frontier justice: A contribution to the theory of child battery," *American Journal of Psychiatry,* 127 (September 1970), pp. 375–379.

8. Bishop, op. cit.
9. B. Justice and R. Justice, "A psychosocial model of child abuse: Intervention strategies and group techniques," paper presented before the Clinical and Research Training Seminar, Texas Research Institute of Mental Sciences, Houston, Tex., February 15, 1974; and Justice and Duncan, op. cit.
10. R. L. Jenkins et al., "Interrupting the family cycle of violence," *Journal of Iowa Medical Society,* 30 (February 1970), pp. 85–89; and M. H. Lystad, "Violence at home: A review of the literature," *American Journal of Orthopsychiatry,* 45 (April 1975), pp. 328–345.
11. M. Bowen, "The use of family theory in clinical practice," *Comprehensive Psychiatry,* 7 (October 1966), pp. 345–374.
12. Anonymous, "Toward the differentiation of a self in one's own family," in J. L. Framo (ed.), *Family Interaction* (New York: Springer, 1972), p. 121.
13. Ibid., p. 119.
14. Bowen, "The use of family theory in clinical practice," pp. 360–361.
15. Bowen, "Family therapy and family group therapy," p. 398.
16. C. Whitaker, Family Therapy Workshop. Presented at the Southeast Institute Second Annual Spring Conference, Raleigh, N.C., March 21, 1975.
17. Bowen, "The use of family theory in clinical practice," p. 360.
18. Justice and Justice, op. cit.
19. Bowen, "Family therapy and family group therapy," p. 398.
20. Bowen, "The use of family theory in clinical practice," pp. 359–360.
21. Ibid.
22. T. Gordon, *Parent effectiveness training* (New York: Wyden, 1970), pp. 121–138.
23. H. Martin, "The child and his development," in C. H. Kempe and R. E. Helfer (eds.), *Helping the battered child and his family* (Philadelphia, Pa.: Lippincott, 1972), p. 104; and Helfer, op. cit.
24. O. J. Keller, "Hypothesis for violent crime," *American Journal of Correction,* 37 (March-April 1975), p. 7.
25. W. Sage, "Violence in the children's room," *Human Behavior,* 4 (July 1975), p. 47.
26. B. F. Steele, as quoted in Kempe, op. cit., p. 30.
27. A. W. Schiff and J. L. Schiff, "Passivity," *Transactional Analysis Journal,* 1 (January 1971), p. 71.

28. E. Fromm, as quoted in H. B. English and A. C. English (eds.), *A comprehensive dictionary of psychological and psychoanalytical terms* (New York: Longmans, Green, 1958), p. 538.

29. Schiff and Schiff, op. cit., p. 71.

30. Ibid.

31. Ibid., p. 72.

32. Ibid., pp. 72–73.

33. E. Berne, *Principles of group treatment* (New York: Oxford University Press, 1966), p. 220.

34. C. Steiner, *Games alcoholics play* (New York: Grove Press, 1971), pp. 3–4.

35. Schiff and Schiff, op. cit., p. 72.

36. E. Berne, *What do you say after you say hello?* (New York: Grove Press, 1972), pp. 106–107.

37. F. Perls, *Gestalt therapy verbatim* (Lafayette, Calif.: Real People Press, 1969).

38. C. H. Kempe, "The battered child and the hospital," *Hospital Practice*, 4 (October 1969), pp. 44–57.

39. M. L. Blumberg, "Psychopathology of the abusing parent," *American Journal of Psychotherapy*, 28 (January 1974), p. 25.

40. M. B. Paulsen, "The law and abused children," in R. E. Helfer and C. H. Kempe (eds.), *The Battered Child* (Chicago: University of Chicago Press, 1968), p. 165.

41. Kempe, op. cit., p. 56.

42. Berne, op. cit., p. 36.

43. B. Justice and R. Justice, " 'Siamese-twinning' in scripts of child batterers." Paper presented before the International Transactional Analysis Association Summer Conference, San Francisco, Calif., August 1973.

44. Steiner, op. cit., p. 29.

45. J. Dollard et al., *Frustration and aggression* (New Haven, Conn.: Yale University Press, 1939), p. 1.

Chapter 4

EPIDEMIOLOGICAL FEATURES OF CHILD ABUSE

Since epidemiology is concerned with the magnitude and distribution of health problems, along with their antecedents and consequences, a systems approach is particularly useful for exploring features of the host, environment, agent, and vector involved.[1] This chapter elaborates on the characteristics of parents who abuse, on the child who is abused, the cultural scripts that influence interaction between them, and the setting in which abuse occurs. Since historical practices and tradition are part of the antecedents to abuse, we will take a brief look at the past as it bears on the problem.

HISTORICAL PREVIEW

Child abuse is as old as the history of man. Even in mythology, children were murdered, sacrificed, beaten, abandoned, or mutilated.[2] There have been many justifications for abuse: religious beliefs, birth control, cultural rituals, superstitions, discipline, and monetary gain. The early Greeks' attitude toward children was expressed by Aristotle as follows: "The justice of a master or a father is a different thing from that of a citizen, for a son or slave is property, and there can be no injustice to one's own property."[3] The 1633 *Bibliotheca Scholastica* repeated the Old Testament admonition not to "spare the rod and spoil the child."[4]

The Roman rule of *Patria Postestas*—which stated that a father owned his child and therefore had the right to treat the child as he saw fit[5]—is no longer legally sanctioned, but it still is unofficially in effect. In colonial America, a father had the right not only to kill his child but to call on colony officers to assist him.[6] It was "also common to flog children without provocation ... to 'break them of their willfulness' and make them tractable, ostensibly for the good of their souls."[7] Until the nineteenth century, "dead or abandoned infants were almost commonplace on city streets. As late as 1892, 200 foundlings and 100 dead infants were found on the streets of New York City alone."[8]

There are still countries (including the United States) where infants are discarded because the family is too large or they are defective or unwanted. There are also countries where children are beaten and mutilated for a variety of reasons.[9] In Houston, Texas, a young couple made front-page headlines after being accused of trying to sell their three-month-old baby for $100. An assistant district attorney determined there was no law in Texas against selling a baby.[10]

Efforts to curb child abuse date back many centuries. Radbill cites seventeenth-century publications that pleaded for more lenient treatment of children. But it was not until the late 1800s that preventive action was taken in the United States. When nine-year-old Mary Ellen was found chained to her bed in a dingy tenement in New York City, the American Society for the Prevention of Cruelty to Animals intervened because no society for the protection of children existed. It was only after the case gained wide public attention that the first American organization concerned with children's rights—the New York Society for the Prevention of Cruelty to Children—was established.[11]

Public and other private agencies began entering the field of child welfare shortly after the turn of the century when the first White House Conference on Child Health and the American Association for Study and Prevention of Infant Mortality convened in 1909.[12] Recently, perhaps as a result of widely publicized findings on the prevalence of child abuse,[13] the federal government established a National Center for Child Abuse and Neglect. As Radbill notes: "[Because] of this recent surge of interest, the problems of the battered child are taking on a new phase in our history. The progress made in the last decade is only a beginning of man's attempt to change the life of these unfortunate children."[14]

INCIDENCE AND PREVALENCE OF CHILD ABUSE

The epidemiology of child abuse underscores the fact that such violence is a public health problem—community-wide in scope, not only in the United States but overseas.[15] Bishop reports that "the number of children at risk appears to be increasing . . . to the point where it would appear that their plight and number constitute the largest single public health problem awaiting solution."[16] Whether child abuse is the "largest" public health problem yet to be solved is debatable, but the evidence tends to confirm predictions of a rapid increase in the incidence—if not prevalence—of child abuse.

A central registry established by Gil for all reported cases of child abuse that occurred in 1967 and 1968 revealed 5,993 cases for the first year and 6,617 cases for the second. These figures represent an incidence rate per 100,000 children under the age of 18 of 8.4 and 9.3, respectively, for the two years. Kempe estimated that between

30,000 and 50,000 cases of child abuse (or 6 per every 1,000 live births) occur each year in the United States, based on reported cases in Denver and New York in 1971.[17] Note the difference in bases between Kempe's and Gil's estimates.

An increase in the incidence of abuse is being reported not only on the national level but on the local level. For instance, in Texas—which Gil's survey indicated had the highest number of reported cases in the nation—the Child Welfare Unit in Harris County, the state's most populous county, investigated an average of 30 reports of abuse per month in 1972, 60 per month in 1973, and 80 per month in 1974.[18] Projections for 1975 were 187 reports per month, the increase related in large part to a statewide public information campaign on child abuse (see Chapter 8).

As for the prevalence of abuse, both Kempe's and Gil's estimates are based on reported cases and therefore do not include children who (1) were not treated by a physician, (2) were treated by a physician but were not identified as abused, or (3) were identified as abused but were not reported. These factors lend credence to the statement that there are at least 100 unreported cases for every reported case.[19] In 1973 Lynch estimated that reported cases represented only 1 to 10 per cent of the total.[20] In addition, Kempe estimated that roughly 25 per cent of all fractures seen in children under the age of two are caused by child abuse and that 10 to 15 per cent of all children under three years of age treated for trauma in hospitals have been abused, regardless of what their parents say or what social class they belong to.[21]

As we have noted, estimates of how much child abuse exists vary considerably. The highest estimate—3,726 to 5,994 cases per 100,000 children a year—is based on a national survey conducted in 1965. Interviewers asked people whether they knew of any cases of child abuse that had occurred during the previous 12 months.[22] Because the results of the survey were based on what people believed were cases of child abuse rather than on confirmed cases, it probably overstated the problem. When school authorities throughout the United States were asked about the amount of child abuse they observed, the result was 40 per 100,000 *school-age* children.[23] Kempe's estimate, when converted to a base of 100,000 children between the ages of one day and 18 years, amounts to 49 to 63 per 100,000 children. (Gil placed the figure at 8.4 to 9.3.) The Texas Department of Public Welfare estimated the number of cases to be 51.8 per 100,000 children; in Connecticut the estimate was 37.8 per 100,000 children.[24] Until states establish central registries based on uniform standards and reporting laws, and use a uniform definition of child abuse, disagreements about the size of the problem will continue.

Helfer estimates that the number of reports are increasing at the rate of 30 per cent a year and that between 1973 and 1982 there will be 1.5 million reports, 50,000 deaths, 300,000 permanent injuries, and 1 million potential abusers.[25] Based on a 15 to 20 per cent increase per year, Ryan predicted 500,000 cases of child battering and 50,000 deaths would occur between 1973 and 1977.[26] Fontana arrived at an estimate of 1.5 million cases of child abuse for 1973.[27] If this figure is correct and if the number of cases is increasing at a rate of 30 per cent a year, the amount of abuse that will occur in 1982 is staggering.

CHARACTERISTICS OF ABUSIVE PARENTS

Relationship to Victim

Perhaps the most extensive data on the epidemiological characteristics of abusing parents was collected by Gil,[28] who found that 86.8 per cent of the perpetrators of child abuse in his sample were parents or parent surrogates. The mother or mother substitute inflicted the abuse in 47.6 per cent of the cases; the father or father substitute did so in 39.2 per cent. In 12.1 per cent of the cases the abuser was another relative, and in 1.1 per cent the perpetrator was unknown.

Our sample is somewhat different because we work with only couples who have abused their children. Therefore, statistics on abuse by nonparents are not applicable. Among the abusing parents or parent surrogates in our group, the mother was the perpetrator in 50 per cent of the cases while the father or father substitute was the perpetrator in 45 per cent of the cases. In 5 per cent of the cases, both parents inflicted the abuse. Our figures are based on a sample of 20 couples.

In Gil's study, 71.1 per cent of the abuse was committed by biological parents, 13.6 per cent by step-parents, 0.4 per cent by adoptive parents, and 14.9 per cent by foster parents, siblings, relatives, nonrelatives, or persons whose relationship to the victim was unknown. In our group, the biological parent was the abuser in 75 per cent of the cases; the step-parent, in 20 per cent; and the biological and step-parent, in 5 per cent. In no instances did the adoptive parent inflict the abuse. In Gil's sample, the child's biological father lived in the home in 46 per cent of the cases; in almost one-fifth of the cases, a stepfather was in the home. The home lacked a male parent in 29.5 per cent of the cases. The child's biological mother was not present in 12 per cent of the cases, and no female was present in 1.74 per cent of the cases.[29]

Having two parent figures in the home was a condition for acceptance into our group. Thus there are no cases of absent male or female figures in our sample. In a child abuse project involving 376 children, it was found that 68 per cent lived with two parents.[30] In our sample, biological fathers were present in 75 per cent of the cases and stepfathers or father substitutes were present in 25 per cent. The biological mother was in the home in 95 per cent of the cases, and stepmothers were present in 5 per cent.

Sex of Abuser

Gil's findings indicated that the perpetrator of the abuse was more likely to be female than male.[31] Zalba, however, found an even split between male and female abusers.[32] Of ten cases reported by Bennie and Sclare, seven abusers were women; in 50 out of 57 cases reported by Steele and Pollock, the child's mother was the abuser.[33] In our sample of 20 couples, 50 per cent of the abuse was inflicted by women, 45 per cent by men, and 5 per cent by both a man and a woman. Gil, however, notes that 29.5 per cent of the children in his study lived in fatherless homes.[34] Fathers or father substitutes were the perpetrators in approximately two-thirds of the incidents that occurred in homes containing a male parent, whereas mothers were the perpetrators in slightly less than half the cases in homes containing female parents. Thus in Gil's study men perpetrated the abuse more often than did women, when a male parent was present, a finding supported by our data as well.

Age of Abuser

Not surprisingly, most abusers range in age from 20 to 40, the typical child-bearing, child-rearing ages. In Gil's sample, 71.2 per cent of the mothers or mother substitutes and 65.9 per cent of the fathers or father substitutes were in this age bracket.[35] The parents in our group were comparable: 75 per cent were between 20 and 40 years old at the time of the reported incident and 25 per cent were under 20. Less than 10 per cent of the mothers and less than 3 per cent of the fathers were younger than 20 in Gil's sample.

Socioeconomic Factors

Bennie and Sclare reported that eight out of ten cases in their study were in low-income families.[36] Seventy-seven per cent of the fathers in Gil's sample were skilled or semi-skilled workers, 9.5 per cent were white-collar workers or professionals, and the occupations of 13.5 per cent were unknown. Thirty-nine per cent of the mothers were employed (68.3 per cent in skilled or semiskilled jobs and 12 per cent in white-collar or professional jobs).[37] Thus there is a general pattern of low occupational status among parents involved in *reported* cases of child abuse, which our data also reflects to a lesser degree. As we pointed out in Chapter 2, *reported* cases of abuse give a misleading impression as to the socioeconomic and educational status of persons who inflict violence on children. This is so because "upper-class persons are able to get help from private doctors who are sometimes willing to let the abuse go unreported, while lower-class persons must go to the public hospital, which is required to make a report."[38] Although private physicians are required to report cases of abuse, they are less likely to do so.

Eighty-five per cent of the men in our group held skilled or semiskilled jobs and 15 per cent were in white collar or professional occupations. Forty per cent of the women were members of the labor force: 88 per cent of these women held skilled or semiskilled jobs and 12 per cent were in white collar or professional positions. Two out of the 20 families were receiving welfare when the abuse occurred and an additional 10 per cent received other public assistance grants. Nearly 60 per cent of the families in Gil's sample received or had received public assistance.[39] Although Gil's figures are high compared with those of

other studies, unemployment *is* disproportionately prevalent among parents who inflict violence on children. Light
found that "the variable that shows up most frequently as
somehow related to child abuse is father's unemployment. This finding confirms a widely held theory that family
stress . . . related to unemployment ties in to incidence of
abuse."[40]

Gil's sample and ours differ in terms of education: our
group tended to be better educated. The majority of parents in Gil's study were not high school graduates: 57.7 per
cent of the women and 48.5 per cent of the men had between nine and 13 years of education; only 4.8 per cent of
the women and 8.5 per cent of the men had college degrees
or graduate training. Approximately 24 per cent of both
women and men had less than nine years of education.[41] In
our sample, 20 per cent of the men and women had college
or graduate training or degrees; 70 per cent were high
school graduates; and 10 per cent had a grade school education.

Eighty-five per cent of the members of our group were
Caucasian and 15 per cent were black. (In Houston 62 per
cent of the population is white, 26 per cent is black, and 12
per cent is Mexican-American.)

Emotional History

By definition, abusing parents have problems concerning
effective parenting, which may be related to lack of information and cognitive skills or to emotional factors that
result in what Kempe calls "serious problems in mothering."[42] The problems in emotional functioning of some of
these parents extend beyond the area of parenting and
predate adulthood. Gil reported that the histories of abusing parents include foster home placement, hospitalization
for mental illness, juvenile court experience, criminal
records, and deviant intellectual functioning.[43] Both au-

thors found that abusing parents tend to have experienced deprivation, if not actual physical abuse. Eighty-five per cent of those in our sample indicated similar deprivation. Fourteen per cent of the mothers and 7 per cent of the fathers in Gil's sample were victims of abuse in childhood.[44] In our sample, 30 per cent of the abusers had been severely beaten when disciplined as children; 13 per cent had been in foster care.

Ten and one-half per cent of the mothers and 9.6 per cent of the fathers in Gil's study had suffered medical problems during the preceding years. Social and behavioral deviance appeared in almost 43 per cent of the mothers and 45 per cent of the fathers.[45] Kempe found that approximately 5 per cent of abusing families have one parent who is psychotic; another 5 per cent have a parent who appears to be an aggressive psychopath.[46] In our group, 5 per cent seemed to be borderline psychotic. According to the classifications in the *Diagnostic and Statistical Manual II* of the American Psychiatric Association, the remainder fit no category at all or fell into various categories, the most common being "explosive personality."

Other Personality Characteristics

As indicated in earlier chapters, parents who abuse their children have a variety of personality characteristics in common. A profile of the abusing personality includes features such as isolation from others, poor self-image, a high need for nurturing, and a tendency to discount the importance of problems and solutions as well as other people and their feelings. Other features might include problems with alcohol.[47]

Abusing parents report that they lack support from family and friends. Since they do not reach out to others, to help or to be helped, this is not surprising. As Helfer says, abusive parents are unable either to use or to help others.[48] Furthermore, they "have no one they feel they can turn to for advice or help, and have few social contacts that might be developed as such a resource."[49] Because abusing parents are likely to have been subjected to deprivation or abuse in their own childhood, they never learned how to give and receive love in a normal manner. They hunger for dependence and frequently choose mates with similar backgrounds and emotional difficulties.[50]

These parents also have unrealistic expectations concerning their children. They seek satisfaction of unmet needs for comfort and nurture from their own child. When the child fails to deliver, the parent interprets this failure as a rejection and his anger and frustration mount.[51]

Unmet needs for love and comfort are highly significant factors in the personality profile of people who abuse and underlie the high demands they place on their children's behavior. "Not only is the demand for performance great, but it is premature, clearly beyond the ability of the infant to comprehend what is wanted and to respond appropriately. Parents deal with the child as if he were much older than he really is."[52] In other words, these parents behave like children themselves and want their children to act like parents.[53] This phenomenon has been referred to as role reversal.[54]

The same pattern can be found in the abusive parents' family histories. Similar premature demands were placed on them when they were children, and they were deprived of basic mothering and a deep sense of being cared for. Thus they learned to comply to their parents' demands and, because their needs were unmet, they never learned to trust or to turn to others for help. This pattern goes back even farther: "It appears that the grandparents, too, were subjected to a constellation of parental attitudes similar to that described above."[55] Thus the pattern may be seen as a script for behavior that has been transmitted from parent to child for at least three generations (see Chapter 3).

Characteristics of the Abused Child

Child abuse is sometimes termed the "battered baby syndrome," suggesting that it is a problem involving infants and very young children. Kempe stated that abuse was most common among children under three years of age; Galdston found the problem most frequently among children aged three months to three-and-a-half years. According to Bennie and Sclare, two- to four-month-old infants are the primary target of abuse; Resnick reported that child murder is most common in the first year of life.[56] But when Gil studied the problem from an epidemiological rather than clinical viewpoint, he found that only about one-third of the victims of abuse were under the age of three, while almost half were six or older. However, the first year of life remained the highest risk year—approximately 13 per cent of the cases occurred during the first 12 months.[57] Other investigators also note that abuse occurs more frequently after early childhood. Lynch, for example, found that 51 per cent of child abuse cases occurred among children ages six to 17 years. "Recognition of child abuse as a phenomenon of the older child—the school child—has been slow."[58] It may be that "although the most dramatic abuse occurs in the younger child, the most frequent abuse occurs in the school-age child. These children have been battered but managed to survive the high-risk years."[59]

There is little doubt that abuse is a problem among school-age children as well as infants and babies. Our findings, however, agree with those of investigators who have found that the very young are at highest risk. Among the children abused by parents in our group, 67 per cent were between four months and three years of age. When four-year-olds are included, the percentage jumps to 79 per cent. Our data agree with those of Gil, who found that although the first year of life is a high-risk year, two- and three-year-olds are at equally high risk.

In a study of 376 abused children in Buffalo, New York, Thomson et al. compared the percentages of abused children found in various age brackets with the percentages of children in each age bracket in the total population.[60] The findings were as follows:

Age groups	Percentage of total child population	Percentage of abused children
5 years or under	35	49
6–9	25	22
10–17	40	29

Gil reports that more than half of the abused children in his studies were male (73 per cent in 1967 and 51 per cent in 1968).[61] Forty-one per cent of the abused children in our sample were male and 59 percent were female.

Although high-risk groups of children will be discussed in Chapter 8, we will note here that Bishop identified six groups of children that are in special risk of abuse: (1) illegitimate children, (2) premature babies, (3) congenitally malformed babies, (4) twins, (5) children conceived during the mother's depressive illness, and (6) children of mothers with frequent pregnancies and excessive work loads.[62] Few (17 per cent) of the abused children of parents in our group were illegitimate, and one-fourth were born to depressed mothers. Zalba reported that 50 per cent of the abused children in Massachusetts were conceived out of wedlock.[63]

Bennie and Sclare found that abused children are usually the youngest or only child in the family, but Gil reported that abused children were twice as likely to come from families with four or more children than was true for the population at large.[64] Several studies in the United States, England, and New Zealand indicate that "the average family size for abusing families substantially exceeds the national average."[65] In our sample, none of the abused children came from families with four or more children. The largest percentage (38) come from families with two children.

Thomson et al. determined that one specific child is the target of abuse in an overwhelming percentage of abusing families: in 88 per cent of the 376 cases he studied, only one child was involved.[66] In our group, only one child was abused in 80 per cent of the cases.

As to seriousness of injuries, in 90 per cent of Gil's sample (N=1380) and 95 per cent of ours (N=20), no lasting physical effect on the children was expected. Although over half the incidents in both samples were not considered serious, 3.4 per cent of Gil's samples were fatal. None of the incidents of abuse from our sample was fatal.[67]

Harrington reports that children contribute to their own abuse in the following ways:

> There is evidence that children who are battered show disturbances of sleep and feeding, cry excessively and respond poorly to attempts to comfort them. How far these features are a direct result of parental attitudes and how far they contribute to abuse is impossible to say, but there is a strong presumption that irritable babies are more likely to fall victims than placid ones. Premature babies, hypersensitive babies, colicky and unresponsive babies are especially vulnerable.[68]

As mentioned in Chapter 3 (see also Chapter 8) difficult babies and children apparently contribute to the likelihood of abuse. Some have "a particularly grating quality to their crying; nurses and social workers have confessed understanding why a parent might batter 'THAT CHILD.' "[69] The literature implies that even normal parents may abuse a particularly irritating or difficult child.[70] Martin states that the aggressive child "perpetuates the notion that many of these children would invite abuse from the most normal of parents," and Flynn comments that "the obnoxious child" is a likely target of abuse.[71]

The question is whether some children are constitutionally and temperamentally so difficult that the average parent may be moved to use excessive measures of management. The presumption has been that "children are neither good nor bad. . . . If they are usually irritable, fearful, obstinate or sly, their parents have helped to make them that way."[72] This problem will be discussed in greater detail in Chapter 8.

DEMOGRAPHIC PROFILES OF THE ABUSED AND ABUSING

Although the findings on demographic features of the abused child and abusing parents vary, Solomon offers the following composite picture:[73]

Abused child

Average age is under four years; most are less than two.

Average death rate ranges from 5 to 25 per cent; average age at death is slightly less than three years.

Average duration of exposure to abuse is one to three years.

Child's sex is not a factor.

Abusive parents

Overwhelming majority are married and living together when abuse occurs.

Average age of abusive mother is 26; average age of abusive father is 30.

Father is the abuser slightly more often than the mother.

Mother commits the serious abuse more often than the father.

Most common instrument of abuse is the hairbrush.

Family dynamics

Thirty to 60 per cent of the abusing parents say they were abused as children.

High proportion of abused children were conceived before their parents' marriage.

Parents tend to marry young.

Forced marriages and unwanted or illegitimate pregnancies are common.

Parents tend to be socially isolated.

Emotional problems in the marriage are common.

Financial difficulties are prevalent.

Two additional demographic findings can be added to Solomon's composite, based on a large study by Lenoski, who compared 674 abusing parents with a control group of 500 nonabusers.[74] Sixty-five per cent of the abusers in his sample reported early exposure to violence in the home, compared to 43 per cent of the nonabusers; 80 per cent of the abusers claimed religious affiliation, compared with 62 per cent of the nonabusers.

SCRIPTING

As we pointed out in Chapter 3, a psychosocial systems model of child abuse is appropriately depicted in public health terms. One influencing factor is the vector from agent (child) to host (parents). The vector in our model is the cultural scripting of the parents—the behavior produced by culturally sanctioned messages, injunctions, and myths about how parents should think, feel, and act toward their children.

We commented that the "Madonna-child" myth has a deleterious effect on interactions between mother and child because it leads the mother to believe she must be infinitely patient and loving 24 hours a day. Equally insidious is the "bundle-of-joy" or "Gerber-baby" myth, which gives rise to expectations that a baby is a constant joy—a clean, cuddly creature who smiles lovingly at his mother and sleeps peacefully in her arms. This myth is promoted by television commercials and advertisements in women's magazines. Mothers who believe it are in for a rude awakening—often accompanied by frustration and anger—when the baby turns out to be fussy, smelly, and wiggly.

Another product of cultural scripting is the ancient idea that children are property of their parents. As we pointed out, in many early societies parents had the right to sell or kill their children at will. Residual attitudes can be seen in the results of the National Opinion Research Center Survey, in which a majority of people interviewed said that even if a child is undeniably beaten and abused, he should be removed from his parents' custody only as a last resort.[75]

Physical punishment of children is another practice included in the cultural scripting of many American parents as well as those in other countries. There is considerable evidence that

> physical violence toward children is acceptable in our society. "Spare the rod and spoil the child" is the philosophy of many people, including teachers, social workers, doctors and judges. There is societal sanction for corporal punishment, but there are no specific rules to distinguish discipline from abuse. Parents can feel justified in using a certain amount of force.[76]

Even nursery rhymes give subtle sanction to physical punishment. For example:

> There was an old woman who lived in a shoe;
> She had so many children, she didn't know what to do.
> She gave them some broth without any bread
> Then whipped them all soundly and sent them to bed.

In the minds of many abusing parents, this type of cultural endorsement gives a degree of legitimacy to physical abuse of children because it is sometimes difficult to delineate sharply where corporal punishment ends and physical abuse begins.

The effect of these cultural scripts is to intensify the impact of the stress the child creates for the scripted parent and to make the parent respond more harshly toward the child. These scripts also tend to contribute to outside intervention since parents are scripted to believe that children are their property and that discipline is their right. Thus parents suspected of abuse "feel blamed, picked on, and interfered with in an area that they regard as no one's business but their own—how to raise their children."[77]

Setting, Circumstances, and Type of Abuse

The home is the most common location for child abuse. More than 90 per cent of the cases of abuse in Gil's study occurred in the child's home,[78] and all the incidents of abuse in our sample took place in the home.

The environment of the home in which abuse occurs will be discussed in more detail later. Briefly, abuse is more likely to occur in a crowded home, in one in which the family is large, or one in which unemployment is a problem. There is also the part played by excessive change (characteristic of a "throw-away society"), and the constant readjustments it requires a family to make often leaves the family without resources to bail itself out.

> Many mothers, and some fathers, in today's crowded and often shifting home environments, without the advantages of the extended family or the understanding neighbor, simply reach a breaking point. Someone to take over for an hour —even someone to talk to for a few minutes—can make the difference. That person may be less likely to be there today than in the past.[79]

The factor of mobility was more pronounced in our group than in Gil's. Nearly all (85 per cent) of the couples in our sample had lived in their present home for less than one year at the time of the reported abuse. In Gil's sample less than half the families had been living in their present home for one year or less.[80] Forty per cent of our families owned their own home, 55 per cent rented an apartment, and one family (5 per cent) lived with relatives. Twenty per cent lived in trailer homes. None of the families lived in public housing. Nearly 12 per cent of Gil's families lived in low-cost public housing, approximately 51 per cent lived in privately rented apartments, 18 per cent rented homes, only 13 per cent owned their own homes. More than 14 per cent shared their living quarters with another family.

Abuse takes place most frequently around dinner time. According to Gil's study, 19 per cent of the incidents took place between 3 and 6 P.M., 20 per cent between 6 and 9 in the evening, and 9 per cent between 9 P.M. and midnight. During the remaining three-hour periods, the incidence of abuse varied from 1 and 9 per cent.[81] Our findings were similar to Gil's: 30 per cent of the incidents occurred between 3 and 6 P.M., 50 per cent between 6 and 9 P.M., and 20 per cent in the morning between 7 and 10.

With regard to the circumstances surrounding the abuse, Thomson et al. found that 57 per cent of the incidents were an "immediate or delayed response to a specific act of the child . . . [such as] crying, failure to eat, wetting the bed, normal developmental problems."[82] The abuse followed serious misconduct—such as stealing, running away, playing on railroad tracks—in only 10 per cent of cases. In 13 per cent of the cases the perpetrator was drunk, and in 11 per cent the abuser viewed himself as a "stern, authoritarian disciplinarian."

In Gil's study, the most common injuries were bruises and welts (67 per cent), which were usually inflicted by hand or with instruments.[83] Bruises and welts accounted for 85 per cent of the injuries in our sample; 5 per cent involved skull fractures; 5 per cent involved other types of fractures; and 5 per cent involved burns. Gil reported fewer skull fractures (4 per cent) and more "other" fractures (10 per cent). Injuries were inflicted by hand in 65 per cent of our cases and with an instrument, usually a belt, in 35 per cent. In Gil's study, children were beaten with instruments in 44 per cent of the cases and by hand in 39 per cent of the cases.

In summary, abuse is most likely to be inflicted upon a young child, in his home, by his parent(s), who beat him in response to his behavior. As we saw earlier, without considering all of these elements—the child, the parents, the environment, and the interaction among them—an understanding of child abuse will be incomplete. In Chapter 5 we will look at how intervention can be made by focusing on these different elements and their interaction.

NOTES

1. B. Justice and D. Duncan, "Physical abuse of children as a public health problem," *Public Health Review*, 4 (April-June 1975), pp. 183–200.
2. S. X. Radbill, "A history of child abuse and infanticide," in R. E. Helfer and C. H. Kempe (eds.), *The battered child* (Chicago: University of Chicago Press, 1968), pp. 3–21.
3. R. J. Light, "Abused and neglected children in America: A study of alternative policies," *Harvard Educational Review*, 143 (November 1973), p. 559.
4. Ibid.
5. E. Gibbon, *The decline and fall of the Roman Empire* (New York: Collier, 1899), pp. 352–353.
6. Light, op. cit., p. 559.
7. S. Zalba, "Battered children," *Trans-Action*, 8 (July-August 1971), pp. 58–61.
8. W. Sage, "Violence in the children's room," *Human Behavior*, 4 (July 1975), p. 42.
9. V. J. Fontana, *Somewhere a child is crying* (New York: Macmillan, 1973).
10. *The Houston Post*, April 3, 1975, p. Al.

11. Although the New York Society for the Prevention of Cruelty to Children has been in existence for a century now, the latest reports indicate that the Society for the Prevention of Cruelty to Animals still has more contributors; Light, op. cit., p. 559.

12. S. X. Radbill, op. cit., pp. 3–21.

13. C. H. Kempe, "Paediatric implications of the battered baby syndrome," *Archives of Disease in Childhood*, 46 (February 1971), pp. 28–37; Justice and Duncan, op. cit., pp. 184–185.

14. S. X. Radbill, op. cit., pp. 3–21.

15. Justice and Duncan, op. cit., pp. 184–185.

16. F. I. Bishop, "Children at risk," *Medical Journal of Australia*, 1 (March 1971), p. 623.

17. D. G. Gil, *Violence against children* (Cambridge, Mass.: Harvard University Press, 1970); and Kempe, op. cit., pp. 28–37.

18. "Child abuse statistics," Harris County Child Welfare Unit, Houston, Tex., 1974.

19. R. Burns, as quoted in V. J. Fontana, op. cit., p. 19.

20. A. Lynch, "Child abuse in the school-age population," *Journal of School Health*, 35 (March 1975), pp. 141–148.

21. Kempe, op. cit., pp. 28–37.

22. See Gil, op. cit., pp. 58–60.

23. K. Drews, "The child and his school," in C. H. Kempe and R. E. Helfer (eds.). *Helping the battered child and his family* (Philadelphia, Pa.: Lippincott, 1972), p. 117.

24. *Houston report on children* (Houston, Tex.: Child Care Council, February 1, 1975), p. 3; and J. B. G. Trouen-Trend and M. Leonard, "Prevention of child abuse: Current progress in Connecticut," *Connecticut Medicine*, 36 (March 1972), pp. 135–137.

25. R. E. Helfer, *A self-instructional program on child abuse and neglect* (Committee on Infant and Preschool Child, American Academy of Pediatrics, Chicago, Ill., and National Center for Prevention and Treatment of Child Abuse and Neglect, Denver, Colo., 1974), p. 2–4.

26. T. H. Ryan, "Child abuse among blacks," *Sepia* (November 1973), pp. 27–30.

27. V. J. Fontana, as quoted in Light, op. cit., p. 559.

28. Gil, op. cit., pp. 58–60.

29. Gil, op. cit., pp. 108–109 and 115–118.

30. E. M. Thomson et al., *Child abuse: A community challenge* (East Aurora, N.Y.: Henry Stewart, 1971), p. 108.

31. Gil, op. cit., p. 117.

32. Zalba, op. cit., pp. 58–61.
33. E. Bennie and A. Sclare, "The battered child syndrome," *American Journal of Psychiatry*, 125 (January 1969), pp. 975–979; and B. F. Steele and C. Pollock, "A psychiatric study of parents who abuse infants and small children," in R. E. Helfer and C. H. Kempe (eds.), *The battered child* (Chicago: University of Chicago Press, 1968), pp. 89–133.
34. Gil, op. cit., p. 116.
35. Ibid., p. 109.
36. Bennie and Sclare, op. cit., pp. 975–979.
37. Gil, op. cit., p. 111.
38. M. H. Lystad, "Violence at home: A review of the literature," *American Journal of orthopsychiatry*, 45 (April 1975), p. 334.
39. Gil, op. cit., p. 112.
40. Light, op. cit., p. 588.
41. Gil, op. cit., pp. 110–111.
42. Kempe, op. cit., pp. 28–37.
43. Gil, op. cit., p. 113–114 and 117.
44. Ibid., p. 114.
45. Ibid., p. 113.
46. Kempe, op. cit., pp. 29–30.
47. B. Justice and R. Justice, "A psychosocial model of child abuse: Intervention strategies and group techniques." Paper presented before the Clinical and Research Training Seminar, Texas Research Institute of Mental Sciences, Houston, Tex., February 15, 1974; Justice and Justice, "TA work with child abuse," *Transactional Analysis Journal*, 5 (January 1975), pp. 38–41; and C. G. Murdock, "The abused child in the school system," *American Journal of Public Health*, 60 (January 1970), pp. 105–109.
48. Helfer, op. cit., Unit 1, p. 12.
49. Justice and Duncan, op. cit., p. 193.
50. Justice and Justice, op. cit., p. 38; and Justice and Duncan, op. cit., p. 193.
51. Helfer, op. cit., Unit 1, p. 12.
52. Steele and Pollock, op. cit., p. 95.
53. Justice and Duncan, op. cit., pp. 187 and 193; and Helfer, op. cit., Unit 1, p. 12.
54. M. G. Morris and R. W. Gould, "Role reversal: A necessary concept in dealing with the battered child syndrome," in *The neglected-battered child syndrome* (New York: Child Welfare League of America, 1963).
55. Steele and Pollock, op. cit., pp. 89–133.

56. C. H. Kempe et al., "The battered-baby syndrome," *Journal of the American Medical Association,* 181 (July 1962), pp. 105–112; R. Galdston, "Observations of children who have been physically abused," *American Journal of Psychiatry,* 122 (October 1965), pp. 440–443; P. Resnick, "Child murder by parents: A psychiatric review of filicide," *American Journal of Psychiatry,* 126 (September 1969), pp. 325–334; and Bennie and Sclare, op. cit., pp. 975–979.
57. Gil, op. cit., p. 105.
58. Lynch, op. cit., p. 141.
59. *Lift a finger: The teacher's role in combating child abuse* (Houston, Tex.: Education Professions Development Consortium C, 1975), p. 35.
60. Thomson, op. cit., p. 109.
61. Gil, op. cit., p. 104.
62. Bishop, op. cit., p. 623.
63. Zalba, op. cit., pp. 58–61.
64. Bennie and Sclare, op. cit., pp. 975–979; and Gil, op. cit., p. 110.
65. See Light, op. cit., p. 574.
66. Thomson, op. cit., p. 116.
67. Gil, op. cit., pp. 118–119.
68. J. Harrington, "Violence: A clinical viewpoint," *British Medical Journal,* 1 (January 1972), pp. 228–231.
69. I. D. Milowe, as quoted in Gil, op. cit., pp. 29–30.
70. Justice and Duncan, op. cit., pp. 29–30.
71. H. Martin, "The child and his development," in C. H. Kempe and R. E. Helfer (eds.), *Helping the battered child and his family* (Philadelphia, Pa.: Lippincott, 1972), p. 106; and W. R. Flynn, "Frontier justice: A contribution to the theory of child battery," *American Journal of Psychiatry,* 127 (September 1970), pp. 375–379.
72. J. M. Smith and D. E. P. Smith, *Child management: A program for parents* (Ann Arbor, Mich.: Ann Arbor Publishers, 1966), p. 1.
73. T. Solomon, "History and demography of child abuse," *Pediatrics,* 51 (April 1973), p. 775.
74. E. F. Lenoski, "Translating injury data into preventive and health care services." Unpublished paper, Division of Emergency Pediatrics, University of Southern California Medical Center, Los Angeles, Calif., 1973.
75. See Gil, op. cit., p. 65.
76. Thomson, op. cit., p. 32.
77. B. F. Steele, "Working with abusive parents—a psychiatrist's view," *Children Today,* 4 (May–June 1975), pp. 3–5.
78. Gil, op. cit., p. 118.

79. C. A. Smith, "The battered child," *New England Journal of Medicine,* 289 (August 1973), pp. 322–323.
80. Gil, op. cit., pp. 112–113.
81. Ibid., p. 118.
82. Thomson, op. cit., pp. 123–124.
83. Gil, op. cit., pp. 118–121.

Chapter 5

INNOVATIVE INTERVENTIONS IN THE ABUSING FAMILY

The optimal goal in child abuse is to keep the abuse from happening—to prevent the explosive elements in a potentially abusing family system from ever coming together so that violence never occurs. This is primary prevention, which will be discussed in Chapter 8. Once child abuse has occurred, the goal is to keep it from happening again—to defuse the abusing family so that violent behavior is eliminated. This is secondary prevention. When effective, it can have a significant impact on the prevalence of child abuse in a community. More than 50 per cent of the children who are abused will be abused again if there is no intervention.[1]

There are a number of secondary prevention—or therapeutic—strategies of intervention (see Chapter 7). The one we use features group therapy with abusive parents and a technique of setting goals and measuring effectiveness. One question that is often asked about traditional treatment of abusing parents (as well as everyone else in psychotherapy) concerns its effectiveness—do the techniques employed actually work? We place considerable emphasis on this compelling question in our approach. In this chapter and in Chapter 6, we will discuss the intervention techniques we use with parents and describe how they work.

THE COUPLES AND THEIR PROBLEMS

The parents we work with are couples—the adults in the household who are responsible for the child. As we noted earlier, the family functions as a system and the spouses represent the principal subsystem. Because the spouses are basically alike and are tied to each other in a symbiotic relationship like Siamese twins, it is essential to work with both of them to defuse the potential for abuse.

If only one spouse enters therapy, the other will do all he can to maintain the symbiosis and to sabotage the changes made by the other. In any spouse subsystem, it is impossible for one person to change without affecting the other, and the other will stoutly resist those changes as the symbiosis is threatened. Thus we have held firmly to a policy of treating only couples. Other therapists also insist on this policy. As previously noted: "Both parents are the same. They should be treated. It doesn't matter which one actually did the battering."[2]

If there is only one parent in the home—these represent a minority of cases—progress can be made by doing group therapy with that parent. But it is necessary to investigate the symbiosis that this person probably has with her mother, father, or some other relative in the family of origin. We also check on symbiotic relationships with families of origin, but when we speak of our interventions with parents, we are referring primarily to the nuclear family consisting of two spouses, both of whom are equally invested in the abuse.

All couples in our parents group are referred by the local child welfare agency (Harris County Child Welfare Unit, Houston, Texas). In 75 per cent of the cases, the child has been removed from the home by order of the court.[3] The couples are told that their chances of getting the child back are likely to be greatly enhanced if they undergo therapy. Thus most couples are resentful when they enter the group because in effect they have been forced to come. Usually this resentment is expressed covertly in the form of a subtle lack of cooperation, passivity, or finding excuses not to come to group meetings. This phase lasts about three to five weeks; the couples then find they are beginning to benefit from coming, enjoy the experience of belonging to a group of people who are like them, and feel that the world looks brighter.

Group cohesion, a sense of belonging, and positive individual changes can develop to the point where many couples find reasons to continue therapy after we have told them they can quit coming. When evaluation of results shows that a couple is ready to terminate, we inform child welfare authorities, who in turn inform the court. The child returns home a minimum of one month before the parents terminate in group so that new problems can be solved, the changes the parents have made can become more firmly entrenched, and the new techniques of child management they have learned can be applied.

The average length of our group treatment is four to five months. While Helfer works with abusing parents from six to nine months, Kempe often sees considerable improvement after only three to six months and rarely continues intensive treatment longer than eight months: "80% of our parents have their children back in eight months' time."[4] Arvanian points out that for the social worker who is the sole source of treatment (because psychotherapy resources are lacking) "a year's treatment is really very short-term in an abuse case. . . ."[5]

A maximum of five couples are members of our group at any one time. Four are preferable, but since there is a waiting list we have raised the limit to five. The group is conducted at the Texas Research Institute of Mental Sciences (TRIMS) once a week from 7 to 8:30 in the evening.[6] Couples join the group after we have interviewed them individually in depth and discussed the case with the chief of adult services (a psychiatrist) at the institute.

To encourage couples to begin reaching out to others in time of crisis or need, we give them our office and home telephone numbers and urge them to call. We also ask them to let us know whenever they are unable to attend group (few couples have missed more than three sessions). As they begin to develop trust in others, they call us more frequently. As group cohesion grows, they also phone and visit other couples in the group.

We believe that group therapy is more advantageous than individual therapy for persons who abuse children because abusive persons are isolated people who lack a basic trust in others. In a group setting with persons who have the same problem, they gradually learn to trust others and to express their feelings and needs. And as they begin to release long pent-up feelings and problems they have never discussed with anyone before and discover that others will not reject them, their ability to trust grows and they begin to risk reaching out to others, form friendships, and break down their wall of isolation.

This process contributes to the amelioration of another problem common to abusing parents—low self-esteem. Acceptance, new friends, trust, and the feeling that their opinions and ideas matter to others—all these new experiences greatly enhance a parent's self-image. As therapists, we encourage the contributions that the group makes to its members, knowing that to change, a person must feel he has "permission" to do so, that he will have "protection" while experimenting with new behavior and feelings, and that there is "potency" or strength on the part of those encouraging the changes. One of our functions as therapists is to help provide the "3 P's."[7] Our ability to do so is greatly enhanced by the backing of a cohesive group.

Group therapy is also advantageous because it reaches more people than individual therapy does. One of our strategies is to train others (e.g., child welfare supervisors and caseworkers) to conduct groups so that all those who need therapy can obtain it without waiting for an opening in our group. Nine additional groups were started after we began this training in 1975.

Our objectives in group therapy for abusive parents are threefold.[8] The first and paramount objective is to promote changes in the parents and the family environment that will ensure the child's safety when he returns home. Again, this is secondary prevention: i.e., it is designed to keep abuse from recurring. Our second objective is to enhance the problem-solving capacities of these couples. In this sense, we are engaged in primary prevention because we attempt to increase their ability to withstand harmful influences of all kinds and keep dysfunction from occurring.[9] Our third objective is to promote the couples' satisfaction with life and their emotional well-being. If we are successful, the child is bound to benefit.

The steps necessary to achieve these objectives involve an analysis of the psychosocial influences in the family system and the isolation of factors that can be dealt with in group therapy. In other words, we try to (1) identify the psychological and social dynamics of the spouses and their subsystem, (2) determine the deficits in the couple's knowledge of child development and management, and (3) assess the role played by their environment. These steps are embodied in the theoretical framework we use for group intervention into the problem of child abuse. The theoretical concepts were presented in earlier chapters.

We rely on the following therapeutic methods to accomplish these steps: transactional analysis, which is a theory of personality organization as well as a therapeutic tool for change; behavior therapy, using techniques developed by Lazarus, Wolpe,[10] and others, and hypnosis, when indicated; child management techniques and information on the needs of children during specific developmental stages; and group dynamics, which promotes group support of the changes made by individual members.

To determine whether our methods are effective, we place considerable emphasis on evaluation. The evaluative technique we use is Goal Attainment Scaling (GAS), which measures outcome not only while the couples are in group treatment but at six-month intervals after they have terminated.[11] GAS can also be used as a therapeutic tool. GAS involves identifying the main areas of concern of abusive couples and setting goals in each area to be attained in therapy. We identify these problem areas by (1) asking couples to rank their problems on a checklist when treatment begins, (2) interviewing each parent in depth individually, (3) borrowing from our own experiences with other abusive parents and their common problems, and (4) taking into account what the literature says about such parents.

Six Areas of Concern

Typical problems we work on with each spouse involve Symbiosis, Isolation, Talking and Sharing with Mate, Impatience/Temper, Child Development and Management, and Employment. A GAS Follow-Up Guide is constructed for each group member, based on the goals to be reached in each area of concern within a three-month period. The same guide is used during follow-up interviews after a couple leaves the group.

Figure 5–1 presents a Goal Attainment Follow-Up Guide, showing the six and the five goal levels (–2 to +2) problem scales to be filled in for each parent.

The weight assigned to each scale varies, depending on the person. The weights are used to designate the relative importance of each area of concern; they do not necessarily add up to any fixed total. Since we believe that Symbiosis is the central problem in child abuse, we invariably give it more weight than the other areas of concern. While one couple may have more of a problem with Isolation than with Talking and Sharing with Mate, the reverse may be true for another couple.

Generally, Isolation receives considerable weight—often second only to Symbiosis—because it is such a severe problem for most abusing families. When Lenoski compared 674 abusing parents with a control group of 500 nonabusers, he found that 81 per cent of the abusers, compared with 43 per cent of the nonabusers, preferred to resolve crises alone; 43 per cent of the abusers compared with 20 per cent of the nonabusers, preferred to be alone, and almost 90 per cent of the abusers did not have listed telephone numbers, whereas 88 per cent of the nonabusers did.[12] Elmer found that the most striking difference between abusing and nonabusing parents was in the extent of associations outside the home. The abusive mothers belonged to few groups, such as church, PTA, a lodge, or a union, and had almost no close friends who might be companions or sources of help.[13]

We include Impatience/Temper in the list of problems, based on our finding that 85 per cent of the abusing parents we work with consider it a problem. Clearly, persons who act out or behave violently are expressing some form of agitation. Many describe this agitation as impatience or temper that they are unable to control.

Level at Intake: ✓

Level at Follow-up: *   GOAL ATTAINMENT FOLLOW–UP GUIDE

SCALE ATTAINMENT LEVELS	SCALE 1: Symbiosis (weight$_1$=)	SCALE 2: Isolation (weight$_2$=)	SCALE 3: Talking & Sharing with Mate (weight$_3$=)
most unfavorable outcome thought likely (−2)			
less than expected success (−1)			
expected level of success (0)			
more than expected success (+1)			
most favorable outcome thought likely (+2)			

Figure 5–1   Goal Attainment Follow-Up Guide

Level at Intake:

Goal Attainment Score
(Level at Follow-up):

SCALE 4: Impatience/Temper (weight$_4$=)	SCALE 5: Child Management (weight$_5$=)	SCALE 6: Employment (weight$_6$=)

Figure 5–1   (continued)

117

Employment is listed as an area of concern for several reasons. Unemployment often plays a part in abuse, particularly among males, because it frequently is a source of day-to-day pressure, which contributes to the abusive climate at home.[14] Employment, on the other hand, has the potential to help husbands—and particularly homebound wives—achieve a sense of growth and competence.

We also place great emphasis on Child Development and Management because we agree with Lystad that "it has been amply documented that parents who abuse children often are woefully ignorant about child development."[15] Although they may not be significantly more ignorant than nonabusing parents, the lack of knowledge and skills in this area, when combined with other problems, greatly reduces their ability to manage their children without harsh physical discipline.[16] Unless parents learn what a child needs at different stages of development and how his behavior can be managed without the use of physical force, all the therapy in the world is unlikely to guard against the recurrence of abuse.

To avoid conveying the idea that every parent in our group is treated in terms of the same six problem areas, we should point out that Goal Attainment Scaling allows for the addition of new goals as we learn more about an individual and his problems. Symbiosis, Isolation, Talking and Sharing with Mate, Impatience/Temper, Child Development and Management, and Employment are the *typical* problems we address. Other problems that a person complains about during his intake interview often clear up when the major problems are relieved.

For instance, a number of abusing parents are depressed. But as we work on Isolation and Talking and Sharing with Mate and help a person change his stroking profile, his depression often lifts. The same thing frequently happens to a person's poor self-image, particularly when the areas of his life involving symbiosis and employment begin to improve. Or, a couple's sexual difficulties and marital conflict are alleviated as each partner works on Symbiosis and Talking and Sharing with Mate.

The six major problem areas do not always cover subsidiary problems, however. Thus special problems are also listed on the Goal Attainment Guide, and goals are set for being reached in three months. An evaluation is made at the end of that time, and new goals are set for another three-month period.

Before illustrating what is done therapeutically about each problem area, we will describe how goals are set and how the GAS can be used to arrive at quantitative evaluations of outcome. Figure 5–1 contains five levels of predicted attainment for each problem area. The goals should be specific enough to enable a follow-up worker to determine whether they have been met. For example, under Isolation, the "most unfavorable outcome" likely for a couple might be the following: has no phone, no friend, does not go out socially. The "expected level of success" might be: has telephone, has one friend, goes out socially at least once a month. The "most favorable outcome" might be: has telephone, has at least two friends, goes out socially at least once a week. These goals would be checked after three months in group therapy and then at six-month intervals after the couple leaves the group.

For successful termination from the group, the expected level of success—as a minimum—must be achieved in each problem area. The GAS lends itself to a composite Goal Attainment T score, based on a formula derived by Sherman, which uses the numerical values attached to each level of outcome (from –2 to +2) and takes into consideration the weights designated for each scale.[17] The composite GAS score for each spouse must be at least 55 before the couple can terminate therapy. Using these criteria for termination, abuse has not reoccurred among the 15 couples who have completed group therapy since May 1973.

Furthermore, six-month follow-ups show that expected levels of outcome and composite GAS scores of at least 55 are holding up.[18]

When Is It Safe for the Child To Return Home?

As we have pointed out, we use a quantitative method called a goal attainment score to determine whether a couple has changed enough so that the child can return home —our primary objective. What kind of profile must a couple have to indicate the necessary amount of change? Helfer adheres to the following criteria to determine when a home is safe for a child: a helpful neighbor or relative is available, the husband is understanding and helpful, the family has a telephone and someone to call, the mother views herself as helpful, the couple has friends, the amount of role reversal has been reduced, the parents are willing to let the child be a child, there is no scapegoating, there are fewer family crises, and so forth.[19] Kempe believes a child will be safe in the home when (1) the self-image of the parents improves ("We can sense this by the way they dress and when they have any kind of social life"), (2) they view their child in a more positive way, (3) they demonstrate that they can reach out to others in moments of stress, (4) they demonstrate that, emotionally, they can handle the child.[20] In 11 three-year demonstration projects funded by two federal agencies in 1974, "the client's progress is measured against indicators thought to be associated with the potential to abuse or neglect—lack of awareness of child development, the way in which anger is expressed, for example—as well as against the individual treatment goals established for the client."[21]

Although these indicators of progress and Helfer's and Kempe's criteria are helpful, we wanted a more objective means of determining the amount of change that parents must make to provide a safe home for their child. Clinical impressions are necessarily subjective, and one therapist's impressions may not agree with those of another. Goal Attainment Scaling allows us to set goals that the client himself can observe and confirm so that his progress is not a matter of our opinion alone. Follow-up studies on group members since 1973 have confirmed that when clients obtain a goal attainment score of 55 or more, it is safe for the child to return home.

Although our first objective is to make certain that the home is safe for the child, we should emphasize the fact that the changes the parents make while accomplishing this goal result in other important benefits for the child. For instance, we devote considerable attention to whether the parents adopt a different way of disciplining the child and drop their excessive expectations of him. Much work is done with parents on child development and management.

Martin and Beezley have argued that although

> most abusive parents can benefit from therapy, in terms of their own personality, their self-esteem, their capability to adapt to stress, and their ability to utilize people and agencies for their own needs, . . . [there is little change in] the attitudes and behavior of these parents toward their children. . . . [In other words,] the child remains in a home where he is viewed in a distorted way, where punitive and corporal punishment remains the mode, and where unduly high expectations remain and little positive reinforcement takes place.[22]

Our experience has been that when the parents change their behavior with respect to all six major areas of concern, the child returns to parents who not only are no longer abusive but are more understanding and giving. By itself, the work on child development and management contributes greatly to specific changes in parental attitudes about the child and the way he should be treated.

By the time couples leave the group and their children have been returned to them, the overall changes they have made will have taken the following form: (1) their symbiotic relationship has changed to the point where each can meet his or her own needs and provide mutual support for one another, (2) their isolation has been dispelled to the extent that they mix with people, telephone people, and reach out to others for help when they need it, (3) their ability to talk and share with one another has increased so that they can exchange positive strokes regularly and provide mutual support, (4) their enhanced ability to control their impatience and temper has resulted in more relaxed behavior, (5) the information they have obtained in group concerning child development and management has helped them to understand their child's needs at different stages of development and thus they know how to respond to him and to manage his behavior without resorting to physical discipline, (6) their difficulties in the area of employment have been reduced to the degree that they have found a job, have learned how to keep from getting uptight at work or using work to avoid relationships at home.

Thus Helfer's criteria for determining whether the home is safe for the child are covered by these changes in the six areas of concern. By breaking up the symbiosis, the parents no longer have to depend solely on each other or the child to meet their needs, which eliminates the problem of role reversal. By breaking up the isolation, the parents can develop sources of help such as neighbors or friends, (but preferably not relatives) to call on for help. By learning to talk and share with one another, each spouse is able to give the other help and support. By learning about child development and management, the parents recognize that the child is a child and needs their support. By learning how to relax (and by eliminating the symbiosis), the parents can stop scapegoating the child. In short, by making changes in all six problem areas, the couples experience fewer crises and we achieve our second objective of increasing their problem-sharing capacities.

The specific changes that couples make in each area depends on the individual goals set up for each spouse. For example, the Goal Attainment Guides for one couple in the group are presented in Figures 5–2 and 5–3. Their problems in each area of concern were as follows:

Symbiosis. Dianne's and Al's symbiotic relationship was almost classic in the sense that Dianne did virtually all the thinking as well as talking for Al, and he took the Child position of being taken care of along with their two small daughters. Typically, Al made few decisions for himself and could not make up his mind about his job.

The symbiosis shifted rapidly, however, whenever Dianne was overwhelmed by the responsibilities she was carrying. At that point, she became the feeling Child and often became hysterical and lost control. Al would then act the part of the strong male decision-maker and try to take care of her. But usually he was too late; she had already turned to their two small daughters to be cared for and, when disappointed, beat them both.

Isolation. The couple had only one another and their children. They had no outside friends and had contacts only with relatives from their families of origin. In an extreme crisis, they called these relatives, with whom they were usually fighting.

Talking and Sharing with Mate. Al generally sat in front of the television set, watching some mindless western, and told the children he was too tired to play with them. He had little to say to his wife during supper or afterwards. She did the talking, which consisted primarily of nagging and criticism.

Impatience/Temper. Dianne had the greater problem in this area. She not only lost her temper easily with her children but also at work, which sometimes left her jobless. Al, on the other hand, became cross and impatient with the children.

GOAL ATTAINMENT FOLLOW–UP GUIDE

√ Intake level

* Level 3 months later

Scale Headings and Scale Weights

Levels of Predicted Attainments	SCALE 1: Symbiosis (weight$_1$=25)	SCALE 2: Isolation (weight$_2$=15)	SCALE 3: Talking & Sharing with M (weight$_3$=15)
most unfavorable outome thought likely (−2)	Make no decisions on own; do virtually no thinking or talking for self at home. √	Make no friends; meet no neighbors; call no one in time of crisis √	Neither talk to wife nor share feelings except to complain √
less than expected success (−1)			
expected level of success (0)	Make own decisions about job & other major areas; do own talking, thinking & acting	Make 1 "outside" friend; meet neighbors; call either in time of crisis	For at least 10 minutes daily talk about good things that happened during day, share feelings with wife *
more than expected success (+1)			
most favorable outcome thought likely (+2)	Make own decisions in all areas & offer suggestions, when asked, to wife; take responsibility, when asked, for care of children *	Make at least 3 "outside" friends; meet neighbors; call them when needed; take wife dancing *	For at least 15 minutes daily, talk about good things that happened; share feelings & support wife

Figure 5–2 Goal Attainment Follow-Up Guide for Al

Level at Intake = 19.36

GA Score 3 months later = 62.25

SCALE 4: npatience/Temper (weight$_4$=10)	SCALE 5: Child Development & Mgmt (weight$_5$=15)	SCALE 6: Employment (weight$_6$=20)
ontinue to feel tight and take out on children d wife √	Learn no child development or management techniques; continue present disciplining √	Continue present job – long hours, low pay; much pressure √
earn relaxation chniques so won't xpress tension in aling with children *	Learn development needs; use "I messages" and reinforcement techniques; assume responsibility for any "swatting" on rear of kids *	Seek & get better job with less pressure *
earn relaxation chniques so won't xpress tension toard children, wife on job	Use "I messages" and reinforcement techniques; leave off all physical discipline	Seek & get better job with less pressure, shorter hours & more pay

Figure 5–2 (continued)

125

√ Intake Level   GOAL ATTAINMENT FOLLOW—UP GUIDE

* Level 3 months later   Scale Headings and Scale Weights

Levels of Predicted Attainments	SCALE 1: Symbiosis (weight$_1$=25)	SCALE 2: Isolation (weight$_2$=15)	SCALE 3: Talking & sharing with m
most unfavorable outcome thought likely (−2)	Talk, think, act for spouse; turn to children to be cared for √	Stay in house all day; visit no one; call on no one for help √	Criticize & nag spouse; give no positive strokes √
less than expected success (−1)			
expected level of success (0)	Do no talking, thinking, acting for spouse; seek no nurturing from children *	Get out of house each day; visit neighbors; call on them or friends in crisis	Give positive strokes instead of nagging & criticism to mate while talking and sharing for at least 10 minutes *
more than expected success (+1)			
most favorable outcome thought likely (+2)	Meet own needs, give support when requested to spouse; support two children	Get out of house each day; go somewhere with a friend; go out with husband; call people in crisis *	Give positive strokes to mate while talking & sharing for at least 15 minutes

Figure 5–3   Goal Attainment Follow-Up Guide for Dianne

Level at Intake = 19.36

GA Score 3 months later = 54.59

SCALE 4: Impatience/Temper (weight$_4$=20)	SCALE 5: Child development & mgmt (weight$_5$=15)	SCALE 6: Employment (weight$_6$=15)
Outbursts of temper & impatience at husband, children, & persons outside the home √	Continue present disciplining; learn no child development or management techniques; children not allowed to be children √	Continue to remain idle at home and demonstrate "job phobia" √
No outburst of temper or impatience at children or husband *	Learn developmental needs; use "I messages" and reinforcement techniques; let husband do any physical disciplining; children allowed to be children *	Overcome "job phobia" by getting & keeping job at least 3 months *
No outbursts of temper or impatience in home or elsewhere	Learn developmental needs; use "I messages" and reinforcement techniques; leave off yelling at kids	Overcome "job phobia" by getting & keeping job at least 6 months

Figure 5–3   (continued)

127

Child Development and Management.   Neither parent knew anything about child development or child management; physical punishment was their principal method of discipline.

Employment.   Al complained about the pressure and long hours of his job and his supervisor's unjust treatment. He brought the stress home with him. Dianne, on the other hand, was idle most of the time. After child welfare authorities removed the children from the home, she was extremely bored and restless, but claimed she had a job phobia, based on fear that she would "blow up" on the job (as she once had), embarrass herself and others, and be fired. Her self-image was poor and she needed a means to grow and develop a feeling of competence as well as an outlet for her restless energy.

As illustrated in the GAS Follow-Up Guides for Al (Figure 5–2) and Dianne (Figure 5–3), goals were set for each problem area. The most unfavorable outcome was likely to be no change or improvement in their level of functioning. The entry level is designated on the GAS guides with check marks. The goals the couple reached after three months in the group are indicated by asterisks.

For instance, Al tackled the problem of symbiosis by making his own decisions, offering suggestions to his wife when asked, and taking responsibility for care of the children when asked. Dianne made an effort to stop talking, thinking, and acting for Al and turning to her children for care. Because symbiosis is the abusing family's central problem, it receives the most weight as a scale heading. Weights for the other scales vary as illustrated by the GAS guides for Dianne and Al. In the area of impatience and temper, a problem for Dianne, she moved from an entry level of outbursts of temper and impatience at home and work to no outbursts at home. Employment was a critical problem for Al, and he moved from continuing his present job, with its long hours, low pay, and pressure, to finding a better job with less stress.

Although we will discuss each problem area separately in terms of what happens in therapy, in almost all these areas we use behavioral prescriptions, which the parents assume responsibility for carrying out by making a verbal agreement to practice certain behavior between therapy sessions. For instance, to break up their isolation, Al and Dianne agreed to meet their neighbors and call on people in time of stress. To break up their symbiosis, they agreed to practice consciously new kinds of behavior: Dianne refrained from talking and acting for her husband and Al begin doing his own talking and acting. At the end of three months in group therapy, their GAS guides were checked to determine what level of goals has been reached. As Figure 5–2 indicates, Al achieved the goals expected on four scales: Talking and Sharing with Mate, Impatience/Temper, Child Management, and Employment—and gained the most favorable goals on two scales: Symbiosis and Isolation. As Figure 5–3 shows, Dianne reached the expected level of outcome in five areas and the most favorable level in one.

As we noted earlier, each goal level bears a numerical designation: –2 for the most unfavorable, 0 for the expected, and +2 for the most favorable. Each problem area also carries a relative numerical weight. The numerical goal levels, scale weights, and the changes the parents make between entry into the group and follow-up are plugged into the following formula to compute the composite goal attainment score:[23]

$$T = 50 + \frac{10\Sigma w_i x_i}{(1-\rho)\Sigma w_i{}^2 + \rho(\Sigma w_i)^2}$$

Thus Al's goal attainment score after three months was 62, while Dianne's was 55. Based on our experience with couples who abuse and their goal attainment scores, we believed it was safe for the children to return home. The couple remained in group for several months after the children returned, however, because they believed they could accomplish even more. At the end of six months, both Al and Dianne had reached the most favorable goals on their GAS guides.

We mentioned earlier that in group therapy we rely on transactional analysis and behavioral therapy and modification, supplemented by child development and management techniques and enhanced by group process and dynamics. Chapter 6 will describe these techniques and the results obtained in terms of the six problem areas.

First, however, we will turn to another aspect of therapy concerning questions and considerations that therapists must face when working with abusing parents.

CONSIDERATIONS FOR THERAPISTS

A number of questions come up in terms of what abusing parents need from the therapist, how they perceive him, and how the therapist can best handle his feelings toward these parents. We will consider five such issues here and describe how we deal with them.

Mothering of Abusive Parents

Kempe and Lascari believe that the therapist must provide abusing parents with mothering because they never experienced mothering in their own childhoods.[24]

We translate mothering into caring, into "unconditional positive regard." A child who receives mothering can go to his parents (mother or father) and get not only the care he needs but a sense of acceptance, of being OK as a person. In transactional analysis terms, the best mothering provides unconditional positive strokes for the child as a person. At times, the child's behavior—what he does—may warrant different treatment: criticism and negative strokes. But whether the child's behavior is condoned or criticized, the child has a sense of being accepted as a person, of being OK and worthwhile. Parents can best impart this feeling.

For people who have never had a relationship in which they were considered unconditionally OK, therapy should provide them with this sense of OKness. Abusive parents grew up in homes where their OKness depended on their being caretakers of their parents or being overly compliant, obedient, or nondemanding. Because many failed to please their parents, they never received a sense of even conditional acceptance. As a result, they grew up doubting their own self-worth.

In our view, mothering consists of providing abusive parents with a relationship in which they are accepted as OK people. What they have done, how they behave, is considered separately—as something that can change. We agree with Ellis that it is important to separate the "doing" part from the "being" part.[25]

The first order of business is to impart a sense of unconditional OKness. This can be accomplished through parent aides (see Chapter 7) or lay therapists as long as the stroking communicates to the parents that they are worthwhile and have a right to exist. We offer this type of relationship in a group setting rather than on a one-to-one basis (although we often deal with the crises of group members on an individual basis when they call us for help). The message we communicate is the same: "You're OK, you count. Even if you have done 'bad' things, you are important as a person and you can change. You have a right to exist."

This does not mean that we unconditionally accept negative behavior. We do not, but we accept the person. It is this acceptance of a person, of his OKness, of his being worthy of regard, that we view as a basic element of mothering and believe is important in therapy with abusing parents.

However, we disagree with those who believe that it is important to allow these parents to become dependent on the therapists for extended periods in order to meet their deep hunger for dependency. We view our job as helping the parents become aware of their needs and giving them the tools to meet them so that they will not turn to their child as a source of nurturing or become unduly dependent on their therapist.

If the therapist is available for only a few months, the client must acquire the strength to meet his needs long after he has left therapy. Therefore, we equip him to find sources of strokes in his mate and in others. We also teach him to ask for what he needs, to be straightforward about what he wants from his spouse in terms of comfort and nurturing.

Abusing parents must understand that it is impossible to make up for what their parents failed to give them as children. Although they can learn how to obtain nurturing, love, unconditional stroking, and support, they must realize that no therapist or parent aide can make up for what they missed as children. They needed love and nurturing then, but that time is past. They are adults now, and they have the potential to learn, with help, how to meet their needs as adults. It is time to make use of this potential, to forget or forgive those who did not give them what they needed and to make the present as satisfying and productive as possible. We do not hold out to these parents the hope that they will get from the therapist what they never got before. Instead, we offer them acceptance, unconditional regard, and methods of meeting their own needs without being dependent like a child.

Relinquishing the Child as a Source of Satisfaction

According to Lascari, therapy must help the parent let go of the child as a source of satisfaction and transfer these needs to someone else: a therapist, parent aide, social worker, visiting nurse, or some other adult who is working with the parent.[26]

Although a child is one source of satisfaction and strokes for the parent, abusing parents must accept the fact that there are different kinds of strokes and a child, because he *is* a child, cannot be the source of nurturing strokes. This does not mean the parent cannot obtain such strokes; it means he must be aware of other sources of strokes— other adults, such as spouses, who will provide nurturing when it is asked for or contracted for, not because they have been manipulated into doing it.

Parents can still enjoy their children and accept the kind of strokes that children have to offer—love, praise, respect, joy. Getting across to abusive parents the idea of alternative sources of strokes is so important that we spend a large amount of time in group teaching marriage partners how to stroke each other, to ask for what they need, and to give what they are asked to give without burdening themselves or feeling put upon.

We teach parents four rules of stroking.[27] First, all the strokes they need are available. Second, they must ask for the strokes they need. This does not mean they should reject strokes that are given without asking (e.g., a compliment or a friendly gesture); it means that they should not use the fact that they are not receiving strokes as an excuse for feeling deprived. If they need strokes, they should ask for them from people who are most likely to give them. Many individuals grow up believing that those who love them will somehow know what they need and provide it. We teach parents that this is a romantic myth; nobody automatically knows what another person is feeling. The only sure way an individual can let others know what he needs is to tell them. Therefore, we encourage parents to tell their spouses directly in words what they need.

The third rule we teach about stroking is that when asked for a stroke, a person can answer yes or no in response. In other words, no one is obligated to comply with other people's wishes all the time. This idea astonishes most abusing parents because it is a radical departure from what they learned while growing up. We show them how to avoid burdening themselves with continual compliance to the demands of others and to feel OK about turning down a request every now and then when doing so will be best for them. Finally, we teach parents that, when offered a stroke, they can either accept or refuse it. We illustrate how they reject positive strokes by pointing out the ways they refuse to accept compliments or friendly gestures from other group members. We then ask them if they will begin accepting positive strokes, mechanically at first if they must. Most agree to do so but feel awkward initially. Later, they like the results because they feel less deprived.

On the other side of the coin, we teach parents that they do not have to accept negative strokes. When someone criticizes them, they have the right to reject the criticism, to "run it through their computer" and determine whether it has merit. Obviously, we do not encourage abusive parents to reject all criticism, but we do ask them to evaluate whether the criticism is justified or whether they accept it because it fits their poor self-image and justifies their continuing to feel not-OK.

By learning about the different kinds of strokes and the rules that govern them, parents begin to realize that their children are not the only source of satisfaction and that they cannot rely on them to provide all the strokes they need. Others, including the therapist, can be turned to, but they must assume responsibility for taking, giving, and asking for strokes in a straightforward, above-board manner. Parents soon learn that there are many people around them who can become sources of strokes and satisfaction. At first they may turn to the therapist, but group members are

soon recognized as sources, then neighbors, fellow workers, and so on.

Handling Personal Feelings About Abuse

Sanders states that "before any person becomes involved
with battering parents he should try to recognize his own
feelings about the problem."[28] Or, as Pollack points out,
the first difficulty in starting therapy with parents is "management of the therapist's own feelings about a parent who
has hurt a small baby."[29]

How do we tackle this problem of handling our feelings? We begin with the premise that we are like most other
people in terms of our attitudes and feelings (unconscious
as well as conscious) toward children and people who abuse
them. Typically, the initial reaction toward abusive parents
is outrage. As Pollack notes: "There is disbelief and a denial, horror, a surge of anger towards the abuser."[30]

We can become angry by reading a caseworker's account of what a parent has done to his child. A certain
amount of intense anger is natural when one hears about
an adult who assaults a defenseless child. However, continuing outrage is not natural and probably has its roots in
other feelings, such as wanting to deny that a parent can be
angry enough to abuse a child. People prefer to believe that
they always love their children. But anyone who has had
children or been around them for any length of time knows
that they can be exasperating and incite fierce anger because "a child often interferes with his parents' pleasures;
and few children live up to all the expectations and demands which parents make on them. Therefore, most parents also have hostile and negative feelings. These feelings,
however, are often totally unconscious."[31] Yet the feelings
are there.

One way to deny these hostile and negative feelings is
to regard abusive parents as completely different from one-

self and be enraged by what they have done. Thus many people look upon these parents as sick, crazy, or maniacs. A person who persists in clinging to an intense sense of outrage cannot be an effective helper. He will only compound the abusing parent's anxiety, guilt, hostility, and low self-image. He wants to punish the parent, not help him. As therapists, we must be certain, when we begin work with an abusing couple, that we are not holding on to our outrage or letting the feeling cover our own repressed hostility toward children.

We must be equally careful to avoid the other extreme of rationalizing the behavior of abusive parents: e.g., "They couldn't help it. They had all these pressures on them. What do you expect since they had poor parenting themselves?" Rationalizations may serve the same function as outrage in defending a person against his own unacceptable negative feelings toward children.

But whatever the reason for such a position, it is no more helpful than outright rejection of abusive parents. Those who reject are inclined to punish; those who rationalize, to dismiss. Although it is important to be aware of the stresses in the lives of abusive parents and how pressure may be a precursor to abuse, these stresses do not justify their behavior. It is possible to understand how abuse occurs without condoning or dismissing it. People who inflict violence on children need to learn that although they have not taken responsibility for themselves in the past, they will be expected to do so now. This is part of being mature. They are not children, and no matter what their parents did to them, they now have adult responsibilities, and it is time to accept those responsibilities. Although we recognize that this is easier said than done, we are convinced that growth and strengthening the personality are possible and that abusive parents can learn how to assume responsibility for themselves and their lives.

To make certain that we can work with abusive parents without antagonism or hostility, we separate ourselves as much as possible from the children who have been abused and spend little time focusing on the actual abuse. After obtaining the essential details about the abuse in the initial intake interview, we seldom refer to the subject again. This "separation" not only prevents our own feelings about the abuse from being activated but helps us to focus on the parents.

We do not see pictures of the child's injuries, we do not testify in court against the parents, and we do not act as therapists to their children. We believe that it is extremely difficult, if not impossible, to be effective with the parents and the child at the same time. Others agree with this position. For example, Davoren states that when the therapist also treats the child, the parents tend to believe that he is concerned with the child and not with them and feel rejected and pushed aside as they have felt so many times before.[32] Therefore, for this reason as well as others we have mentioned, we treat only the parents. Although we do arrange for the children to receive services or treatment, we do so through the parents or caseworker.

When parents regain custody of their child and are nearing the end of therapy, we invite them to bring the child to group, which is usually a proud occasion for them. We also attend social functions such as picnics together, where group members bring their children and we bring ours.

Holmes states that if a therapist has "a warm, ongoing relationship with the parent, [he will want to] deny the abusive act and see only the pleasant side of the parent . . . , forgetting that, in order to help, he must be able to accept the rage as well as the love in the client."[33] In our opinion, it is possible to accept the parent as a person, along with his feelings and passions, but not to accept what he does. In other words, it is important to keep the person and his behavior separate—to recognize the human being and the influences that have shaped him, but avoid using his background or problems as an excuse to condone his behavior.

We impress upon parents their right to feel anger, rage, resentment, and other negative emotions, but at the same time we emphasize that expressions of these feelings must not interfere with the well-being of anyone else. We encourage them to express their strong feelings in a safe setting such as the group, but make it clear that having these feelings is entirely different from acting on them.

One way to deal with abusive parents with understanding rather than anger is to think in transactional analysis terms: to focus on the Child part of the parents that wants to be taken care of, to obtain help, reassurance, and guidance. These parents are hurting and in need, and anger is not an effective therapeutic tool at this stage, although it may be therapeutic later. Anger may serve to meet the therapist's needs, but it does not help the client. So what feeling of anger we may have initially quickly passes and our feeling then is one of sadness that these families have such problems, coupled with a hopefulness that their lives will be different in the future as they learn to make changes in themselves.

Identity as an Authority Figure

Another factor to consider is that parents often identify therapists as authority figures who have the power to take away the child.

We have found that this can be a problem in certain situations. For example, the protective services caseworker, through the court, does have the authority to remove the child from the home and often has exercised it by the time a couple comes to therapy. Despite the fact that we do not have this authority, parents often perceive us as having it to some extent. Therefore, any structure we can set up to separate this power from the therapy is useful. We agree with Davoren that the person who works with abusive parents should be free of the obligation to remove the child or even tell the parent that the child will be removed.[34]

Parents are referred to our group only after the child welfare authorities are involved and usually after they have decided to petition the court to remove the child. We make this clear to the parents by telling them that we had nothing to do with child welfare authorities getting involved in their lives, that we were not involved in the court action, and we are not employed by the child welfare agency. In addition, we make it clear to parents that although the caseworker and the judge will place heavy emphasis on our report about their progress in the group, we are not directly involved in the disposition of the case.

At this point we tell the parents that it is their responsibility to do what is necessary to regain custody of their child and to get their lives straightened out so that the child welfare authorities can be assured that the child will be safe in their home. Once the parents have accomplished these things, the child will come home and the welfare department will leave them alone. We try to function as friends with the parents rather than as power figures. Parents are likely to view Rita (who is called by her first name) as someone to give comfort and warmth. Blair, whom some group members address by his first name while others call him Dr. Justice, is turned to more often for advice and information. In either case, we recognize that we exercise some control over the lives of these parents and that they know this. We attempt to minimize our roles as authority figures but, do not deny that we may be viewed this way to varying degrees.

Advantages of Using Two Therapists

Investigators at the University of California at Los Angeles take the position that it is important to provide a male and female therapist for a parents' group to facilitate the members identifying with a father and mother figure.[35] Since we play down our role as authority figures, we do not encourage this identification. But we do believe it is important to provide adult role models for both men and women in the group. Both sexes bring up questions that they believe members of their own sex can best answer. Although they may be incorrect in their assumption, it reassures them to have both a male and female therapist present. For example, one man in the group phoned Blair to ask if he could see him privately to discuss a personal problem. The problem concerned homosexual encounters the man had had as a teen-ager, which he claimed kept him from performing certain sex acts with his wife. At Blair's suggestion, the man presented the problem to the group. If a male therapist had not been available, the man probably would not have mentioned the problem at all.

There are other advantages to using two therapists. First, as Helfer has noted, if a parent is angry at one therapist, he can let off steam to the other.[36] The anger may be inappropriate, but it is important to express it. Abusing parents are often reluctant to tell someone they are angry with him and instead nurse their resentment or pout in silence. But if another person they have some rapport with is available, they will express their feelings to him. Some parents in our group follow this pattern when dealing with their anger at one of us. Because the other therapist is present, the parent learns how to deal with his anger effectively and resolve the problem.

Another value in having co-therapists is that one may see things the other misses. This is especially true when one therapist is bogged down or involved in a game with a group member. At these times, the co-therapist can point out what is going on. Also, with two therapists, two different points of view are available on an issue. When we differ, we regard it as therapeutic for group members to see how we settle our differences and then proceed, without hurt feelings or resentment. When one therapist and a group member differ, which actually may represent a power struggle, the co-therapist can be more detached.

Still another advantage is that in working with the difficult problem of child abuse and with parents who have committed it, the co-therapists can talk the problems over and give each other support when the going gets rough. Having someone to turn to is important because there are moments in any group when the battleline seems to be drawn between clients and therapists. This is particularly true in a new group of abusing parents. It is also reassuring for the therapists to have someone to check with about what is going on in the group or what therapeutic approach is best.

Finally, working with abusing families can be emotionally draining, and it is extremely comforting to know that someone else appreciates the toll it can take and understands how the therapist feels.

NOTES

1. V. J. Fontana, "The neglect and abuse of children," *New York State Journal of Medicine,* 64 (January 1964), p. 218.
2. S. Isaacs, "Neglect, cruelty and battering," *British Medical Journal,* 3 (July 1972), pp. 224–226.
3. In the majority of abuse cases in Harris County, the court does not intervene and attempts to alleviate the problem are made by child welfare workers who counsel parents while the child remains in the home. In the most serious cases, however, the child is removed.
4. R. E. Helfer, *A self-instructional program on child abuse and neglect* (Committee on Infant and Preschool Child, American Academy of Pediatrics, Chicago, Ill., and National Center for the Prevention and Treatment of Child Abuse and Neglect, Denver, Colo., 1974); and C. H. Kempe, "Paediatric implications of the battered baby syndrome," *Archives of Disease in Childhood,* 46 (February 1971), p. 34; and Kempe, Panel discussion, "Symposium on Child Abuse," *Pediatrics,* 51 (April 1973), p. 791.
5. A. L. Arvanian, "Treatment of abusive parents," in N. B. Ebeling and D. A. Hill (eds.), *Child abuse: Intervention and treatment* (Acton, Mass.: Publishing Sciences Group, 1975), p. 95.
6. TRIMS, located at the Texas Medical Center in Houston, is the research and training arm of the Texas Department of Mental

Health and Mental Retardation and is one of the largest mental health outpatient facilities in the country.

7. P. Crossman, "Permission and protection," *Transactional Analysis Bulletin*, 5 (July 1966), pp. 152–154.

8. B. Justice, "Group therapy for abusing parents." Paper presented before the Mini-Conference on Child Abuse and Neglect, Texas United Community Services, Houston, April 11, 1975.

9. See G. Caplan and H. Grunebaum, "Perspectives on primary prevention: A review," in H. Gottesfeld (ed.), *The critical issues of community mental health* (New York: Behavioral Publications, 1972), p. 128.

10. A. A. Lazarus (ed.), *Clinical behavior therapy* (New York: Brunner/ Mazel, 1972); and J. Wolpe, *The practice of behavioral therapy* (New York: Pergamon Press, 1969).

11. T. J. Kiresuk and R. E. Sherman, "Goal attainment scaling: A general method for evaluating comprehensive community mental health programs," *Community Mental Health Journal*, 4 (December 1968), pp. 443–453.

12. Lenoski's study also suggested that abusing parents not only avoid other people but were raised to shun pets. Only 4 per cent of the abusive parents reported early exposure to pets, compared with 86 per cent of the nonabusers. E. F. Lenoski, "Translating injury data into preventive and health care services—physical child abuse." Unpublished paper, Division of Emergency Medicine, University of Southern California Medical Center, Los Angeles, 1973.

13. E. Elmer, "Child abuse: A symptom of family crisis," in E. Pavenstedt and V. W. Bernard (eds.), *Crisis of family disorganization: Programs to soften their impact on children* (New York: Behavioral Publications, 1971), p. 54.

14. See R. J. Light, "Abused and neglected children in America: A study of alternative policies," *Harvard Educational Review*, 43 (November 1973), pp. 587–588; and E. J. Merrill, "Physical abuse of children: An agency study," in V. DeFrancis, *Protecting the battered child* (Denver: American Humane Association, 1962).

15. M. H. Lystad, "Violence at home: A review of the literature," *American Journal of Orthopsychiatry*, 45 (April 1975), p. 338.

16. Light, op. cit., p. 595.

17. Kiresuk and Sherman, op. cit. 448–449.

18. Three couples dropped out of group therapy. The children of two had not been removed from the home and have since been abused again and taken from the parents' custody. The child of the third couple was returned and the parents lost custody of him permanently.

Although results of treatment programs in child abuse are difficult to find, which is one reason we emphasize evaluation, Helfer stated that "some families (somewhat less than 20–25%) do not respond to treatment with our present methods and understanding of the problem." Helfer, op. cit., pp. 4–12.

19. Helfer, op. cit., pp. 4–10.
20. C. H. Kempe, "A practical approach to the protection of the abused child and rehabilitation of the abusing parent," *Pediatrics,* 51 (April 1973), p. 809.
21. A. H. Cohn, S. S. Ridge, and F. C. Collignon, "Evaluating innovative treatment programs in child abuse and neglect," *Children Today,* 4 (May–June 1975), p. 12.
22. H. P. Martin and P. Beezley, "Prevention and the consequences of child abuse," *Journal of Operational Psychiatry,* 6 (Fall–Winter 1974), p. 72.
23. Kiresuk and Sherman, op. cit., p. 449.
24. C. H. Kempe, "The battered child and the hospital," *Hospital Practice,* 4 (October 1969), p. 52; and A. D. Lascari, "The abused child," *Journal of Iowa Medical Society,* 62 (May 1972), p. 231.
25. A. Ellis, *Humanistic psychology* (New York: Julian Press, 1973), pp. 17–19.
26. Lascari, op. cit.
27. *See* N. R. Haimowitz and M. L. Haimowitz, "Introduction to transactional analysis," in M. L. Haimowitz and N. R. Haimowitz (eds.), *Human development* (New York: Thomas Y. Crowell, 1973).
28. R. W. Sanders, "Resistance to dealing with parents of battered children," *Pediatrics,* 50 (December 1972), p. 855.
29. C. Pollack, as quoted in C. A. David, "The use of the confrontation technique in the battered child syndrome," *American Journal of Psychotherapy,* 28 (October, 1974), p. 547.
30. Ibid.
31. Sanders, op. cit., p. 855.
32. E. Davoren, "The role of the social worker," in R. E. Helfer and C. H. Kempe (eds.), *The battered child* (Chicago: University of University of Chicago Press, 1974), pp. 142–144.
33. S. A. Holmes et al., "Working with the parent in child abuse cases," *Social Casework,* 56 (January 1975), p. 5.
34. Davoren, op. cit.
35. A. B. Savino and R. W. Sanders, "Working with abusive parents: Group therapy and home visits," *American Journal of Nursing,* 73 (March 1973), p. 483.
36. Helfer, op. cit., Unit 3, p. 14.

Chapter 6

GROUP THERAPY TECHNIQUES
WITH ABUSING PARENTS

Once goals have been set with abusing parents in each of the six problem areas, how do we go about the actual therapy? The literature on child abuse is virtually nonexistent with regard to *specific details* on therapeutic concepts and approaches to the treatment of parents who have inflicted violence on children. In Chapter 3 we presented our psychosocial systems model and the topic of symbiosis, which provide the central theoretical framework for our approach. Chapter 4 described our objectives, the problems we are concerned with, and how we measure results.

This chapter provides specific suggestions on what we do in each problem area. Although Child Development and Management and Employment may not appear to be the kinds of issues customarily addressed in psychotherapy, we believe that social concerns are inextricably linked with psychodynamics and that to ignore them is to invite failure or, at best, less than optimal success. The material we present concerning what a child needs at what age and how his behavior can best be managed is largely didactic, but the questions raised and the group dynamics generated are extremely therapeutic. The same can be said about Employment when viewed from the standpoint that an isolated, homebound abusive mother can often improve her self-image and sense of mastery by finding a job. In any event, the key concept that underlies much of our therapy begins with the symbiotic relationships in the abusing family. Thus we will begin our discussion with this topic.

SYMBIOSIS

When we set about breaking up the symbiotic relationship of a husband and wife, we attempt to strengthen two separate personalities and confront the discounting that keeps abusive parents locked into the symbiosis. In Chapter 3 we said that discounting, the thought process that underlies symbiotic behavior, consists of devaluing (1) the existence of a problem, (2) its significance, (3) its solvability, or (4) the person's ability to handle it. In transactional analysis terms, we want each partner to begin using all three of his or her ego states—Parent, Adult, and Child—and stop "using" certain ego states of the other.

We also mentioned earlier that one typical way a spouse "uses" the partner's ego state is to pretend he cannot make decisions effectively, thus discounting (or devaluing) his own Parent and Adult, and leaving the decision-making responsibility to his mate. This was reflected in our survey of parents (see Chapter 1), which indicated that abusive parents find it extremely difficult to get their spouses to make decisions. One spouse adopts the Child position (feelings only) while his partner is forced to be Parent and Adult: that is, using his own opinions and facts to make a decision without any help from the mate.

For example, Dianne made all the decisions about the discipline and care of the children as well as the decisions about finances, recreation, and home management. In other words, she was Parent and Adult to her husband's Child until she "couldn't stand it any more." At that point, she would burst into angry tears and demand that Al take over, which he did—for a while. Then the cycle would begin all over again.

Breaking up their symbiotic relationship began with a verbal contract in which Dianne agreed to *ask* Al for help with decisions and child care when she *felt* she wanted or needed it. This contract resulted in replacing their old Child-to-Parent and Parent-to-Child pattern with Adult-to-Adult communication. The contract also gave Dianne permission to feel, to have needs, and to take action to meet those needs, thus confronting her discounting of herself and her own ability to meet her needs directly. Al, on the other hand, was delighted to assist his wife at her request rather than be treated like a naughty child who had neglected his mommy, and as a result he stopped discounting his ability to help solve household problems.

Often, when a woman in our group does not work, she is discounting her worth as a wage-earner and is adopting the Child stance in the symbiotic relationship to force her husband into the Parent and Adult roles. To stop her discounting and force her to use her Adult more often, we typically contract with her to find a job. The process of seeking employment, being organized enough to go to work each day, actually working, and getting paid all tend to strengthen her total personality and stop the discounting of self. Women who never believed they had value begin to change when they find that someone is willing to pay them for their services. Also, because they are able to help cover family expenses, they gain an even greater sense of responsibility and importance. Because work is an important means of meeting psychological needs as well as material ones, we emphasize employment and treat it as a separate area of concern.

Sheryl had never worked and was terrified when we suggested that she get a job. She was certain no one would hire her and that she had no skills that would enable her to find work. With the group's encouragement and repeated urging, Sheryl did find a job, discovered that she enjoyed working, and was proud that she could buy things for herself and her child. Her husband, Jimmy, had long wanted her to get a job, but because of their Parent-to-Child relationship, Sheryl had responded to his pleading with rebellion and stubborn resistance. It took the group's urging and support, as well as an Adult-to-Adult contract with Jimmy, before Sheryl was able to confront her self-discounting and find a job.

Ethyl maintained her Child position by refusing to obtain a driver's license. She discounted the problem by saying she did not need a license because she could drive in an emergency if she had to, and she discounted the solvability of the problem by insisting that it was impossible to leave work to take the test; furthermore, their car was not safe enough to take the test in. After a group contract and persistent confrontation of her discounting, Ethyl obtained a driver's license and took more responsibility for chauffeuring their child, driving herself to work, and in general providing the transportation necessary to run a household and raise children.

When working with a spouse who stays in the Parent and Adult role most of the time, as Dianne did, we work on getting him to show, use, and acknowledge his feelings more often: in other words, we confront his discounting of feelings. For example, Robert sat rigidly erect in group, arms and legs crossed. He began to learn about feelings when we told him about body language and asked him to experiment with using more relaxed body postures. As Robert changed his body positions, he got in touch with his fear and anger and gained insight into why he was holding on to himself so tightly. We also ask the "feeling" partner to provide the nonfeeling mate with body contact by rubbing his back, for instance.

Although our approach varies, our overall objective is consistent: we try to teach group members to use parts of their personalities that they have never used successfully before. We achieve this goal by confronting their discounting. Touching, working, driving, thinking—all these activities teach people to grow beyond symbiosis into whole people.

ISOLATION

Abusive parents are often lonely, cut off from others both in fact and in feeling, and have few contacts with people outside their immediate families. So we focus on ways to break up their isolation and help them initiate successful contacts with others. Membership in the group is an important first step in breaking up the isolation of these parents. Once a week, for one and one-half hours, parents are with other people—people who share a common problem, talk about intimate matters, and listen in return.

But because group meetings are not enough to break up life-long patterns of isolation, we use behavior modification contracts for changes that will increase the parent's contacts outside the group. The get-a-job contract serves this function in addition to breaking up symbiosis. The homebound housewife who gets a job makes new friends at work and sees someone other than the deliveryman or newspaper carrier. We also ask members to contract to socialize in their own neighborhoods. Many abusive parents do not know their neighbors well enough to visit or call on them in an emergency.

Sheryl and Jimmy had no mutual friends, although both were young, friendly people who had been sociable as high school students. After their marriage, however,

Sheryl's social life consisted of visiting her mother on weekends, and she bitterly resented it when Jimmy went out with his friends. Thus one contract they made was to go dancing with another couple and invite couples to their home. Sheryl agreed not to sulk when Jimmy went out with his friends and to find some friends of her own. At her new job, she did make some friends.

It is not uncommon for abusive parents to live in isolated areas and to have no telephone even when they can afford one. Sheryl was proud that her father never had a telephone and was never called to work overtime at the factory. So she was opposed to the idea of having one. After contracting with the group, she and Jimmy did get a telephone and listed their number. After announcing "I don't know anyone to phone and no one will phone me," Sheryl was surprised to discover how much she enjoyed using it.

Some parents maintain their isolation by rejecting positive strokes and then feel lonely and deprived. Kim refused to accept positive strokes from her husband, Raymond, or anyone else in the group. To change this pattern, we introduced Kim to the Stroking Profile board.

The Stroking Profile, a group process and research tool, is a graphic index by which people can evaluate themselves and be evaluated by others in terms of their willingness to give, take, ask for, and refuse to give both positive and negative strokes.[1] Most people find it easy to rate themselves on each dimension and can measure changes when they occur.

As a "homework assignment" for five nonconsecutive weeks, Kim contracted to give and take an agreed-on number of positive strokes from Raymond and to ask for at least one positive stroke from him every day. As Kim learned to accept and ask for positive strokes, she not only felt less isolated but learned to meet her own need for stroking more directly and effectively. Her stroking profile changed dramatically: the "take," "give," and "ask for" bars depicted in Figure 6–1 rose as Kim learned the value of strokes. Prior to her work with the Stroking Profile, Kim's score had been extremely low (Never to Seldom) in terms of giving, taking, and asking for positive strokes.

The group itself also helps to break up the isolation of its members. This is especially true when members decide to visit each other outside of group. All we do is request that parents write down one another's phone numbers, so that they will have several people to call during an emergency. It is a happy occasion when some of the couples, wives, or husbands report that they got together over the weekend and had a good time. Sometimes they reach out by offering help to each other. Gary knew little about cars; Chuck was an experienced mechanic. Both men were thoroughly pleased with themselves and one another when they

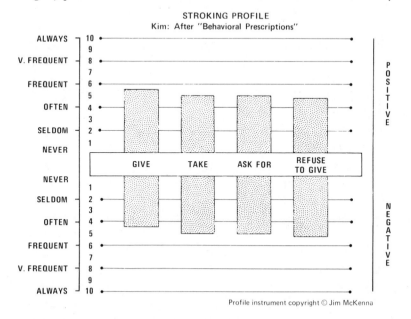

STROKING PROFILE
Kim: After "Behavioral Prescriptions"

Profile instrument copyright © Jim McKenna

Figure 6–1   Stroking Profile

told the group how they had fixed Gary's carburetor the previous Sunday.

The warmth and closeness that developed among five couples in one group resulted in a Sunday picnic, with group members, therapists, and everyone's children joining in for a day of fun together. (The children had either just been returned to their parents or were visiting for the weekend.) Socializing with a group of people other than relatives was a new and enjoyable experience for many of these parents. From experiences such as these, parents learn that loneliness is not only painful but unnecessary and usually decide to break the pattern of isolation for good.

TALKING AND SHARING WITH MATE

All couples who enter our group have marital problems. The most common complaint is "We don't communicate" or "He (she) never talks (listens) to me." This tension is also reflected in the sexual problems that abusive parents report. Typically, both partners feel unrewarded and dissatisfied with their marriage and have accumulated a large amount of anger that is not expressed openly.

Initially the couples deny they have any problems, but by the time the first few group sessions end, the problems and hostilities are usually out in the open. One way we bring out marital disharmony and get partners to begin talking to each other is to ask each one to name three likes and dislikes about the other. This opens the door for contracting between the mates for change. Della complained that Robert never talked to her when he came home from work but instead turned on television, read the paper, or went outside to mow the lawn (which he did two times a week). Robert was unhappy because Della never wanted to visit his friends. The two contracted that Robert would spend 15 minutes a day with Della before turning on the television set or mowing the grass and Della would visit his friends once a month. Although this contract was only a crack in the wall they had built up between them over the years, it was a beginning.

When Greta joined the group, she reported, with terror in her voice, that she had taken their toddler to the doctor for treatment of bronchial asthma and was afraid that her husband, Jerry, who was sitting beside her in group, would be angry because she had spent the money. We suggested that Greta ask Jerry directly how he felt. Jerry replied that he was hurt and angry that she had not called him at work to discuss what she thought needed to be done. They talked a little longer, hugged one another, and began working out how they would handle the children's illnesses in the future so that neither of them would feel hurt or left out. This situation is typical of the marital relationships of abusive parents in our groups: because each assumes the other is or will be displeased, he acts independently rather than checking out his assumptions, and thus virtually ensures his mate's anger or displeasure. In group, parents learn to share on a Child-to-Child and Adult-to-Adult basis, instead of having Parent-to-Child dialogue and controversy.

When Chuck and Sandy were angry with each other, he sulked and went out to the garage to work on his truck. After several futile attempts to force Chuck to talk to her, Sandy pouted and felt sorry for herself. In group, they learned that there is a reason for unhappiness, something can be done to solve the problem, and it is their job to figure out what they need to feel happy again. Chuck and Sandy agreed to think about their feelings when they had marital disputes, figure out what they needed or wanted, and talk over their conclusions with each other. They put this plan into effect, were successful, and had fewer fights as a result.

To get couples to talk and share with each other, we teach them the value of strokes and point out that both partners need stroking in positive ways to have a happy relationship. Once they learn that people will seek negative strokes when they think positive ones are not available, they decide to start supplying one another with the positive kind. Contracting for positive strokes is common. David contracted with Denise for back rubs, and she asked for and got his help in preparing meals and caring for their infant son. Our overall goal in the area of Talking and Sharing with Mate is to teach people that their spouses can be a rich source of pleasure and strength once they learn to give, ask for, and receive strokes from each other.

IMPATIENCE AND TEMPER

The tempers of people in the group range from explosive to an inability to show anger at all. The partner who acts out often has a short fuse and a hot temper, while the passive partner finds it difficult to express anger. Therefore, we teach parents that anger is a natural emotion and has a useful purpose but that it can be misused. Our goal is to teach the members to use anger effectively.

Initially, some group members ask for tranquilizers to help them control their explosive tempers. These are prescribed by the examining psychiatrist if he believes that medication will be helpful. Once in group, we teach parents relaxation techniques to help them control their violent outbursts and impatience. Since controlling temper and impatience is a common problem for group members, everyone participates in the relaxation exercise at times. It is a unique experience to be a therapist in a room full of apparently sleeping people!

The most common relaxation technique consists of having each person imagine a scene that is peaceful to him

—usually a place where he has felt relaxed and calm. He then takes three deep breaths, holds them, and, while exhaling, imagines the peaceful scene. The scene is commonly at the seashore, in the country, or deep in the woods. As simple as the technique sounds, many parents report that the technique calms them down when they begin feeling explosively angry or impatient. Moreover, their self-confidence increases as they discover they can control their own emotions.

Sometimes veteran members will demonstrate for newcomers the effectiveness of the relaxation exercises. Pam, after one or two tries, was able to go into an extremely deep state of relaxation, literally in seconds. When a new member was leery or skeptical about the exercise, Pam would illustrate how simple the process was and others were soon following suit. She used the technique both at home and at work. While in therapy, Pam became much more relaxed, got her children back, managed them successfully, and was promoted twice at work.

Occasionally we use hypnosis when a parent is unusually tense, suffers from headaches, or has some other physical complaint. Suggestions given during the hypnosis reinforce the value of using the relaxation technique when first signs of tension appear, and group members have reported encouraging results.

With spouses who are timid and the target of their mate's outbursts, we focus on assertive training. One goal is to teach them to express anger when they feel it. Ethyl was a quiet, reserved woman who quaked in the face of her husband's violent outbursts of temper. After hearing over and over in group that anger is a natural emotion but needs to be expressed verbally, not physically, Ethyl finally mustered the courage to express her anger at us. It was a banner day when Ethyl told us she felt we had been slighting her and her husband, Gary, for the newer group members, which was in fact true. We stroked and complimented her for telling us about her anger and adjusted our timetable so that everyone was more equally included. Meanwhile, Gary, who initially relied on medication to control his temper, became so adept in the use of relaxation techniques that his violent outbursts ceased. His expressions of anger now consisted of shouting, an obvious improvement over the violent beatings he gave his small son before joining the group. In turn, Ethyl felt freer to tell Gary when she was angry with him. This freedom was the result of learning that it was all right to be angry and seeing that Gary had better control of his temper.

The point we stress when working on the problem of temper and impatience is that people become angry and impatient when their needs are not met and they feel frustrated. Thus we teach parents to identify their needs and meet them effectively so that they will have less reason to feel angry and impatient. Most important, we teach them not to hold onto past angers in order to justify getting even. In this sense, we use the Gestalt approach of dealing with the here and now: past wrongs cannot be righted; only the present is available to work with. So we must figure out why we are angry or impatient *now*, what we want the other person to *do*, and how we can get what we need or will be satisfied with. In other words, our goal is to get group members to get on with the business of solving their problems and enjoying life.

CHILD DEVELOPMENT AND MANAGEMENT

In our comparison of abusive and nonabusive parents (see Chapter 1), we said that the abusive parent feels he has difficulty getting his spouse to discipline the children. The most common pattern is that one parent carries most of the responsibility for disciplining the children. When working on the child management problem, we try to help the parents distribute this responsibility more evenly.

Dianne, for example, carried most of the burden of disciplining her small daughters. When her strength and tolerance ran out, she screamed at Al when he came home from work, demanding that he spank the girls. Al, knowing little or nothing about what the children had done, would obediently beat them with a belt—because Dianne punished them this way. This system broke up when Al contracted to handle decisions about disciplining the girls when he was home, not wait until Dianne instructed or forced him to do something. When he did spank them, he was to swat them once with the flat of his hand on the buttocks. We find that we must be specific about what constitutes a spanking, because the "spankings" many abusive parents experienced as children were actually severe beatings.

In instances where one parent alone is responsible for the actual abuse, we contract with him not to discipline the child physically under any circumstances. If he feels a spanking is necessary, he is to ask his spouse to do it at the time the child misbehaves. After making this contract, Dianne said she felt as though a weight had been lifted from her shoulders because she knew she would not harm her little girls and would have Al's help. Surprisingly, the parent who has done the spanking has little difficulty keeping this contract. The difficulty comes for the nonacting-out parent who has been pushing off on the mate the burden of punishing their children.

Many parents, abusive or otherwise, are ignorant of techniques of child management other than physical punishment. So a portion of the group's time is devoted to talking about behavior management and other techniques, such as token systems, for modifying children's behavior. We also present practical problem-solving exercises dealing with child management. Techniques used in Parent Effectiveness Training, such as "active listening," "I messages," and resolution of need conflicts, have been most effective.[2]

After learning about token systems, Greta and Jerry devised a creative method of rewarding their two little girls. The system consisted of one large bowl of jelly beans and two smaller, empty bowls, one for each daughter. Whenever a child did something her parents approved of, she received a jelly bean. If she did something they did not approve of, a jelly bean was placed in the empty bowl. To get another jelly bean, she had to do enough good things to empty the "bad" bowl. The parents soon reported that after some modifications for extra good or bad behavior, the system worked extremely well and the entire family was much calmer.

We also provide parents with developmental information: that is, what children need at different ages and what appropriate and inappropriate parental responses are (see Figure 6–2). We deliberately make our presentation simple and practical. When the parents become familiar with transactional analysis, we supplement the information by explaining at what ages the different ego states develop and why a child has no Adult available to respond in a healthy way to discipline and parental expectations before the age of two. We also emphasize that some children are slower or more advanced than others and therefore will complete the various developmental stages at different times. Because few stages are completed entirely, the child will attempt to fulfill the unmet needs of previous stages when he is much older. We point out that adults also continue to seek fulfillment of unmet needs from childhood.

We present this information on a blackboard and incorporate it, along with material on child management, into our weekly group therapy meetings. Many questions are generated. For instance, Donna and Dean were concerned because their two-and-a-half-year-old son masturbated, until they learned that this was normal for a child his age. Sue and James did not know what to do when four-year-old Tommy insisted that monsters exist. After we reassured them that most children his age believe in monsters and need to believe in them, they thought of a clever way to reassure the boy that it was safe to go into his room at night. James brought out a can of "monster spray" (room deodorant) and sprayed under the boy's bed. This procedure reassured Tommy and allowed everyone to sleep in peace.

Frequently the parent who has not been disciplining the children finds that he feels inadequate to the task when asked to do so. In this situation we work with him on increasing his effectiveness as a disciplinarian. One technique is to have a group member role-play the child; the parent then attempts to correct him. The group's feedback on the interaction is valuable. When Greta tried to make her 18-month-old daughter (role-played by a woman in group) stop playing with a dangerous object, the group commented that Greta began fighting with the child right away, rather than attempting to distract her with something more interesting. This solution had never occurred to Greta, and she found the group's insight invaluable. This is another example of group dynamics at work.

The overall goal when working on Child Development and Management is to give parents the information they need to be effective parents, insight into the maladaptive parenting techniques they may now be using, and permission to change their ways of parenting.

EMPLOYMENT

In addition to the points we have already made about employment and how it can help break up symbiosis and isolation, there are other reasons for examining the subject. Members of our group sometimes are experiencing some type of stress connected with their jobs at the time they abuse their children. Some have been laid off; others work

Age	Stage	What the Child Needs
0 – 6 months (or crawling)	Early Oral (Existential)	To establish symbiosis Food and physical stroking To find that he/she has impact on the environment Talk
6 months – 1½ or 2 years	Late Oral (Exploratory)	Move around Get into things Drop things Self-feed
1½ or 2 – 3 years	Anal (Separation)	To test and oppose To be negative Break symbiosis Learn to consider needs and feelings of others
3 – 6 years (can be 2½ – 5)	Genital (Imaginative)	Identify differences in self and others: sex, color hair, eyes Ask questions Move away more from par- ents physically Invent monsters
6 – 12 years	Latency (Creative)	Argue, compete, achieve Do things, have companions Join community activity
12 – 18 years (puberty through teens)	Adolescence (Recycling)	Be contradictory Be part child, part adult Say, in effect: "Go away closer" and "Tell me what to do – I dare you." Recycle previous stages

Figure 6–2 Developmental Stages and Needs

What Parent Needs to Do	What Parent Shouldn't Do

ed, fondle, talk to baby
hen baby cries, check to see
  what is wrong
y out different things to
  soothe child
	Don't withold strokes
	Don't feed on schedule
	Don't spank
	Don't hover over baby
	  when there's no discomfort

ntinue giving unconditional positive strokes aby-proof" the house ovide protection	Don't restrict mobility Don't force toilet training Don't spoon or force-feed Don't spank

pect child to start con-
  sidering others
pect child to use cause-and-
  effect thinking and problem-
  solving
stitute disciplining
gin toilet-training
	Don't fail to discipline (not
	  punish) and give reason to
	  convey expectations
	Don't make expectations too
	  high or be too demanding
	Don't be inconsistent toward
	  child

swer all questions with
  reasons
courage problem-solving
ach how to get strokes
	Don't answer questions with
	  "because I said so"
	Don't get uptight over mas-
	  turbation
	Don't tease

scuss values and state
  rules
sten to child's reasons
courage task completion
  and setting priorities
	Don't make rules and values
	  too rigid
	Don't fail to discuss rules
	  and values

ick by rules and values
courage independence but
  still offer "protection"
  and guidance
	Don't give up
	Don't be over-protective
	  or under-protective

Figure 6–2 (continued)

at several jobs or on double shifts; still others are unhappy with their jobs. These job problems are reflected in the frequent financial changes in abusive families, as measured by the Social Readjustment Rating Scale (see Chapter 1).

Because the kinds of stress related to employment vary, the contracts related to the problem also vary. For example, Mickey was able to give up his second job when Pam decided, with the group's support, that she could get a job. Jimmy was able to shop around for a less dangerous and stressful construction job when Sheryl went to work.

Joe's situation was somewhat different. He had hated his engineering job for months, especially because he was frequently required to work overtime. However, until he and his wife joined the group, he had been unaware of the damaging effect the job had on his wife and his marriage. Feeling secure in the group, his wife, Lannie, finally confronted Joe with the pressure his long hours placed on her in trying to raise their infant son virtually alone. When her confrontation forced Joe to recognize that changing his job would not be only for his benefit, he worked out a more reasonable schedule with his employer.

Some of our work on the employment problem consists of providing information. Dean was unemployed and was unsure of his ability to work because of an old eye injury. We gave him information about a vocational rehabilitation agency that would test his job aptitude and give him a stipend while he was enrolled in a training course. On the other hand, mothers who enter the job market for the first time may need information about day care facilities.

Group dynamics come into play when one person uses the experiences of other group members to make a job decision. One night Al asked the other men what they thought about his moving from one job to another. Together they weighed the advantages and disadvantages of each, and Al felt more secure about making the decision to change jobs. Without the group's help, Al probably would have worried for a long time about his situation and would have felt uncertain about his final decision. The group's support helped him to solve his problem more quickly than he could have done alone.

Although everyone is not fortunate enough to have a rewarding and enjoyable job, no one in our opinion, has to stay in a job that is emotionally destructive. Therefore, we work with group members to minimize the tension and dissatisfaction connected with their employment. Also, as we noted in the section on symbiosis, employment can provide people with a sense of growth, competence, and satisfaction.

THE SIX PROBLEM AREAS REFLECTED IN ONE CASE STUDY

The following personal account was written by a 22-year-old college graduate who participated in our parents group. She had been married to an engineer for four-and-a-half years and had a 10-month-old son, who was removed from the home two months before she and her husband joined the group. Her narrative illustrates how the six problem areas we have been discussing affected the lives of one couple.

Denise's Story

For as long as I can remember, I have tried very hard to please everyone, but particularly my parents. One incident occurred when I was about 11. From the time I was about three I loved horses. I collected models of them and saw all the "horsy" movies. My biggest thrill was to go to a stable and rent a horse for an hour. When I was about eleven, my parents gave me a horse. I think they paid $75.00 for her, a saddle, and bridle. We had about an acre of land and I kept her stabled out in the back yard. After about six months, my parents felt I was losing interest in her and decided to sell her. Afraid to displease them, I went along, putting my own enjoyment of her out of my mind.

Soon after that my sister ran away from home. I don't know what her reasons for leaving were, but I do know that my mother was a very critical person, and she always expected a great deal from us. I remember vividly my parents' anger at my sister after she was returned to us. I was frightened by their anger and more determined than ever to please them and go along with their desires.

This behavior continued until my junior year in high school. I was 15 when I met David and had managed by then to block out my own feelings completely. My mother had been pushing since about seventh grade for me to have a greater interest in boys, so when we first started dating she was delighted. I was glad that she was pleased, but more important was the fact that at last I felt my own feelings and opinions were important. When David *asked me* to go out with him and what I wanted to do, I felt important. This meant everything to me.

When I continued to date David almost solely, my mother began to put the pressure on again. This time she wanted me to date other boys. This caused a great deal of confusion in my mind. I felt shame, guilt, and fear for having displeased her again. I also felt defiance for the first time, but this made me feel even more guilty. I had convinced myself that *good* girls did not disagree with their parents on anything; therefore I must be bad.

The pressure continued to build along with all my pent-up emotions until our wedding. On two occasions, my emotions got the best of me. The first happened a few months before our wedding. My mother, an extremely nervous, impulsive person, vented her emotions through constant criticism and bickering. We had driven downtown and on our way back home, mother was "discussing" something (I don't remember what) with me. I finally had enough of her criticisms and opened the door and got out before she could even stop the car. Luckily for me we were in the outside lane and not going too fast. She tried to get me back into the car, but I wasn't about to, so she drove home. By the time I had walked the two or three miles home I was really tired. We never seriously discussed the incident after that, but mother made a joke out of it to tell the family and her friends.

The next time I lost control was more severe. The constant bickering continued, until finally about a month before our wedding my pent-up emotions emerged again. My mother had been doing the wash, and as she came in and out she complained about everything I did. She finally made some remark (I don't remember what it was) which by itself was very minor, but it was the last straw for me. I began to scream as loudly as I could and couldn't stop. I remember my mother's shock and she yelled at me to make me stop. When I didn't stop, she called her sister and asked her to come over and talk to me. My aunt came over, but I was too ashamed of myself and my real feelings to talk to her honestly.

All this time, I was looking forward to a marriage which I expected would be a somewhat continued courtship. I realized that it would be give and take and that it wouldn't be a "bed of roses," but I felt that at last my own feelings and opinions would be important.

By this time I had become a very emotional person internally and had many self-doubts and needs which had been ignored. Most couples go through a learning period in terms of their sexual relationship: a period of finding out what each person wants and needs and how these can best be fulfilled. But to me, it was a particularly tense time. When at first we didn't succeed, I felt it was my fault and that I had expected too much. My husband took the ostrich approach to the problem. He found other things to do (TV, paying bills, etc.) or was too tired. Many nights I would cry myself to sleep, feeling the same shame and guilt as before but a different fear—a fear of losing my husband and adding another failure to my parents' long list of my deficiencies.

I soon began to block out my feelings again. We moved to a college town and became so wrapped up in the time-consuming process of a college education that we had little time for anything else. I used to look back on those two years as being the happiest in my life, but now they seem like a fantasy. We never talked about our own feelings about each other, our goals for marriage, or anything more serious than whether our team would win the conference.

After my husband graduated and got a job, I had more time to think about our marriage and myself. My husband didn't seem to want to share anything with me that had to do with our emotional needs. It seemed to me that all he needed was a live-in maid.

I had always heard that a baby would strengthen a marriage and hold it together, so I looked forward to the day that I would become pregnant. I knew that a baby would require a lot of care, but I couldn't foresee any major problems. I thought all babies were soft and cuddly and would sleep when they were tired and eat when they were hungry. When I became pregnant, my husband and I were both delighted. I made plans and expected myself to be the perfect mother.

Our baby arrived three weeks early and was a fussy eater from the beginning. I wish one of the nurses had explained that many newborns are not big eaters and that it was definitely not my fault, for this is what I felt. I was too ashamed to mention my feelings of failure to anyone. I thought that with David's help, things would work out by themselves at home. He had told me that he would take three or four days off from work when the baby came home to see that we got settled. But lo and behold! David went back to work immediately, and I was left alone again to find my own way.

Our baby continued to be a fussy eater after we brought him home. He also had colic (although I didn't realize it was colic until much later) and never seemed comfortable until he fell asleep. My pediatrician advised me not to take the baby out until he was about six months old so my husband and I rarely got away from home. The baby had an eye infection and jaundice when we brought him home from the hospital. His umbilical cord failed to heal correctly, and then at three weeks he caught his first cold. Somehow I thought I was responsible for all his troubles. We went to the doctor every week for the first six weeks after the baby was born. All along I felt more and more inadequate, more shame, more guilt, and feared that I had failed the baby as well as everyone else.

During this period, all my husband's thoughts were about the baby. He seemed to expect me to know what each sound the baby made meant and how to comfort him. He never understood what a trying time this can be for new mothers; in fact, he seemed not to care about me at all. He thought mothers were prepared instinctively to care for their children perfectly. Not once did he say he wanted to be alone with me or that it would be nice to get off by ourselves for awhile. Being new at parenting and extremely insecure, I interpreted this to mean that a good mother never needs or wants to be away from her child. My mother-in-law brought her children up that way and they seemed to have been happy children and adults, so I tried to be like her. I convinced myself that it would be selfish to spend time on things I wanted to do that didn't involve the baby.

Because our baby continued to be a fussy eater and was sick a good deal of the time, my feelings of failure multiplied. Three times I lost control, and my feelings of despair and complete failure as a daughter, wife, and now mother took over.

Day by day, I became more and more depressed. I gradually got to dread feeding times, which I'm sure the baby sensed. I tried harder and harder and got nowhere until I finally dreaded even getting up in the mornings. At the same time, I tried to give everyone the idea that everything was fine, that I was the perfect mother.

One morning I dragged myself out of bed to feed the baby. I warmed the bottle and mixed the cereal, and then went in to get him. I tried not to show my emotions to him or displease him. We went to the kitchen table and I held him as I gave him the bottle. He took about half of the milk and was finished so I tried a spoonful of cereal. He didn't want that at all and began to cry. All the while my stomach felt like a vibrator was attached to it. Tears came to my eyes, and I took him back to the nursery, changed him, and put him back in his crib. I shut the door and after about fifteen minutes he was asleep.

The rest of the morning I criticized myself for not comforting him and for feeling so insecure. I tried to suppress my feelings of despair and failure but there were tears in my eyes all morning.

By the time the noon feeding came around I was exhausted physically as well as mentally. The closer the feeding time came, the more I trembled, the more I doubted my capabilities. Needless to say, when the baby did awaken I was unable to comfort him. He immediately sensed my tension and could eat no better than he had that morning. My life seemed so useless, nothing seemed to matter. Nothing.

Again the tears flowed, the baby's and mine. We were both miserable. I ran with him back to the nursery and carelessly and hurriedly put him back in his crib. I remember thinking, "I've got to get away from the crying." He was lying with his head too close to the front of the crib and in my haste to get out of the room, I grabbed his right leg and jerked him down in the crib. Then I ran out of the room and shut the door. After about fifteen minutes the baby was asleep again.

The rest of the day I criticized myself even more for treating the baby so horribly. I had given his leg a tremendous jerk, and I felt so ashamed I couldn't keep out of his room for very long after he fell asleep. Every few minutes I would tiptoe in and check on him, but everything seemed OK. I convinced myself that if he'd been hurt, he would cry or look pale or run a fever, but he didn't do any of these things and I was relieved.

The evening feeding was like the morning feeding, except that I had to look secure and in complete command to my husband. The baby had his one half ounce of milk and was soon back in bed asleep. I remember looking at his leg closely before I picked him up that evening, but he seemed fine and in no pain. Nor was there any swelling.

That evening we watched the TV and avoided talking to each other, which was not new. That night my husband slept like a log while I tossed and turned.

The next morning my husband went to work as usual. The baby awakened and seemed OK, still no symptoms of any kind. I decided to forget the cereal that morning. I was rocking him in the nursery as I fed him when he fell asleep. As I tried to get up and put him back in bed without awakening him, he did wake up and cried. I was so exhausted that the sudden noise startled me and he rolled from my lap to the floor as I got up. He only fell a couple of feet onto thick carpet, so when I picked him up and he stopped crying, I checked him again, found nothing, and put him back to bed.

Around eleven or so I went in to check on him again and this time I noticed swelling in the upper part of his leg. I was so ashamed and felt guilty, but I wanted to make sure the baby got the help he needed so I called my husband at work and asked him to come home because the baby had been dropped and I was afraid his leg had been broken.

The baby's leg was broken and the next few weeks were pure torture. The shame and guilt I felt were almost overwhelming. But again I clung to the hope that things would get better, that somehow I would find the strength to overcome my doubts and inadequacies.

The next few months I tried even harder to hold in my feelings. I tried especially hard to keep them from the baby. I went very slowly with solid foods, at times stopping them entirely when he protested. He began to take the bottle a little better, but hated the solids. I felt he would come around to liking solids as he grew older. But my pediatrician told me that the baby wasn't eating solids well because he was taking too much milk. He advised us to limit the amount of milk the baby was given. The baby was three to four months old then and underweight. Looking back, it seems like the doctor gave us ridiculous advice. If the baby was getting too much milk, why was he underweight? But being a new mother, I took the doctor's advice.

The baby did begin to take solids better, but then he started catching a lot of colds and his eating fell back down. All of my doubts surfaced again. I felt responsible each time he sneezed or coughed or ran a fever. When the baby was about five months old, I began to notice how exhausted and depressed I was. I tried to get through one day at a time. My doubts about myself continued until I finally was at the end of my rope. Several times over the next couple of months, when the baby refused to eat, I lifted him out of the high chair and, with my hands about his waist, shook him. I didn't think it would hurt him physically. Everything I read said babies are stronger than you think, they're not fragile. I did worry afterwards that it was not good for him emotionally.

When the baby was about six months old, he was hospitalized with a staph infection and the doctors found many hairline fractures over his body, arms, and legs. I knew shaking him so hard had caused them, but our pediatrician told us that if it turned out to be child abuse there would be quite a hassle; someone would come to our house to investigate us and it would be very unpleasant. I was so confused. On the one hand, the baby needed so much help, but on the other I was so afraid he'd be taken away from us. My husband was still burying his head in the sand, so I had nowhere to turn. Again I convinced myself I'd be better. I'd be so careful, so perfect. But inside were all my doubts.

Somehow we were allowed to return home. The next month was better for the baby. I did succeed in hiding my tension from him and his eating improved. But then my husband began to pressure me to go on a trip. We were to be gone six days in all, but four of those days consisted of from eight to twelve hours of driving time. The baby had a tendency to get overly excited when we were away from home and spit up his food, so I felt we should wait awhile before taking the trip. I told my husband the trip would be too hard on the baby, that we weren't ready for such a trip yet, but he wouldn't listen. We went on the trip and it was a disaster. The baby couldn't sleep in the car and was physically worn out before the trip was half over. So was I. The baby was also so excited by the new surroundings and people that he began spitting up from one fourth to one third of each meal.

By the time we got home, the baby and I were miserable. I was exhausted before the trip, and afterwards we both were. I felt unloved as a wife and incapable as a mother. I was also disappointed in my husband for insisting that we go on the trip when I thought it was a bad idea.

The baby's eating did not improve after we got back home. He continued to spit up and then got another cold. After about a month of feeling more and more depressed, I struck my baby and hurt him again. This time as usual it happened when the baby refused to eat. It had gotten to the point by then where I had to awaken the baby for his meals.

The fact that he didn't wake up on his own worried me. One morning after I had awakened him for breakfast and he didn't eat, I struck him with my open hand on the top of his head. He was in his high chair at the time and I remember how pitifully he cried. I felt like my life had been, was, and always would be a terrible nightmare. I picked the baby up and we rocked for awhile in the nursery. I cried the whole time. I felt so guilty and so alone. It seemed like everything was against me and I had nowhere to turn. That was Thursday.

Somehow the rest of the week went by. But I grew more and more certain that something was wrong as the days passed, and sank deeper and deeper into myself. I truly felt that I was a despicable person.

By Monday I was certain of what I had done. The baby didn't play at all and slept about 80 per cent of the time— much too long for a nine-month-old. By Monday he'd even lost his desire to raise his head. I called my husband and he said he'd go with me to the doctor's office. On the way to pick him up at work, my guilt and shame and, most of all, fear for the baby's health overwhelmed me. My thoughts rambled and I couldn't concentrate on driving. I lost control of the car and drove into a ditch. We weren't hurt nor was the car damaged, but I felt even more that I could do nothing right. I called my husband again and he got a friend to drive him to me. From there we went on to the doctor's office. Later that day the baby went into the hospital. The next day a clot was removed from the tissues surrounding his brain. Thanks to modern medicine, but mostly thanks to God, the baby lived and will be a normal, healthy, and beautiful child.

Strange as it may seem, we now can look back to that time and see that it was not the end but, in reality, the beginning of a new life for the three of us. We have a long road ahead of us and it won't be easy, but with the help of some very dear people at the welfare office and the guidance of God, we will get there. To us, our nightmare has become a lesson, and we will be better parents and people as a result.

Case Analysis

All six problem areas that are typical of abusing families were creating stress in Denise and her husband. The following are points that can be made about each problem area as it related to their situation.

Symbiosis. The relationships in this family illustrate the concept of shifting symbiosis. Denise played the role of Child, feeling and wishing but doing little thinking or decision-making. For example, she did not want to go on the trip with their small son, but David decided to do it anyway. This type of interaction is typical of such couples: that is, Denise verbalized what she wanted but did not take the necessary steps to get it. David, on the other hand, ignored her wants and acted on the basis of his own opinion.

Denise's description of her relationship with her mother illustrates how the symbiotic pattern is passed from generation to generation. Denise played the Child role while her mother assumed the Parent and Adult roles. Jumping out of the car and screaming hysterically demonstrated how she stayed in the feeling Child position, allowing her mother to be the thinking Adult and opinionated Parent. Denise transferred her symbiotic relationship with her mother to David, hoping that in marriage she would be more fulfilled. The symbiosis in the marriage is illustrated by Denise's statement, "We never talked about our own feelings about each other. My husband didn't seem to want to share anything with me that had to do with our emotional needs." In a symbiotic relationship, there is not and cannot be any emotional sharing since only one person uses the Child, or feeling ego state.

When her relationship with David was unsatisfying, Denise turned to their child for fulfillment and, of course, was even more dissatisfied. One result was repeated abuse.

Because the infant did not meet her needs any better than her mother or husband had, Denise was as enraged at him as she had been at the others. This time, however, she allowed herself to act out her rage by attacking the child. She adopted the Child role even with her infant and attempted to beat him into "taking care" of her by eating well and not being sick.

As in most abusing families, the symbiotic relationships here were not static. David agreed to be Parent and Adult to Denise's helpless Child in times of crisis. For example, he came to get her when she could not think clearly enough to drive the car. Denise also called on David to do something about the damage she had done in her emotional outbursts. But there were times when David was Child and Denise was forced to be Parent and Adult. The vacation trip is an example. In this battle for the Child position, David won. David wanted to go, and Denise was forced to put aside her needs and serve his. Another way David claimed the Child role was to arrange things so that he be taken care of when he was home. Denise's statement that David wanted a live-in maid reflects the fact that she was the Parent and Adult to his Child at home.

Denise's dramatic descriptions of trying to get the baby to eat illustrate how quickly the symbiosis shifts. The Parent role, "I awakened him for breakfast and he didn't eat," shifts to the Child position, "I struck him with my open hand on the top of his head," then back to the Parent, "I picked the baby up and we rocked for awhile in the nursery," and finally back to the Child again: "I cried the whole time. I felt so guilty and so alone." Sadly, the frantic shifting reflects the desperate efforts of many abusive parents to obtain love and nurturing.

Isolation. Denise's story illustrates the isolation of abusive parents. First, both Denise and David were emotionally isolated. Denise reported that since childhood she had kept her emotions to herself, letting them out only in ourbursts of temper after the pressures had become too great. David too held back his feelings. Early in their marriage, Denise and David pulled away from each other, rather than discuss sensitive subjects such as their sexual difficulties. As Denise says, they blocked out their feelings and in the process blocked themselves off from each other.

Denise and David were also socially isolated. Although they socialized some while they were in college, after David began working they rarely saw friends. The isolation became even more acute when the baby arrived. When the pediatrician advised Denise "not to take the baby out until he was about six months old," Denise decided this meant she should also stay home. No arrangements were made so that she would have time away from the child. Instead, all three were trapped in an atmosphere of increasing tension and frustration.

Because Denise and David seldom went out, they had few friends they could turn to in times of crisis. And even if they had known people, Denise was unlikely to request help from anyone but David. Her description of her child-hood reflects the fact that she learned early not to ask for what she wanted or needed, and until she joined the group, she continued to operate on that basis. Thus, asking a neighbor to help her out with her baby or relieve her for awhile was antithetical to the way she perceived herself and others. Consequently, she and David remained isolated and had no resources available to alleviate the stress that finally culminated in repeated abuse of their child.

Talking and Sharing with Mate. This problem overlapped partially with Isolation. The problem began with their marriage. Denise reports that when she and David had sexual difficul-ties, she blamed herself and David "took the ostrich ap-proach to the problem." Neither one felt free to talk about the problem with the other, so they attempted to ignore it—or, in Denise's case, keep the hurt and guilt to her-self.

When the baby came, David and Denise continued to avoid talking about their problems and feelings. Although David promised to help Denise take care of the new baby, he went back to work. Rather than confront David at the time, Denise buried her anger and disappointment. She did the same thing with her insecurity about taking care of the baby. Because she believed David expected her "to know what each sound the baby made meant and how to comfort him," she was reluctant to share her doubts with him. Therefore, he "never understood what a trying time this can be for new mothers." Most important, Denise never told David about the nightmare of trying to get the child to eat. Instead she tried to "look secure and in complete command." Although it is doubtful that David was oblivious to the tension and pressure Denise was experiencing, he chose to go along with Denise's pretense rather than experience the discomfort of sharing with her about sensitive or intimate subjects.

Talking about personal matters is difficult for many married couples, in part, perhaps, because they want to keep up a pleasant front and, in part, because they are afraid of being attacked, criticized, or ridiculed. But because abusive parents avoid talking about minor as well as major concerns, before long an all-but-impenetrable wall has been built up between them. Not surprisingly, the partners feel more and more isolated, lonely, frustrated, and angry. These were the feelings Denise had built up behind her wall, and they began to disappear only as the wall was torn down.

Impatience/Temper.   In this family, impatience and temper were more of a problem to Denise than to David, which is fairly typical of many abusive parents in our groups. One spouse is prone to express his anger in emotional outbursts, while the other handles anger in a passive manner. As Denise illustrates, her outbursts of temper developed during interactions with her mother.

Denise is hardly what one would call "hot-tempered," but because she allowed her anger and frustration to reach the boiling point, she exploded. Jumping out of the car when her mother criticized her illustrates how she handled her anger. Screaming when her mother criticized her while washing clothes is another example. Denise tried "very hard to please everyone," an understandably impossible task, and when she failed, she stopped trying and went in the opposite direction—acting out her frustration and anger.

When Denise was a mother, she attempted to please everyone by being a "good" mother, which meant having a baby that was happy, cute, and well-fed. Here, too, she was thwarted just as she had been thwarted in her efforts to please her mother. But this time, her frustration and anger was expressed as rage toward her infant son. He, like everyone else, was dissatisfied with her. As she admitted, "I made plans and expected myself to be the perfect mother," and then was faced with a new baby that was premature, a fussy eater with an eye infection, jaundice, an umbilical cord that failed to heal properly, and a cold at age three weeks. Not surprisingly, Denise felt she had failed miserably to live up to her own and others' expectations. As her feelings of failure multiplied, she eventually lost control and expressed the rage that had built up inside by repeatedly abusing her baby.

Temper and impatience are closely interlocked in abusive parents like Denise. She expected a certain kind of behavior from her baby and, when it was not forthcoming fairly quickly, she became both angry and guilty. When the baby would not eat promptly, she was terrified he would not eat at all, which increased the tension both she and the baby felt and in turn reduced the chances he would eat. When her panic reached a certain point, she acted impulsively, e.g., ran with the infant to the nursery and "carelessly and hurriedly" put him in the crib, jerking him by the leg. At other times when the baby would not eat, Denise lifted him out of the high chair and shook him. Her impatience led her to expect him to eat faster, and shaking him was an expression of her temper. But it was difficult for her to draw a line. Drawing the line between impatience and temper is not, it seems, nearly as important as drawing the line between *feeling* and *acting* out impulsive anger. Denise did not draw that line.

Child Development and Management. As Denise's account vividly illustrates, she and David had unrealistic expectations of a baby, as do many abusive parents. "I had always heard that a baby would strengthen a marriage and hold it together. . . . I thought all babies were soft and cuddly and would sleep when they were tired and eat when they were hungry." Thus the reality of a premature infant was overwhelming. When the child did not fit her preconceived expectations, Denise alternated between frustration and guilt. "Somehow I thought I was responsible for all his troubles."

In addition to having unrealistic expectations of the baby, Denise—reinforced by David's beliefs—had unrealistic expectations of herself. David assumed that mothers "were prepared instinctively to care for their children perfectly." Believing he must be right, Denise felt guilty about not knowing what to do and about wanting some time to herself.

Like so many young parents, not just abusive parents, David and Denise knew little more about parenting than what they had learned in the process of being parented. David learned from his mother that mothers devote all their time to their children, so he assumed that Denise should behave that way. When Denise made herself miserable trying to live up to his expectations, she felt even more guilty, angry, and depressed.

Denise and David were also woefully lacking in accurate information on infant behavior and child care in general. She complained that the nurses in the hospital did not explain to her that many newborns are fussy eaters. She was unaware that her baby had colic until he had cried for weeks. And she assumed she was responsible for all his illnesses—illnesses that are common among premature infants. She was confused about when and what to feed him and about what to do when he would not eat. At some level, she believed the baby would eat if he was punished for not eating. Her lack of information forced her into futile but frantic attempts to make the child comply with her efforts at parenting.

It is hard to imagine that two people with college educations would have so little information about child care, but Denise and David are not exceptional. Like many parents, their ideas of parenthood are formed by mass media presentations of families and mother-child relationships. Thus it is not surprising that so many young parents are unprepared for the unpleasant aspects of child rearing. In Denise's and David's case, their lack of information was almost fatal to their small son.

Employment. Unlike many abusive parents, employment was not a source of stress for Denise and David. Yet it was a problem. David liked his work, was reasonably well paid, and got along well with most of his co-workers. But he used his job as an escape. "He had told me that he would take three or four days off from work when the baby came home to see that we got settled. But lo and behold! David went back to work immediately and there I was left alone to find my own way." David was just as nervous about the prospect of caring for a new infant as his wife was, so he used his work as a way out. In that respect, David's work was a source of stress to Denise, not because it forced him to be away from home, but because David fled to his work to get away from the tension at home.

Denise had never worked before her marriage or before the birth of their son. For her, a job probably would have been a relief from the stress of 24-hour child care. She had a college degree and was personable and outgoing. Finding a suitable job would not have been difficult and would have given her an opportunity to arrange for someone else to care for the baby part-time. Unfortunately, neither Denise nor David had considered the possibility of her working. They were not opposed to the idea; they simply had not considered alternatives.

Case Outcome

In the course of group therapy, Denise and David made many dramatic changes in their lives. In terms of breaking up the symbiosis, Denise made some important decisions about her worth. After realizing how self-destructive her relationship with her mother had been, she decided to stop seeing her mother for a few months until she was certain she could be around her without assuming the Child role. By breaking the symbiosis with her mother, she began using her Parent and Adult more often and more effectively. She was able to care for her son with less stress and trauma and, as she stopped playing the Child role so completely, David began showing some of his feelings. In short, Denise broke out of symbiotic relationships in both her family of origin and her nuclear family and began functioning as a complete person, which allowed David to do so too.

Denise returned to school for a master's degree in education and, in the process, made many new friends and interesting contacts with professional people. She and David also began inviting friends over for dinner and going out with other couples. Denise's terror about being trapped alone for hours on end with a crying baby ended. Also, as Denise began to feel better about herself, she was more willing to share her fears and feelings with her husband. As a result, he began to share his feelings more and both realized how unnecessary their self-imposed silence had been.

Temper ceased to be a problem for Denise as her self-esteem improved. She asked for help when she needed it, felt less burdened, and consequently less angry about the burden of child rearing. Relaxation training also helped her control tension when she felt it mounting. The pressure on Denise lessened, too, when she learned more about child development and management. Because of this information, she found that she had blamed herself for things which were not her fault. She also learned how to handle the baby more effectively.

Denise plans to teach after completing her master's degree. Looking back, both she and David see that much of the stress that played a part in abuse might have been avoided if Denise had been able to get away from the baby more often and had had outside interests to break the monotony and burden of child care. Now that they have planned that relief into their lives, both are optimistic about their own and the family's future.

NOTES

1. J. McKenna, "Stroking profile: Application to script analysis," *Transactional Analysis Journal,* 4 (October 1974), pp. 20–24.
2. T. Gordon, *Parent effectiveness training* (New York: Wyden, 1970).

Chapter 7

ALTERNATIVE APPROACHES TO SECONDARY PREVENTION

Much of the treatment of abusing parents in this country is done by lay persons. Many, if not most, suspected cases of abuse are reported by lay persons. Therefore, secondary prevention—providing help to abusive parents and their child so that no further acts of violence will occur—depends heavily on the nonprofessional.

There are several reasons why the lay person plays such a prominent role in secondary prevention. First, treatment of abusing parents on an individual basis with psychoanalysis or related psychotherapy not only takes too long but is probably ineffective. Second, group therapy has not yet been extended to enough people who abuse to help all those who need it. Third, relatively few professional therapists are interested in working with abusive parents, either because they feel unprepared to help these parents or because they can earn more by working with other kinds of clients. Fourth, the lay person is in a better position than the professional to provide some services to abusing parents.

All of these factors apply to the treatment or support-ive side of secondary prevention. But before treatment and support, there must be detection, and the earlier the detec-tion, the more abuse is likely to be prevented. As we have pointed out, more than 50 per cent of the children who are abused once are likely to be abused again if there is no detection and intervention.

Lay persons are at the forefront of detecting suspected cases of abuse. Despite all the programs and materials de-signed to familiarize physicians with early signs of abuse and the importance of reporting suspected cases, most re-ports do not come from physicians. Neighbors, relatives, and friends rank high in terms of those who report abuse. Teachers also need to recognize the importance of early detection and reporting of suspected cases because they see more of the school-age child than anyone else except members of the child's family.

In this chapter we will present the early signs of abuse that teachers and other lay persons can use to detect and report cases and briefly outline some indicators physicians need to be familiar with—in the hope that they will act on those indicators once they have identified them. Next, we will discuss several approaches to secondary prevention, including lay therapy, self-help groups, and supportive ser-vices, as well as the role of casework counseling and some professional psychotherapy programs that differ from ours. Finally, we will discuss how the various approaches to sec-ondary prevention can be linked into an overall, multidisci-plinary delivery system.

EARLY WARNING SIGNS OF ABUSE

Teachers—or, for that matter, any person who has contact with children—should be alerted to the possibility that a child is being abused if the following physical and behav-ioral signs appear:

Physical Factors

Cheek Bruises. "Hands and fists can be used as weapons. Be especially suspicious of cheek bruises. Children fall down and hit their heads, but they seldom hit their cheeks."[1]

Hidden Marks and Bruises. If a child returns to school after an absence of several days dressed in a long-sleeved shirt and long pants, even in warm weather, or is reluctant to change into gym clothes, he may have hidden marks and bruises.[2] If he has marks and bruises in areas other than where children usually injure themselves (knees, elbows, shins), he should be checked.

Unusual Marks. Some parents use electrical cords to beat their children. These cords leave a characteristic mark on the skin. A few burn their children with cigarettes, which leave an oval scar, unlike the usually round scar commonly caused by an infected insect bite or impetigo.

Soreness. If a child hesitates to play at recess or moves unusually slowly, he may have been beaten.

Distended Stomach. A certain per cent of physically abused children are also neglected. One sign that a child is not being fed properly is a protruding stomach. When questioned, the parents may claim that he is a finicky eater or has a vitamin deficiency, or "the doctor doesn't know what's wrong with her."[3] These children often come to school without lunch.

Behavioral Patterns

Withdrawn, Passive Behavior. Some children respond to beatings by becoming quiet and showing little initiative. They try to guard against further abuse by acting as though they are not there: they ask for nothing, say as little as possible, and try to avoid attracting attention. Although the teacher may view this lack of responsiveness as a sign of retardation, an abrupt behavioral change in this direction should make her suspect abuse.

Regressive Behavior. Some abused children revert to infantile behavior, as if bidding for the sympathy or mercy of adults by their very helplessness. They may suck their thumb, wet their pants, or cry a lot.

Aggressive, Bullying Behavior. Other abused children pick fights with or try to beat up their playmates. They may be acting out the anger and hostility caused by being beaten themselves or they may be identifying with those who abuse them. They also may steal trinkets to give to others in an attempt to buy friendship.

Inability to Make Friends. The child who is abused at home often fails to make friends at school. He usually sees himself as unlovable and unacceptable to anyone. Because of his poor self-image, few children want to be around him. If he does try to make friends, his parents discourage him since they "have a vested interest in keeping themselves emotionally isolated."[4] Abusive parents distrust people and want no one around. To maintain their isolation, some move frequently and transfer their child from school to school.

Obviously, one symptom alone does not necessarily indicate child abuse. But if several occur together, and especially if they form a pattern over time, a teacher is justified in suspecting that a child has been abused. If a teacher is unsure about the meaning of the marks or the child's behavior, then he should question the child as casually as possible. Obvious questions will only alarm the child.[5]

The aggressive child who is abused at home often adopts a facade of being wise beyond his years. Ironically, he assumes "a protective attitude toward his parents. Even though his parents are torturing him at night, he will back them to the hilt in the light of day."[6] He does not want to run the risk of worse beatings.

Early detection, then, requires not only knowledge about the warning signs but tact when talking with the child. Although some people find it hard to understand, most abused children will go to great lengths to protect their parents. A child may fear his parents, but he also loves them, and they represent the only security he knows.

The importance of early detection cannot be overemphasized. As the American Humane Association pointed out:

> If children are identified when they show the earliest impact of their families' troubles, help can be made available at a stage when their problems can be more readily resolved. Too often referrals to protective services are not made until the conditions of neglect or abuse become acute and intolerable. Such referrals may come too late to salvage the home.[7]

As for what physicians can watch for to identify abuse in its very earliest stages, the doctor has the parents as well as the child to pick up cues from. And of course he also has the records of physical injuries.

> A potent case-finding lead is a discrepant history. The parent may tell us that the child fell down a flight of stairs, but on examination we find that he has spiral fractures on both arms. There is simply no way that that accident could have produced those injuries; the arms had to be twisted. In general, a history totally out of keeping with the clinical findings, or x-ray evidence of repeated fractures when a history is given of only one injury, is very revealing.[8]

Also, the parents' description of the child and his behavior may not jibe with the physician's observations. A mother may say that her child is clumsy and always bruises or insist he is irritable or retarded; the physician, however, finds that the child is agile and does not bruise easily or that he seems amiable and bright. "These contradictions tell us that the mother or father is seeing the child unrealistically. In general, we have come to believe that any inappropriate viewing of the child can be a valuable aid in diagnosis and prognosis."[9]

When parents bring an injured child to a physician or a hospital, their behavior sometimes indicates that abuse has occurred. Abusive parents act differently from non-abusing ones. Morris and colleagues found that typical parents report the details of the child's injury spontaneously; express concern about the injury, the treatment, and the prognosis; exhibit a sense of guilt; ask questions about discharge date and follow-up care; and visit the child frequently and bring gifts. Abusive parents, on the other hand, do not volunteer information about the injury and are evasive or contradictory; seem critical of the child and angry with him for being injured; do not seem to feel guilt or remorse; show no concern about the injury, treatment, or prognosis; seldom visit or play with the child; do not inquire about discharge date or follow-up care; and are preoccupied with themselves and unconcerned about the child.[10]

The child himself also provides telling clues. The nonabused child usually clings to his parents when they are brought in, turns to them for assurance and comfort during and after examination and treatment, repeatedly expresses in his words and actions that he wants to go home, and is reassured by the parents' visits. The abused child, on the other hand, is likely to cry hopelessly during treatment and examination, but cry very little in general. He does not look to his parents for reassurance, is wary of being touched by his parents or anyone else, and may become apprehensive when an adult approaches another child who is crying. When admitted to the ward, he usually settles in quickly, but he is constantly on the alert for danger and assumes a blank facial expression whenever discharge from the hospital is mentioned.[11]

Once the physician, hospital, teacher, social worker, neighbor, or relative reports the suspected abuse and the case is confirmed, the next step in secondary prevention is to get help for the parents so that they will stop inflicting violence on the child. Although the kind of help offered varies widely across the country, the nonprofessional plays a major role in many treatment and support programs.

LAY THERAPY

It has long been held that much of psychotherapy depends on the warmth, empathy, and respect that one person shows while listening to another. There is also good reason to believe that, to gain maximum results, a person should have the special skills that can only be acquired through professional training. But at least one investigator contends that some persons are naturally endowed with the qualities of a therapist and therefore need no special training to be effective.[12] These individuals make the best lay therapists for abusing parents. Unlike the professional therapist, the nonprofessional goes into the home and provides a warm parent model for the abusing parent, who probably never had this kind of caring relationship. The lay therapist in the field of child abuse goes by many names— parent aide, mother surrogate, family aide, mothering aide, community aide. Some receive brief training and are considered paraprofessionals; others do not. But they all play a significant role in many child abuse treatment programs. Their "training" primarily consists of having been loved by their mothers and fathers and having been a loving father or mother themselves.[13] They are prepared to spend a large amount of time for little or no pay and to become meaningfully involved in the lives of abusing families. Because they are willing to give so much of themselves and their time and because the need is so great, they carry much of the burden in the treatment of abusive parents and, furthermore, appear to be successful.

Parent aide is the term most commonly applied to the person who goes into the home of an abusing family and establishes a caring relationship. In the process, the aide gradually overcomes the parents' suspicion and isolation by proving "that she is available to reach out and offer comfort and concern even when it is not convenient to do so. She must offer the mother a chance to ventilate her feelings about her role as a woman, wife and mother . . . [work] side by side to teach mother abilities . . . [and be] tolerant of any anger the mother expresses."[14]

At Colorado General Hospital, the federally funded Foster Grandparent program has been a main source of parent aides. The program developed when grandparents assigned to cuddle, nurture, and give attention to hospitalized battered children began mothering the abusing parents. Some began making visits to the parents' homes and eventually a program of using parent aides in abuse cases emerged. The program recruited men and women from all walks of life and age groups (24 to 60) and assigned them the task of taking care of deprived adults. Lay workers and parents are matched by social and economic class. In addition to having good parenting and being a parent, the parent aide must be a "mild and loving individual who is not easily upset by an ungrateful, suspicious and often initially unwilling client."[15]

Parent aides spend an average of 15 hours a week in the home during the first week, ten hours the second week, and four hours every week over the next six to eight months.

> The surrogate mother has to be available by phone, day and night. She is the recognized lifeline for that family. She tries to give these people, who are damaged, suspicious, unfriendly, and hurt, their first experience in mothering because these people, for better or worse, missed out with their parents. Later on they missed out with teachers and then friends.[16]

By providing this kind of relationship to abusing parents, the parent aide helps them to acquire some mothering qualities and abilities themselves. They internalize what they see and hear the parent aide doing and begin to act in similar ways with their child.

No matter where parent aides live or what program they are affiliated with, they must be prepared to deal with crises. At some point, being an empathic listener and a good model will not be enough. As one client said:

> I'm cold and I'm hungry. . . . If you aren't going to bring me food, heat and light, why come? We've got to feed my kids first. Let's get rid of all this jazz of worrying about my feelings and how I'm doing and developing a friendship, when you don't even show me how to get food.[17]

Parent aides, then, must be prepared to address basic issues such as what resources can be tapped quickly during a crisis to meet the physical needs of abusing parents. Although psychological needs are important, physical needs come first.

Because working with abusive parents involves much emotional wear and tear, the professional staff of the Colorado General Hospital program conduct regular group meetings so that the aides can ventilate the feelings of frustration, fear, and anger that inevitably arise when working with abusive parents. The professional staff also supervises the aides, does the psychological and psychiatric assessment of each case, and provides the aides with support and information in times of crisis and stress.

The lay workers in the Child Abuse Project of Sinai Hospital in Baltimore are called community aides.[18] In addition to being empathic listeners and behavioral models for abusing parents, the community aides serve as advocates for the parents to ensure they do not get lost or trapped in bureaucratic red tape. Because they are available when needed and are so intensely involved with abusing families, these aides are not only the cornerstone of child abuse treatment programs but often a critical factor in overcoming the isolation that characterizes so many abusive families.

How the lay therapist fits into an overall treatment program is illustrated by the case of Mr. and Mrs. R.[19] They were an attractive, ambitious, upper middle-class Jewish couple that was referred to the Sinai Hospital Child Abuse Project because of kidney damage their seven-year-old son Paul suffered when his father punished him for disobeying his mother. The R's pattern for abuse was typical: Mr. R had been born out of wedlock and abandoned by his mother. He was reared by relatives who treated him with indifference or rage and left him to shift for himself. Mrs. R had loving parents and had suffered little trauma but was locked into a symbiotic relationship with her father and turned to him rather than her husband to meet her needs. She had few friends and experienced much stress in her marriage: Mr. R degraded her, his expectations were impossible for her to meet, and he demonstrated little affection or emotion. Mrs. R responded with manipulative behavior and psychosomatic complaints. Paul became a vehicle for their rage and they used him to manipulate each other. In contrast, they both idealized their daughter. The treatment plan consisted of weekly marital counseling sessions for both parents as well as frequent individual sessions. A community aide helped Mrs. R overcome her isolation and find more effective methods of disciplining the children. In addition, the community aide enabled Mrs. R to experience a warm, trusting relationship while going through her daily tasks. Thus Mrs. R learned that her father was not the only person she could turn to in time of need. Paul was given medication and play therapy. Although Mr. R continued to have difficulty controlling his temper, his outbursts occurred at less frequent intervals and he felt more satisfied. Mrs. R developed outside interests and made new friends. Paul learned to trust adults and to communicate his needs more constructively. This is one example of how professionals and lay persons can work together to change an abusing family into a loving and growing one. Unfortunately, many communities have not developed similar programs to alleviate the problems of child abuse.

SUPPORT SERVICES

The term support services means all the resources that, although not specifically designed to be therapeutic, are a vital part of the secondary prevention of child abuse. These resources include visiting or public health nurse programs, homemaker services, co-op nurseries, crisis nurseries, day care centers, foster home care, classes on child development and management, and telephone hot-line programs. Whether combined or offered separately, they are an important means of assisting parents and children alike and heading off abuse in its early stages.

Visiting or Public Health Nurse Programs

The visiting nurse has long had access to families that ordinarily do not have any contacts with professionals. In terms of training and experience, the visiting nurse is qualified to provide support, aid, and human contact to isolated individuals and thus is well suited to intervene with abusing families. Although some nurses have neither the personality nor disposition to function as friend-therapist to abusive parents, many do and can.[20] By being supportive and caring rather than critical and judgmental, the public health or visiting nurse can establish the kind of rapport with abusive parents that will make them accept new information about child management. In a sense, these nurses "mother" abusive parents in the same way that lay therapists do, and they have the added advantage of being knowledgeable about health care. They can also be a valuable link between the abusing family and the agencies that serve them, establishing sufficient rapport and trust to ensure that the family will take advantage of what the agencies have to offer. Finally, the visiting nurse can follow up abusive families over the long term in a way that agencies cannot. By making periodic visits to families that have been in treatment programs, the visiting nurse can check on their progress and make certain that abuse has not recurred.

Thus the visiting nurse can and does go where other professionals do not—into remote areas of the country where there are no professionals and into homes where other professionals would not be trusted. For this reason, as well as the others we just mentioned, the visiting nurse is a vital link in alleviating child abuse.

Homemaker Services

The homemaker, like the visiting nurse, is sometimes welcome when other professionals are not. She can serve as a model for mothers who never had adequate parenting, teach these mothers the principles of home management and child care, and in the process bring order and structure to homes that are frequently chaotic.[21] But perhaps most important, she breaks up the isolation that so often characterizes abusive families and serves as a link between the family and the community.

However, the homemaker must be aware of the abusive parents' feelings and needs and avoid seeming overly brisk and efficient, thereby increasing the parent's already pervasive feelings of unworthiness and inadequacy.[22] Her most useful role is to gently encourage and reassure the parent. In short, the homemaker must let the parents know that they are not alone and that someone cares about them and the family. In some cases, the homemaker assists in evaluating the family's strengths and weaknesses and provides information that will help determine whether the abused child should remain at home or temporarily be placed elsewhere.[23]

Although homemaker services can be expensive and time consuming, the cost is not great when measured against the alternative. Foster care (if enough good foster homes existed) costs almost as much in financial terms, and the emotional savings of keeping a family intact are incalculable. In the light of these considerations, a homemaker program certainly seems worth the cost. Regrettably, however, homemaker services are either inadequate or nonexistent in many cities.

Child Care Services

Under the heading of child care services are programs that either partially or completely take over the care of abused children: crisis nurseries, co-op nurseries, day care programs, and foster care. All these programs are important for the prevention of repeated abuse, but unfortunately some exist more in theory than in practice.

Crisis Nurseries. Underlying the concept of crisis nurseries is the idea that parents should have a place to take their child when they feel they can no longer manage—resources where preparation, planning, and expense for leaving the child would be minimal. These resources would be available day and night, 365 days a year.[24] Few parents can be loving, kind, and understanding all the time, and they sometimes need relief from the pressures of parenting.[25]

Those who oppose the concept of crisis nurseries believe that parents should bear the burden of child rearing since they chose to have children in the first place and that if parents had the opportunity to let someone else take care of their children, they would misuse the privilege. But Kempe reported that parents have not misused this service.[26] There are only a few crisis nurseries in existence at the present time, and more are badly needed if abusing families are to be encouraged to seek help before abuse takes place or keep it from being repeated.[27]

Emergency Shelter Care.   Even less available than crisis nurseries are emergency shelters. Emergency shelter care has several advantages:

> It can allow the parent to separate from the child for part or all of the day, whichever seems best, but it does not make complete separation necessary as a part of relief and treatment. A shelter staffed by treatment people can observe crisis behavior and either intervene when necessary, at an especially meaningful time, or, in less threatening situations, allow the crisis to run its course.[28]

Co-op Nurseries.   Another type of therapeutic program that does not separate parent and child is the co-op nursery. Usually staffed by volunteers, it is a place where the abusing parent can work and visit, and observe how children can be handled without physical discipline. As one abusive parent said: "I didn't know you could get a kid to do something without hitting him."[29] In Boston and San Francisco, co-op nurseries have been established, using former abusive parents as volunteers. Although these nurseries have been helpful, similar nurseries operated by nonabusing parents who can serve as role models to abusing parents have been even more useful. Teaching parents how to play with children is one important function of a co-op nursery. Abusing parents whose parents never played with them find it threatening to play with children. Through play therapy and "philiotherapy" (as the co-op nursery program is called in Lansing, Michigan) parents get in touch with their own need to have fun and learn to let their children act like children: i.e., their expectations with regard to their children become more realistic.

Day Care Centers.   Although co-op nurseries, crisis nurseries, and emergency shelters are not widely available, various kinds of day care centers are. The majority of these centers are not designed as therapeutic resources, but they can relieve parents from the burden of continuous care of children. The following family in our group illustrates this point:

> Donna is a bright, articulate woman with two small daughters and a husband who works a night shift as a guard. She became so angry and frustrated about the misbehavior of her children that, in addition to spanking them herself, she insisted that her husband beat them with a belt when he got home.
>
> When these parents entered our therapy group, one of our first recommendations was that Donna seek employment and put the children in day care. She was elated and surprised because we considered it acceptable for her not to stay at home all the time with the children. Since she began working, there has been no repeated abuse. A crisis did develop when one child was sick for several weeks, and Donna took a leave from her job to stay home. When the pressure from staying home began to mount again, we recommended that the family find someone to stay with the sick child. They did, and the tension in the family subsided when Donna returned to work.

Realizing that they are not expected to stay at home all day taking care of children enables some parents to cope much better when they are home. Donna is a good example of this. In this sense, any adequate day-care facility becomes a therapeutic facility in terms of the parent's needs.

Even so, it is fortunate that some day care centers are planned therapeutic settings. A center such as the Parents' Center Project for the Study and Prevention of Child Abuse in Brighton, Massachussetts, not only cares for and protects children from further abuse but provides parents with opportunities to interact with their children in a supervised setting and to watch models of good child care. While similar programs do exist in other parts of the country, there are far too few of them.[30]

Foster Care. The scarcity that marks therapeutic day care centers and adequate, inexpensive day care facilities in general also extends to foster care. Since foster care is not at this time either socially attractive or financially rewarding, there are few excellent foster homes where a child not only receives adequate care but is healthier for having had the experience.[31] Yet there is a dire need for facilities where a child can be cared for when it is unsafe to leave him in his own home. Foster parents receive small sums for taking in children who often are difficult to care for, primarily because they have been removed from their own homes. If a child was mistreated by his parents before being removed from their home, the difficulties are compounded. If foster homes are to be a resource in the secondary prevention of child abuse, the situation must improve. At present, children sometimes return home with more problems than they had originally. Any improvements his parents make through therapy will be useless if the child's problems are so severe that the parents cannot cope with them.

Courses on Child Development and Management

A number of treatment programs for abusing parents include a parent education or child management component. The reason for this became apparent during our discussion of the characteristics of abusing parents. Most parents who abuse their children have either erroneous or inadequate information about children's developmental needs and techniques for effective child management. In addition, most abusive parents are products of the "world of abnormal rearing," and parent education is essential to help overcome its effects.[32]

Much education on child rearing is given in conjunction with other programs and interventions of secondary prevention nature. For example, a program for abusive parents established at the Neuropsychiatric Institute of the

University of California at Los Angeles has incorporated a child management class, which is taught by the nursing staff.[33] The staff emphasizes behavior modification techniques and uses Patterson and Gullion's book titled *Living with Children* to help parents modify their maladaptive behavior.[34]

In our work, we use Smith and Smith's *Child Management* and Gordon's *Parent Effectiveness Training.*[35] As noted in Chapter 5, we focus on child rearing and management in the context of group therapy. Although programs such as ours cover the subject in an instructional fashion, learning can also take place in more indirect ways. For example, lay therapists or parent aides can serve as models of adequate parenting and simultaneously establish a relationship of warmth and trust. The visiting nurse program and crisis nurseries are also vehicles for educating parents about child rearing. The reason for combining education (direct or indirect) with other aspects of treatment is clear: unless the other problems of abusive parents—dependency, feelings of inadequacy, marital strife—are taken into account, educational materials will have little effect. Abusive parents are likely to continue their abusive child-rearing patterns until their own needs are met sufficiently so that they can focus on the needs of their children. Thus although educating abusive parents about the developmental needs of children and techniques for child management is essential, this service should be combined with a program that takes into account the dynamics of the abusive situation.

Transportation

One of the biggest problems in implementing secondary prevention programs for abusing parents is transportation. If parents are to participate in group therapy, child-rearing classes, or co-op nurseries, they must be able to get to the service. A number of low-income abusive parents have chronic transportation problems: their cars break down or they live in areas where public transportation is inadequate or nonexistent.

Although parent aides and caseworkers furnish some transportation, the problem is substantial enough to address separately. Thus a "transportation group," consisting of resources for getting abusive parents to sources of help, needs to be organized as a supportive service in secondary prevention programs.[36]

Telephone Reassurance Services

Providing abusive parents with someone to reach out to in times of stress and crisis is a vital link in the prevention of child abuse. Telephone hot lines or reassurance services can provide this link, particularly when parents have no contacts with a parent aide, homemaker, social worker, or therapist.[37] One of the first hot lines that was designed specifically for parents with abuse problems is the Child Abuse Listening Mediation program (CALM), established in 1970 by a housewife in Santa Barbara, California.[38] Manned by volunteers, CALM provides a link between people who need help and those who are willing to provide it. When clients call CALM, they are told that volunteers (who function much as parent aides) are available. Although most of CALM's calls are self-referrals, reports of abuse by third parties are referred to protective service agencies. A number of calls come from parents who fear they are going to abuse their child and the help provided takes the form of primary prevention. Other calls concern cases where recurrence of abuse is threatened or has taken place. Counseling and reassurance are provided.

CALM has stimulated the growth of similar programs across the United States: Home Emergency Lifeline for Parents (HELP) in Phoenix, Arizona; Suspected Child Abuse and Neglect (SCAN) in Little Rock, Arkansas; the Child Abuse Listening Line (CALL) in Santa Monica, Quality of Life Hotline in Palo Alto, Child Abuse Prevention Services (CAPS) in Napa, Parental Stress Service (PSS) in Berkeley, and Help for Upset Mothers in Redding, California; the Crisis Clinic in Aurora, Colorado; Family Focus in Birmingham, and the Child Abuse Resource Exchange in Battle Creek, Michigan; The Citizens Committee on Child Abuse in Vestalk and the Heart Line in New York City, New York; the Child Abuse Study Committee in Salem, Oregon; Child Abuse Prevention Effort (CAPE) in Philadelphia, Pennsylvania; SCAN in Spokane, Washington; and Child Abuse Restraint Effort (CARE) in Green Bay, Wisconsin.

The proliferation of telephone hot lines for parents makes it apparent that the need is there. How much abuse is prevented by these services has not yet been determined, but the approach seems promising. Perhaps their only weakness is that they do not touch the many abusing parents who will not reach out for help.

Another type of child abuse hot line has also emerged. This is the kind sponsored by a public agency, usually a department of public welfare or protective services, designed to make it easy for anyone to report a suspected case of child abuse day and night. The public information campaign to promote the program in Texas emphasized that "it doesn't take much—just a phone call. Lift a finger, report child abuse. You may save a child."[39] The telephone number of the toll-free statewide child abuse hot line has been widely advertised by means of television, brochures, and so forth.

Another example of a telephone service along similar lines is the "24-hour statewide toll-free child abuse prevention and information line." Such a service is operated by the Connecticut Child Welfare Association, a private agency.[40] In 1974 this service, called Care-Line, received 104 calls, which represented 5.3 per cent of the 1,957 reports of suspected abuse that came in that year.

Clearly, the launching of statewide hot lines will have an impact on the number of cases of abuse reported and should lead to more early detection and more effective secondary prevention. These services, however, are still too new to evaluate how beneficial they will be.

Child Abuse Registries and Indexing

Another type of support service that plays an important role in secondary prevention is the statewide central register, which records all reported cases of abuse, regardless of where they occur in the state. The concept of a central register has existed for some time for health problems such as cancer, and registers for child abuse were set up in some states in the 1960s. The register provides local protective service agencies with a central source for determining whether an abusive parent brought to their attention has ever been involved in child abuse elsewhere in the state or nation.

At a time when so many families move from city to city, it is difficult to determine whether abusive parents have had similar problems elsewhere. Some abusing families move deliberately to escape detection. Now, with the registry system, it is easier to determine whether they have a past history of abuse. Because this kind of information can influence decisions about removing a child from his home or attempting to rehabilitate his parents, central registries are an important part of secondary prevention.

For rapid retrieval of information, register systems are now computerized. In Texas, a system called Child Abuse and Neglect Recording Information System (CANRIS) went into effect in 1974.

Eventually, a system that connects all the individual state registries into a single network should be set up. At present, information can be exchanged between states, but the process is slow and needs to be centralized. The Office of Child Development of the U.S. Children's Bureau, which operates the National Center on Child Abuse and Neglect in Washington, D.C., has identified an effective central register of child abuse as an essential element of a comprehensive secondary prevention program.[41]

Just as child abuse registries should be interlinked among cities and states, hospitals need a cross-indexing system to identify suspected high-risk parents and children before injuries escalate. The Vulnerable Child Committee (VCC) was set up in the Brockton, Massachusetts, area to promote early identification of high-risk children, using cross-indexing as one means to alert hospitals and social agencies to the cases. For example:

> A two-month-old boy was brought to a hospital by parents who said the child had fallen out of the crib. A check with the index showed a sibling had been seen a month prior with a slight concussion. In view of this, X-rays were taken of the infant. They revealed five prior fractures of both legs. In the absence of the index, the case might have been dismissed as an isolated and unimportant accident.[42]

As we will see in Chapter 8, the VCC system is useful in primary as well as secondary prevention.

Another method of flagging high-risk cases and promoting secondary intervention is to color code the charts of children who are suspected of being subject to abuse. The South End Community Health Center in Boston uses charts with red covers for children who may be at high risk.[43] This permits easy retrieval and periodic review of the chart without using identifying names or diagnostic terms. Other hospitals and clinics put a star on the chart and stamp it with "TRAUMA X," suspected child abuse.

SELF-HELP GROUPS

The growth of self-help groups in child abuse was stimulated by several factors: (1) the lack of professional help in many communities, (2) the inadequacy of services in general for abusive parents, and (3) the recognition that many abusive parents have a basic distrust of authority figures (including professionals) and some simply feel more comfortable around people who have the same problem. As Helfer points out, the self-help group is "a good way to short-circuit abusive habits."[44] Parents change their behavior by modeling themselves after others in the group who have proved that it is possible to stop inflicting violence on children. There may be no major changes in the parents' feelings toward the child or in their understanding of why they abuse him, but their behavior changes: e.g., "I don't beat him any more, but I cannot really say I have any feeling or love for him."[45] "Since I joined P.A. (Parents Anonymous), I don't beat my kid any more, but I don't like the little bastard any better."[46] Another mother, a founder of a Parents Anonymous organization, said that she still gets angry at her daughter "[and I feel like] clobbering her, but would I? No, I don't have to be afraid of the urge. I can handle it. If not, I could always call my husband or another P.A. member, or go back to kicking the chair."[47]

Learning to deal with anger and to redirect it is a major concern of self-help groups. Although the parent does not always direct his anger toward the child (it may be toward another adult), he often becomes so frightened of his rage, which he has frequently vented on the child, that he is afraid of expressing anger toward anyone. In other words, he is afraid of losing control. "Because he was not allowed to express his anger as a child, he may not know how to express it legitimately as an adult nor even understand that anger is an acceptable, normal emotion."[48] The self-help group offers the parent the opportunity to learn that he can express anger without destroying a relationship with another person or losing control of himself. The following excerpt illustrates this point:

> Mrs. N phoned [her caseworker] to say that she had been hurt by Mrs. O's remarks at the previous Parents Anonymous meeting and felt that Mrs. O did not want her in the group. Mrs. N was encouraged to express just how she felt, and it was then suggested that it was important for her to express these same feelings to Mrs. O at the next meeting.
>
> Supported by the caseworker's acceptance of her feelings, Mrs. N was able, with great difficulty, to repeat to the group what she had said. The worker's role in the group meeting was to help each of the women to clarify how she was feeling and to express these feelings to the others. Mrs. O told Mrs. N that she could accept the fact that her own problems were different from Mrs. N's but that she did want her in the group and she did care for her. As they talked out their misunderstanding, the tension subsided. It was a learning experience for the whole group.[49]

In addition to short-circuiting abusive behavior and redirecting anger, self-help groups are effective for two other reasons: they help break up the isolation of abusing parents and the members bail each other out during a crisis.

Whether self-help groups should admit professionals such as social workers or psychologists to their meetings or ask them for advice is an issue that is addressed differently by different P.A. organizations. Parents Anonymous, Inc., of Los Angeles, which began in 1970 under the name of Mothers Anonymous, does use professionals as chapter sponsors. It also relies on the advice and input of other professionals when necessary.[50] Parents Anonymous, Inc., of New York, founded in 1972, does not rely on professionals for consultation or advice."[51]

According to Helfer, one drawback of self-help organizations is that the members "lack a model of healthy parenting—a person who understands child development and can provide examples of healthy ways to handle problems as they arise."[52] Because abusive parents had poor parenting themselves, many believe it is essential for them to be exposed to healthy parenting. Another possible drawback of P.A. groups is that they do not address the problems of symbiosis and role reversal: teaching parents how to meet their own needs rather than depend on their offspring.

Parents Anonymous of California apparently exposes its members to role models to some degree. Parents Anonymous of New York believes it is essential that parents learn from those who have overcome their abusive behavior and thus serve as effective examples for others who are still struggling with the problem.

Regardless of which position is more valid, self-help groups are proving the value of the Alcoholics Anonymous model, which has led all kinds of people to band together to help themselves—Gamblers Anonymous, Neurotics Anonymous, Schizophrenics Anonymous. The idea of a self-help group for abusing parents was greeted with skepticism and a lack of cooperation from professionals when Jolly K, then 29, wanted to use her understanding of the problem and her leadership ability to help parents like herself. But Jolly went ahead and founded Mothers Anonymous, which later became Parents Anonymous of California. She had been reared in 100 foster homes and 32 institutions, had been raped at age 11, had completed only five years of school, and had been a prostitute. After two disastrous marriages, she tried to destroy both herself and "the little slut" she had brought into the world. "Her 'credentials' and cries for help turned off at least nine established agency 'professionals' who found it difficult to accept this form of 'field work' as a suitable criterion for motherhood, much less leadership."[53] Finally, a social worker challenged her to go ahead and do something about the dearth of services for abusive mothers. Parents Anonymous of California was the eventual result of Jolly's efforts.

In 1974 the initial Parents Anonymous organization received a grant from the Children's Bureau to set up additional chapters. It now has 150 chapters and some 1,500 members. Its goals include (1) redirecting anger onto objects other than children or other people, (2) learning to reach out to other people for help, and (3) altering destructive ways of viewing oneself and one's children.[54] P.A. meetings often deal with the subject of how to handle anger without acting it out toward a child in the form of abuse. As one P.A. member told the other members of her group:

> I did it! Last week . . . I got so teed off at my son! [He is five.] But instead of abusing him I squashed the milk carton I was holding until the milk went all over the place. . . . I released my anger in a more positive way and it worked. Now I know I can do other things besides being abusive when I'm uptight.[55]

Jolly believes her organization serves the typical abusive parent. "We are seeing the very withdrawn, the very aggressive, the isolationist, the uptight, the psychotic. . . . In short, we are seeing human beings displaying a lot of different 'typical human traits.' "[56] The size of these groups at any one time averages six to ten parents, most of whom remain for one or more years. Only 25 to 30 per cent of the members are men. When a group learns that a member has committed an abusive act, it devotes special attention to that parent. If these efforts fail, outsiders are asked to intervene whether the parent agrees to this intervention or not.

One need of self-help groups is a system of evaluation and follow-up. Jolly says that there is no formal follow-up on members, but "recidivism has been very, very low." Nevertheless, P.A. provides a lifeline, particularly in times of stress and crisis, and thus performs an essential service.

Parents Anonymous, Inc., of New York also offers a lifeline to abusing parents in the form of its Heart Line telephone service, which provides information and counseling on a 24-hour basis. Even on slow days, there are at least ten calls, reports Mrs. Gertrude M. Bacon, a former Family Court judge who founded the organization. Through her efforts, 30 other P.A. groups have been formed, based on the New York model. Unlike the California-based P.A., the New York organization does not accept federal or agency funds because "we want to keep emphasizing the self-help concept."[57] In addition to the hot line, the P.A. group holds weekly meetings in a Manhattan office building and sends out posters and other material to parents who are interested in setting up a P.A. chapter.

A third self-help organization is Families Anonymous, which was started in Denver by a public health nurse and her husband, a psychiatric social worker, on an Alcoholics Anonymous model.[58] Groups of abusive parents voluntarily meet on a regular basis, and their sessions are supervised by professional leaders who act primarily as "advisors, counselors and friends." However, when crises arise, the ultimate decisions rest in the hands of the professionals.

The emphasis in Families Anonymous is on sharing experiences, both positive and negative.[59] Parents are provided with a safe place to express their feelings. The structure varies with the parents' needs: e.g., sometimes it is highly directive and at other times quite free flowing. By sharing their feelings and experiences, parents learn they are not unique in their feelings of frustration concerning their children. Information on child management techniques is also an important component of the program.

The therapists or group leaders in Families Anonymous play an active role in teaching, being directive in group, and following up on clients because they find that doing so is vital when working with abusive parents—much more so than with nonabusive clients. For this reason, they feel strongly about including professionals in what is essentially a self-help group. An additional advantage is that professionals can offer the positive "mothering" model that is either lacking or minimal in other self-help groups.

CASEWORK COUNSELING

If any group can be called the infantry in the war against child abuse, it is the protective service agency caseworker. The responsibilities of these men and women run the gamut from investigation of homes and removing children from them to family counseling. They are expected to be many things to many people, and performing all their duties without getting caught between roles is difficult. Some are successful; others are not.

What is necessary for successful casework with abusive parents? Although there is no precise formula, several factors seem to be important.

One of the first hurdles confronting the caseworker is how to establish a relationship with the abusive parent.[60] Since initially abusive parents are likely to be hostile, cold, and defensive, relating to them is not easy. If they are likable, the caseworker may tend to deny the seriousness of the abuse. If he is able to surmount these barriers, the parents' excessive dependency and the crisis they are likely to go through in the course of counseling place a heavy burden on him. In short, abusive families are difficult to work with—a discouraging thought for a caseworker whose caseload is already extremely heavy.

> Often workers can't help but feel accusatory or vengeful for what the parents have done to their child. They also feel uneasy about interfering in the time-honored sanctity of the parent-child relationship. This all adds up to a situation in which workers may find themselves confronted by people who don't like them, who are threatening them, and whom they find it hard to like.[61]

The initial anger and hostility that abusive parents feel when confronted can often be reduced if the caseworker is understanding and empathic. Beneath the parents' anger is fear—fear of what will happen. Therefore, the caseworker needs to show concern for their feelings and demonstrate that their feelings count. This can be done by asking questions such as: What did your child do that upset you? Is your youngster hard to handle? Does your baby need too much attention? The parents' tension can also be relieved by making certain that they clearly understand what will happen. As Davoren points out: "Offering practical and specific help in contacting family members, finding child care for other children in the family and obtaining transportation—or simply thinking through with parents how they can do these things—will help them be more open to treatment."[62]

If the caseworker is successful in establishing a relationship with the parents, one of his first tasks is to explore more fully the factors that precipitated the abuse. Once he has identified these factors, he and the parents can work together to change the situation or at least devise ways that will help the parent control his abusive behavior. That control may develop as a result of learning the techniques of effective child management, learning about their own feelings, or both. In the process of educating the parents, the caseworker must continually keep their needs in mind and help them to modify their child's behavior without making them feel inferior or inadequate.

Practical information on child rearing and how to deal with anger is important, but the caseworker must also demonstrate constantly to the parents that he believes they are worthwhile and that he is willing to listen to them:

> In many situations the first thing parents need is someone who is willing and able to go to a lot of effort just to see them. Home visits are not only useful in themselves, but may

be the only way workers will get to see the parents at all—
at least in the beginning. . . . Sympathetic, responsive, non-
judgmental listening is an extremely valuable service. People who have never been listened to before will find it hard
at first to believe that anyone is interested in what they have
to say.[63]

After the abusive parents have developed trust in the
caseworker, the worker can begin encouraging them to
break out of their isolation and expand their lives by engag-
ing in more satisfying activities. However, when it is clear
to the caseworker that a child is not safe at home, he must
accept the burden of placing the child in foster care or, in
some instances, attempting to terminate parental rights.

What kind of person functions well while carrying out
these varying and sometimes contradictory tasks? Davoren
lists the following characteristics as useful in casework with
abusive parents:

A person with few, if any, managerial tendencies.
Someone who is willing to put himself out for patients, but
who does not go around sacrificing himself much to everyone's discomfort.
Someone who has a fair number of satisfactions in his life
besides his job so that he won't be looking to the patients
to provide these satisfactions.
Someone with a strong working knowledge of child behavior
that can be shared with abusive parents at appropriate
times.[64]

In short, the successful caseworker must be someone who
is willing to give much of himself to abusive parents, but
not to the point where he himself becomes "abused." He
also must understand the dynamics of abuse sufficiently to
know what is reasonable to expect of abusive parents in
terms of change and what they will need in order to change.
Many abusing parents need nurturing, and many communities lack parent aides, mother surrogates, or even home-

makers to help fulfill this need. Thus the job falls on the caseworker.

> Even when workers feel strong within themselves, and have reasonably fulfilling lives of their own apart from their work, the nurturing of abusive parents can be exhausting. The parents' needs are extensive—at times like bottomless pits. Workers calling on their own emotional resources are constantly aware of themselves, their own upbringing and the way they are raising their own children, if they have any. The awareness can be wearing. But the most draining part of caring for these parents is knowing that a child may be seriously injured or neglected, or even die, if the worker misjudges the parents' capacity to care for the child.[65]

Beyond the emotional drain abusing parents often put on the caseworker, they often turn to him also for transportation, money, and child care facilities. "If services are not available elsewhere and workers are able to give some of these services themselves, it can be well worth the time."[66]

Thus being a friend and helper and generating the kind of conditions necessary for effective counseling is a major part of doing casework with abusing parents. In one four-year child abuse project involving 46 parents, "the nature of service was primarily supportive in 28 cases, casework was aimed at the development of insight in 11 cases, and eight were receiving psychiatric services."[67]

Caseworkers do considerable treatment of abusing parents in this country. Some are trained social workers; some are not. Some have parent aides and homemakers to help them; many do not. A few have psychotherapy resources to refer parents to; most do not. Arvanian offers the following approach for social workers who must handle treatment on their own:

> Emphasize caring and acceptance of the isolated, depressed people who feel so worthless. Primarily, our tool is the therapeutic relationship between parent and helping person. The

> therapist becomes the parents' parent; through identifica-
> tion with the therapist—as a loving, caring parent—par-
> enting of their own children is learned. Listen and try to
> help them sort out their feelings—at whom they're really
> angry, how to love, and how to set limits for their child-
> ren. . . .[68]

Alone or assisted, trained or not, the caseworker who works with abusive parents must do so within the context of his agency, where heavy caseloads and frequent turnover of personnel may be a fact of life. Generally speaking, caseworkers never have enough time to do the things necessary for the best results: establishing rapport with and meeting the needs of abusive parents.

In the ideal situation, the caseworker would have psychotherapy resources available. Thus he would be able to function as an "alternate therapist" to the psychologist or psychiatrist doing the therapy.[69] As an alternate therapist, he would be available to the family when the primary therapist is not and would be willing to listen to criticisms and complaints that they may be unwilling to express to the primary therapist. Misunderstandings that arise in the therapeutic situation can be passed through the alternate therapist, and when the family learns that they can express their thoughts and feelings without reproach, they gradually begin to express them directly to the primary therapist. Most important, because abusive parents are so needy and distrustful, having more than one person available can be an enormous resource for change.

Although psychotherapeutic modes will be discussed in the next section, a program in Allentown, Pennsylvania, will be mentioned here because it involves protective service workers.[70] The program is designed to benefit abusive parents by helping their caseworkers. A psychiatrist and psychiatric social worker run groups for protective services caseworkers, using as material the problems these workers encounter in their caseloads. This approach is different than the one we use in our program for child welfare workers, which was initiated to extend group therapy services to more abusing parents by training the workers to conduct therapy groups on their own. However, we do offer therapy to workers in the program who find that material from their own groups is causing them problems.

MODES OF PSYCHOTHERAPY

Essentially, there are three basic approaches to psychotherapy: cognitive, behavioral, and affective.[71] Different modes of professional therapy emphasize different approaches. The psychoanalytic mode emphasizes the cognitive approach: gaining insight into causation. Behavioral modification focuses on what a person is doing that causes a problem: i.e., on his behavior, not on his thoughts or feelings. The affective mode emphasizes feelings and emotions, based on the assumption that if these change, then behavior and thoughts will change.

As we pointed out in Chapters 5 and 6, our therapeutic mode consists largely of transactional analysis. We believe that all three approaches to therapy must be used to engender lasting change in people and that transactional analysis seems to encompass the three. As part of our cognitive approach, we use structural analysis in our work with abusive parents, getting group members to recognize which part of their personality structure—Parent, Adult, or Child —is involved in a particular transaction. We also make minimal use of "script analysis" to determine how parents get scripted to behave and feel in certain ways. We rely heavily on the behavioral approach in making contracts with parents to carry out certain behavioral "prescriptions" such as make a friend, visit a neighbor, interview for a job. In addition to transactional analysis, we use hypnosis and relaxation training to teach parents how to act differently in tense situations. All these methods are combined with Goal Attainment Scaling, which is behaviorally oriented. In the affective mode, we rely on Gestalt techniques and confrontation as well as "permission" and "protection" to bring out underlying feelings of anger or sadness.

Other therapists working with abusive parents have relied on conventional psychoanalytic modes and techniques. Steele found that although "a few parents have been successfully treated by classical psychoanalysis, . . . the general character structure and lifestyle of most abusive parents make this procedure quite impractical and probably unsuccessful."[72]

All psychotherapy suffers from the lack of systematic evaluation, and few, if any, reports have been published on the results of follow-up with abusing parents. Furthermore, as Helfer points out, it is "very difficult to find a psychiatrist willing to take on one of these parents on a one-to-one long-term therapy basis."[73]

However, Steele contends that

> psychoanalytically oriented dynamic psychotherapy in the hands of skilled experienced therapists has been extremely successful in many cases. With most abusive parents, the therapist must be more willing to adapt to patient needs and to allow more dependency than is ordinarily considered appropriate. Intensive psychotherapy which skillfully utilizes the transference neurosis, can stimulate great growth and deep structural change in these patients despite their severe immaturity and developmental arrest.[74]

Another method of individual psychotherapy in child abuse focuses on a confrontation technique in which the therapist tells the parent not to punish his child under any circumstances.[75] This technique is designed to establish the therapist as a significant helper and to reassure the parent that the control he lacks will be provided by a potent outsider. It also is a way to get at the parent's underlying feelings, which must be worked through. Although this approach may be useful during the early stages of treatment, the technique has limited application. It also increases the parent's dependence on the therapist and thus encourages continuance of the symbiosis, something that abusive parents do not need.

Highly directive therapy also involves other risks. For instance, parents may take out their hostility on the child

> because their submission to the therapist reminds them of the unpleasant past. ... Additionally, overdirection may cause parents to say what they know is "right" simply for the therapist's benefit. Because abusing parents generally do not have well integrated identities, they can say the "right" thing and do the "wrong" thing impulsively with little more conflict than they are already experiencing. This kind of behavior reinforces their self-image which consists of a firm concept of where they should be and another of what they actually are—namely, bad people. This destructive pattern of living must be interrupted.[76]

We do not favor intensive psychotherapy on a one-to-one basis for abusing parents. Because we view the problem as both social and psychological, we emphasize the need for treatment to be conducted in a group setting. Membership in a group allows abusing parents to acquire the social skills and the sense of belonging and acceptance they so badly need. Steele too believes that

> for those parents who have the courage and ego strength to enter into group programs, the process helps them express their emotions more openly and also to become desensitized to criticism. ... Groups in which both spouses are present can help solve the common difficulty of getting both spouses involved in treatment. Husbands are notoriously reluctant to get help, but the presence of male workers leads some of them to accept either group or individual treatment pro-

grams. It is important for both partners in the marriage to be involved in rehabilitative efforts if at all possible, regardless of which one was the actual abuser.[77]

One of the first reports of group work with abusive parents was published in 1958.[78] The goals of this group were to provide parents with the opportunity to meet with others who had similar problems, exchange ideas, and have a social experience. Meetings were held every two weeks for six months, with a membership composed of single parents as well as couples. Topics for discussion were proposed both by leaders and members, and considerable time was devoted to child rearing and marital problems. The focus was more educational than therapeutic, and no differentiation was made between abusive and neglectful parents in terms of who was admitted into the group.

Groups have also been used in work with potentially abusive mothers. One group was composed of mothers with infanticidal impulses and one who had actually beaten her child.[79] The group met twice a week for an hour in psychoanalytically oriented group therapy. The reported benefits were that the women found that others shared similar destructive impulses, that there was group support for change, that consensual validation was possible, that there was an exposure to different ways of handling stress, and that there was an opportunity for social interaction that these women rarely had. Thus even some of the earliest groups worked on the problems of isolation, marital stress, and child management that plague abusive and potentially abusive parents.

A more recent group approach specifically designed for abusive parents, implemented at the University of California at Los Angeles, uses interdisciplinary teams consisting of a psychologist, a psychiatrist, public health and psychiatric nurses, and a psychiatric social worker.[80] Therapy groups are conducted by teams composed of a psychiatrist or a psychologist and a nurse once a week for one and one half hours. The program's orientation parallels that of many other group therapy approaches: e.g., sharing and expression of feelings, gaining insight into the motivations for underlying behavior, working through early childhood feelings about authority figures, learning trust, and so forth. In addition, the nurses provide information on child development. Eclectic techniques are used.

Paulson et al. reported that the groups have continually questioned whether their goal is insight, problem-solving, cathartic, or purely social. In other words, the groups have been trying to define their position in terms of the cognitive, behavioral, and affective approaches to treatment. Although this self-questioning was not presented as a problem, it seems likely that valuable group time and energy has been consumed in the process. If so, clearly defined goals, such as those specified in the six problem areas we emphasize in our work, might enhance a group's ability to define its purpose and get on with the important work of change.

Finally, so far as group therapy is concerned, a unique program was started that combines a therapeutic day care unit for children with therapy for parents. This is the Parents' Center Project for the Study and Prevention of Child Abuse in Brighton, Massachusetts. It has a therapeutic day care unit for children who have been abused and weekly group meetings led by social workers for abusive parents.[81] The day care program provides opportunities for parent-child interaction in a protected setting, with the parents acting as participant-observers. The goal is to avoid removing the child from the home and, while protecting the child, allow the parents to view the child from the viewpoint of other caretakers. The parents also obtain valuable child-rearing information by watching others care for their children. The weekly parents' meetings are designed so that parents can share their personal experiences, past and present. The project has reported success in terms of the children's physical and emotional maturation, the pleasure that parents begin to derive from their children and mates, and the smaller number of repeated instances of abuse.

Residential treatment programs for the abusive family are also beginning to emerge.[82] However, these programs serve a relatively small number of families and little information has been published about their operation or results.

In addition to the group approaches just described, more specialized modalities are also being used with abusing parents. One psychotherapy approach that makes use of a social learning model is based on the assumption that abusive parents have not had the opportunity to learn adequate parenting skills. Thus the goal of this approach is to determine the deficits in social learning that result in child abuse and to overcome these deficits.

The child abuse project of the Presbyterian-University of Pennsylvania Hospital involves behavioral analyses, which are conducted in the homes of abusive parents to spot problems related to social learning and teach alternative behavior patterns.[83] For example, the project's staff observed that abusive parents frequently are ignorant about child development and techniques for behavior management other than physical punishment. An outreach staff member teaches parents the techniques of positive reinforcement for child management and serves as a model for appropriate assertive discipline.

A smilar approach was instituted at the Denton County, Texas, Mental Health Clinic.[84] In this Parent-Performance Training program, parents were instructed in child-rearing techniques through a programmed text. Abusive parents were assigned a short text to read and were required to pass a specific number of tests with scores of 90 or better. They had to attend counseling sessions until all the tests were passed. After each test, parents received feedback about the items they missed and were involved in a general discussion about relevant information on child rearing. After passing all the tests, the parents were asked to identify undesirable behavior in their children and were taught how to change those behaviors based on the principles they had learned in the text. As in the social learning model, the goal of this program was to pinpoint weaknesses in parenting skills and gaps in child-rearing information that are likely to result in child abuse.

Although both programs reported success in terms of changing parental attitudes about child rearing, they have definite limitations. It is certainly important to teach abusive parents effective child management techniques, but it is equally important to focus on other problems that influence the family, which are more likely to be emotional in nature than problems related to proper child management methods. For example, changing the symbiotic relationship in the family is essential to stop the pattern of abuse.

We believe that it is necessary to work on all six problem areas discussed in Chapters 5 and 6 rather than concentrate exclusively on child rearing. Although many abusive parents lack information about child development and management, they cannot use this information effectively until they change their own relationship and their feelings about their child.

A COORDINATED TEAM APPROACH

Tying all the elements of secondary prevention together into an effective delivery system requires coordination of the highest order. It demands the teamwork of hospitals, community agencies, the helping professions, and volunteers. One of the biggest problems in the delivery of services is fragmentation and lack of coordination. A number of community agencies may be concerned with child abuse, and if parents are pulled from one to another, the stress in their lives increases and heightens their potential for abuse.[85]

Based on a system outlined by Helfer, the following is one way that a coordinated team approach could work:[86]

Step 1. The problem is recognized when a teacher, nurse, neighbor, policeman, or relative makes a report to a community protective services agency, which in many cities is legally responsible for investigating child abuse cases.

Step 2. The child is taken to the emergency room of a hospital that has a child abuse consultation team. An examination is performed and acute treatment provided.

Step 3. The child is admitted to the hospital for further treatment, which allows time for the case to be investigated. The family physician, if any, is brought in.

Step 4. The hospital-community SCAN (Suspected Child Abuse and Neglect) Consultation Team is notified and checks to ensure that a social worker from the protective service agency will assess the family and the home environment. In addition to the agency social worker, the SCAN team includes a hospital social worker, a public health nurse, a pediatrician, a family physician, and a psychologist or psychiatrist.

Step 5. A diagnostic and treatment planning conference is held by the consultation team three or four days after the case is reported and the child has been admitted to the hospital. By this time, all relevant information on the child and the family has been gathered. The team considers the following questions at the conference: Does the family meet the criteria for abuse? Is there any evidence that either parent is psychotic? What are the major problems of the family and child in terms of priority? Who will take action on each problem listed: e.g., who will arrange treatment for the parents, what kind of treatment or placement should the child receive, who will help the parents with employment or housing problems, who will act as overall coordinator? (Helfer suggests there should be a friendly family coordinator for each case of child abuse because it is so easy for these families to slip through a crack when several agencies and referrals are involved.) Which treatment programs can be used for parents and child? After answering these questions, the team formulates a treatment plan.

Step 6. If it is advisable to remove the child from the home, the protective service agency petitions the court for the authority to do so. If the child was not hospitalized after the report came in on his suspected abuse, the agency approaches the court immediately to obtain temporary custody.

Step 7. The treatment plan is put into action. A parent aide —and a homemaker, if necessary—is assigned to the family. The parents are referred for group therapy or begin receiving casework counseling; they also may be advised to join a Parents Anonymous chapter and to visit a co-op nursery, where they can observe how to play with and manage children. If the abused child remains in the custody of his parents (or if there are other children in the home), the family becomes acquainted with the local crisis nursery or emergency care shelter and the telephone hot-line service. Again, a coordinator must be designated to ensure that all these services are marshalled on the family's behalf.

Step 8. Everyone involved in the treatment program meets regularly to report the family's progress, including medical and psychological follow-ups on the child.

Step 9. When the team agrees that the parents have progressed to the point where the home is safe, the child is returned. The court is petitioned at the appropriate time to return legal custody of the child to the parents. The parents remain in group therapy or continue to receive counseling until the child has been back home at least one month and any problems of readjustment have been overcome.

Step 10. Treatment ends, but the parents remain in a Parents Anonymous group and the family coordinator checks periodically to determine whether the family is functioning satisfactorily.

This is an ideal kind of coordinated approach to secondary prevention. In reality, however, such a cooperative concentration of services and professionals is difficult to find. The program at the University of Colorado Medical Center is similar in terms of coordination; the Sinai Hospital Child Abuse project in Baltimore also has a teamwork program.[87] Other coordinated programs that are not based in hospitals include several of the 11 demonstration programs funded by the federal government in 1974 to "test different strategies for tackling the child abuse problem and to study carefully . . . the successes and failures of the projects."[88]

NOTES

1. *Lift a finger: The teacher's role in combating child abuse* (Houston, Tex.: Education Professions Development Consortium C, 1975), p. 35.
2. Ibid.
3. "Identifying the battered or molested child," *Handbook for School Staff Members* (Palo Alto, Calif.: Palo Alto School District, January 1972).
4. Ibid., p. 226.
5. *Lift a finger*, op. cit., p. 34.
6. Ibid.
7. *Guidelines for schools, teachers, nurses, counselors, and administrators* (Denver, Colo.: American Humane Association, 1971), p. 221.
8. C. H. Kempe, "The battered child and the hospital," *Hospital Practice*, 4 (October 1969), p. 45.
9. Ibid.
10. M. G. Morris et al., as quoted in F. M. Nomura, "The battered child 'syndrome,'" *Hawaii Medical Journal*, 25 (May–June 1966), p. 390.
11. Ibid., p. 389.
12. R. G. Carkhuff and B. G. Berenson, *Beyond counseling and therapy* (New York: Holt, Rinehart & Winston, 1967), pp. 23–24 and 46–48.

13. C. H. Kempe, "A practical approach to the protection of the abused child and rehabilitation of the abusing parent," *Paediatrics*, 51 (April 1973), p. 807.

14. J. Hopkins, "The nurse and the abused child," *Nursing Clinics of North America*, 5 (December 1970), p. 596.

15. C. H. Kempe and R. E. Helfer, "Innovative therapeutic approaches," in Kempe and Helfer (eds.), *Helping the battered child and his family* (Philadelphia, Pa.: Lippincott, 1972), p. 44.

16. Kempe, "A practical approach," p. 808.

17. R. E. Helfer, *A self-instructional program on child abuse and neglect* (Committee on Infant and Preschool Child, American Academy of Pediatrics, Chicago, Ill., and National Center for Prevention and Treatment of Child Abuse and Neglect, Denver, Colo., 1974), Unit 4.

18. G. Barnes et al., "Team treatment for abusive families, *Social Casework*, 55 (December 1974), p. 604.

19. Ibid., pp. 607–608.

20. Kempe and Helfer, op. cit., pp. 45–48.

21. J. Holter and S. Friedman, "Principles of management in child abuse cases," *American Journal of Orthopsychiatry*, 38 (January 1968), pp. 133–134.

22. Kempe and Helfer, op. cit., p. 47.

23. M. J. Paulson and P. R. Blake, "The physically abused child: A focus on prevention," *Child Welfare*, 48 (February 1969), p. 95.

24. Ibid., pp. 47–48.

25. Kempe, "A practical approach," p. 804.

26. Kempe and Helfer, op. cit., p. 48.

27. A. H. Cohn, S. S. Ridge, and F. C. Collingnon, "Evaluating innovative treatment programs in child abuse and neglect," *Children Today*, 4 (May–June 1975), pp. 10–12.

28. E. Davoren, "Working with abusive parents—a social worker's view," *Children Today*, 4 (May–June 1975), p. 40.

29. Helfer, op. cit.

30. Cohn et al., op. cit., p. 11.

31. Kempe, "A practical approach," p. 808.

32. Helfer, op. cit., Unit 1, p. 2.

33. A. B. Savino and R. W. Sanders, "Working with abusive parents: Group therapy and home visits," *American Journal of Nursing*, 73 (March 1973), p. 484.

34. G. R. Patterson and M. E. Gullion, *Living with children: New methods for parents and teachers* (Champaign, Illinois: Research Press, 1968).

35. J. M. Smith and D. E. P. Smith, *Child management: A program for parents* (Ann Arbor, Mich.: Ann Arbor Publishers, 1966); and T. Gordon, *Parent effectiveness training* (New York: Wyden, 1970).

36. Helfer, op. cit., Unit 3.

37. A. H. Cohn et al., op. cit., p. 11.

38. E. Pike, "C.A.L.M.—a timely experiment in the prevention of child abuse," *Journal of Clinical Child Psychology,* 11 (Fall 1973), p. 44; and *Child abuse listening mediation* (Santa Barbara, Calif.: CALM, 1974), p. 27.

39. *Children in danger* (Austin, Tex.: State Department of Public Welfare, 1974).

40. S. M. Sgroi, "Sexual molestation of children," *Children Today,* 4 (May–June 1975), p. 19.

41. F. Ferro, "Combatting child abuse and neglect," *Children Today,* 4 (May–June 1975), inside front cover.

42. H. D. Lovens and J. Rako, "A community approach to the prevention of child abuse," *Child Welfare,* 54 (February 1975), p. 86.

43. Gerald Hass, "Child abuse, the community, and the neighborhood health center," in N. B. Ebeling and D. A. Hill (eds.), *Child abuse: Intervention and treatment* (Acton, Mass.: Publishing Science Group, 1975), p. 15.

44. R. E. Helfer, as quoted in S. Davidson, in "At last! Help for the abusive parent," *Woman's Day* (March 1973), p. 190.

45. Kempe and Helfer, op. cit., p. 53.

46. Helfer, op. cit.

47. S. Davidson, "At last! Help for the abusive parent," *Woman's Day* March 1973, p. 190.

48. S. A. Holmes et al., "Working with the parent in child-abuse cases," *Social Casework,* 8 (January 1975), pp. 3–12.

49. Ibid., p. 8.

50. J. Reed, "Working with abusive parents: A parent's view—an interview with Jolly K.," *Children Today,* 4 (May–June 1975), p. 9.

51. G. M. Bacon, Parents Anonymous, Inc., New York, N.Y., personal communication, June 24, 1975.

52. Davidson, op. cit., p. 190.

53. Kempe and Helfer, op. cit., p. 49.

54. Davidson, op. cit.

55. Reed, op. cit., p. 8.

56. Reed, op. cit., p. 9.

57. Bacon, op. cit.

58. R. Smith, "Now experts are trying to draw out these battering parents," *Today's Health,* 51 (January 1973), pp. 59–64.

59. *Families anonymous.* Film produced by The National Center for the Prevention and Treatment of Child Abuse and Neglect, Denver, Colo.

60. Holmes et al., op. cit.

61. Davoren, op. cit., p. 39.

62. Ibid.

63. Ibid, p. 42.

64. E. Davoren, "The role of the social worker," in R. C. Helfer and C. H. Kempe (eds.) *The battered child* (Chicago: University of Chicago Press, 1974), p. 147.

65. Davoren, "Working with abusive parents," p. 39.

66. Ibid, p. 43.

67. E. M. Thomson et al., *Child abuse: A community challenge* (East Aurora, N.Y.: Henry Stewart, 1971), pp. 139–140.

68. A. L. Arvanian, "Treatment of abusive parents," in Ebeling and Hill (eds.), op. cit., p. 101.

69. Kempe and Helfer, op. cit., pp. 13–14.

70. Helfer, op. cit.

71. R. G. Erskine, "The ABC's of effective therapy," *Transactional Analysis Journal,* 5 (April 1975), pp. 163–165.

72. B. Steele, "Working with abusive parents—a psychiatrist's view," *Children Today,* 4 (May–June 1975), p. 5.

73. Helfer, op. cit., unit 4.

74. Steele, op. cit., p. 5.

75. D. David, "The use of the confrontation technique in the battered child syndrome," *American Journal of Psychotherapy,* 28 (October 1974), pp. 543–552.

76. C. H. Kempe and J. Hopkins (eds.), "The public health nurse's role in the prevention of child abuse and neglect," *Public Health Currents,* 15 (March–April–May 1975), p. 4.

77. Steele, op. cit., p. 5.

78. J. McFerran, "Parents' group in protective services," *Children,* 5 (November–December 1958), pp. 223–228.

79. H. Feinstein et al., "Group therapy for mothers with infanticidal impulses," *American Journal of Psychiatry,* 120 (March 1964), pp. 882–886.

80. M. J. Paulson et al., "Parents of the battered child: A multidisciplinary group therapy approach to life-threatening behavior," *Life-Threatening Behavior,* 4 (Spring 1974), pp. 18–31.

81. R. Gladston, "Preventing the abuse of little children: The Parents' Center project for the study and prevention of child abuse," *American Journal of Orthopsychiatry,* 45 (April 1975), pp. 372–381.

82. See Cohn, op. cit., p. 11.
83. J. Tracy and E. Clark, "Treatment for child abusers," *Social Work,* 19 (May 1974), pp. 339–342.
84. R. C. Hughes, "A clinics's parent-performance training program for child abusers," *Hospital and Community Psychiatry,* 25 (1974), pp. 779–782; and O. L. Sydnor, N. Parkell, and C. D. Hancock, *Controlling Behavior* (Monroe, La.: Children Unlimited, undated).
85. See "Child abuse and neglect reach epidemic levels: Maze of programs may be promoting the crisis, not attacking it," *Houston Post,* July 2, 1975, p. 4AA.
86. Helfer, op. cit., pp. 3–2 to 3–11.
87. H. Delnero, J. Hopkins, and K. Drews, "The medical center child abuse consultation team," in C. H. Kempe and R. E. Helfer (eds.), *Helping the battered child and his family* (Philadelphia, Pa.: Lippincott, 1972), pp. 161–176; and Barnes et al., op. cit.
88. Cohn, op. cit., p. 10.

Chapter 8

PRIMARY PREVENTION OF CHILD ABUSE

We have identified child abuse as a public health problem, requiring public health approaches. Although it fully qualifies for such a designation, the public health profession has largely ignored the problem. One consequence has been that other professions must wrestle with the question of primary prevention—a problem for which public health has traditionally assumed responsibility. Primary prevention consists of heading off a problem before it occurs. Unlike secondary prevention, it reduces not only the prevalence of the problem but also its incidence—the number of *new* cases.

Until recently, the medical, nursing, and social work professions have devoted the most time and effort to the child abuse problem. Each field is chiefly concerned with treatment—helping to ameliorate a problem after it has occurred—not with prevention. The time has come for public health to join the team with more than public health nurses, to focus on the issue of primary prevention, and do something about the epidemic proportions that child abuse has reached. In other words, research must be done by public health professionals, and city, county, and state public health departments must participate actively in the prevention of child abuse.

Enough is now known about the problem to begin instituting some of the programs that will be discussed in this chapter. Although public policy must first be established on the most far-reaching proposals, there are still other services that public health departments can provide, given the necessary commitment. It is in the area of individual rights where public law and policy will first have to be thrashed out before widespread prevention programs can be launched, but much can still be done in the meantime.

One reason that primary prevention of child abuse is such a formidable problem is that it touches on the sacrosanct question of whether parents have the right to raise their children as they see fit. Just about every far-reaching strategy that might be designed runs headlong into the issue of parental rights: the right to bear children (including illegitimate children), the right to have any number of children, the right to be left alone, and the right to be free of investigation as to how the children are doing. But the rights of children to a safe and healthy home and a mother and father with parenting skills must be given equal attention. As one observer puts it: "Every child has the right to his own home. He has a right to live, a right to a good emotional environment, and to a good education, food, clothing and shelter."[1]

A variety of commissions and national and international organizations have issued proclamations on children's rights, but their statements have been largely unheeded. For example, the Joint Commission on Mental Health of Children stated that children have the right to be wanted, to live in a healthy environment, to have their basic needs satisfied, and to continuous loving care.[2] The General Assembly of the United Nations also specified the rights of childhood in its Universal Declaration of Human Rights.[3] Yet public sentiment—and the law—still favors parents' rights.

Kempe has suggested that

> the rights of the child for reasonable care and protection must be balanced against the right of parents to be free to raise their children in their own image. But the child does no longer "belong" to his parents, he belongs to himself in the care of his parents unless he receives insufficient care or protection. . . . We do force all parents to present their 5-year-old child to society for an attempt at basic education under penalty of prison for the parents who refuse. Why would it not be right to force each parent to present their infant to society in the form of an understanding and properly trained health visitor for required basic supervision of physical and emotional health at regular intervals?[4]

To have health visitors check on the development and well-being of babies represents a nonspecific intervention strategy for preventing child abuse. In this chapter, we will discuss both nonspecific and specific prevention programs.

NONSPECIFIC STRATEGIES

What Kempe has proposed is an extensive strategy that represents a form of national health screening. The strategy is extensive in the sense that it involves intervention at all levels of the public health triad described in Chapter 3: intervention at the level of host (parents), agent (child), environment, and vector (culture). The parents would be involved in that the health visitor would consider not only their child-rearing practices but any symbiotic relationships in the family plus other characteristics, such as isolation and unemployment, that might portend abuse. The child would be involved in terms of how irritable, difficult, and provocative he is and how he reacts to his parents. The environment would be examined from the standpoint of overcrowding, poor housing, and other social and physical indicators of potential abuse. The culture would be involved in the sense that any national health screening policy would require changes in public attitudes, particularly with regard to the parental rights and the notion that a man's home is his castle.

Health Visitors Program

While testifying before the Senate Subcommittee on Children and Youth in 1973, Kempe elaborated on his proposals as follows:

> We suggest that a health visitor call at intervals during the first months of life upon each young family and that she become, as it were, the guardian who would see to it that each infant is receiving his basic health rights. . . . It is my view that the concept of the utilization of health visitors would be widely accepted in this country. Health visitors need not have nursing training, and intelligent, successful mothers and fathers could be readily prepared for this task at little cost. . . . In those areas where it is not practical to have health visitors, health stations could be established in neighborhood fire houses.[5]

Two questions have been raised about this proposal. One concerns the cost and the other relates to the implication that firemen are qualified to perform the necessary screening.[6]

If the health visitor is to make effective preventive interventions, he must be trained to recognize the signs of potential abuse. The program is not likely to be inexpensive, but the dividends could be great. With proper inspection and intervention, child abuse is not the only problem a health visitor could head off. This is why the strategy is called nonspecific. As Helfer has suggested, the "world of abnormal rearing" to which the abused child is subjected also involves a number of spin-off problems: failure to thrive, retardation, brain damage, learning disorders, behavior disorders, drug abuse, obesity, neglect, teen-age pregnancy, assassination.[7] What the health visitor should be trained to detect are signs of this "world of abnormal rearing": the parents' isolation, suspicion, and distrust; lack of friends; inability to reach out to others; marital conflict; excessive expectations of the child. Early detection of potential child abuse requires the recognition of signs of symbiotic relationships between parents and between parent and child.

To assess a family's potential for child abuse, the health visitor would ask questions such as the following: "Does your baby cry excessively and does it make you feel like crying? Do you dislike having somebody watch you feed or take care of the baby? Does your older child know when you're upset and does she take care of you at that time?"[8] Persons who abuse are extremely sensitive to criticism because they were criticized by their own parents. Furthermore, they often feel helpless and thus look to others—including their own child—for nurture and rescue. These questions touch on such points.

Although the idea of national health screening may seem far-fetched, we would like to point out that the United Kingdom has both a national health screening program and a health visitors program.[9] The health visitors program, adopted in some cities more than 65 years ago and in a few a century ago, requires public health nurses to visit the home of every newborn and follow the child's physical, emotional, and mental development on a periodic basis. Although the law states that these visits must be made, it does not require parents to admit the health visitor to their home. But because these health visitors have earned a reputation for helpfulness and are trained to deal effectively with recalcitrant families, few if any newborns escape examination. Parents are given friendly tips and useful information on the baby's needs and how to meet them.

> All ... [health visitors are] able nurses who go to every house, rich, poor, middle class, knock on the door and say, "How are you, Mrs. Jones?" They are always courteous to the mother. Eventually they have some tea in the kitchen and eventually they see the child and they then do what amounts to an advocacy job for the child.[10]

A large corps of health visitors would be needed for a similar program in the United States. But if the United Kingdom has been able to bear the expense since the early 1900s, this country can certainly do so. In addition, after a potentially abusing family is identified, it would be necessary to have personnel and resources available to head off the abuse. This may require group therapy, parent aides, homemakers, emergency shelters—or finding a job for the father. As we will point out later, volunteers can do much of this work.

Although opposition to health visitors is likely—even if families are not required by law to admit them to their homes—a truly comprehensive primary prevention program may well require this extensive measure. The home is the only place where all the critical points of the triad of host, agent, and environment can be observed. If children are followed up beyond infancy, early warning signs of other problems can also be detected, including those we have identified elsewhere as warning signals of later violent behavior.[11] The fact that parents are hungry for information on effective child rearing became apparent to us when we produced 80,000 copies of an easy-to-read, illustrated booklet titled *Your Child's Behavior* and held 150 workshops on family problems for parents and teachers.[12] These booklets are now in use in schools and neighborhood centers as well as in many homes.

Parent Licensing and Training

If the health visitors program seems to be a bold measure (despite its long existence in the United Kingdom), an even bolder one would involve the licensing of parents. We do not necessarily endorse such a measure but believe it does deserve more public attention. Margaret Mead has pointed out that although society requires people to get licenses before they marry, no constraints are placed on child bearing, which is an even greater responsibility.[13] When parents are ill-equipped and uninformed, the consequences affect not only the child but in many cases society at large. Lord and Weisfeld made the following statement in support of licensing: "For . . . the protection and welfare of parents, children and society . . . should there not be the requirement that potential parents have at least some rudimentary knowledge and skill in the field of effective parenthood?"[14] Toffler points out the need for proved proficiency in parenting as follows:

> Raising children. . . . requires skills that are by no means universal. We don't let "just anyone" perform brain surgery or, for that matter, sell stocks and bonds. Even the lowest ranking civil servant is required to pass tests proving competence. Yet we allow virtually anyone, almost without regard for mental or moral qualifications, to try his or her hand at raising young human beings, so long as these humans are biological offspring. Despite the increasing complexity of the task, parenthood remains the greatest single preserve of the amateur.[15]

A number of behavioral scientists are convinced that enough is now known about the principles and techniques of child rearing and management to dispel any arguments against the idea of requiring all potential parents to take courses that will teach them these skills. According to Hawkins, for example,

> a training program that will improve the quality of child-rearing and prevent the development of mental health problems should reach parents before their first child is born. Because there is no practical way to identify inept parents in advance, it would be necessary to have a compulsory parent-training course that would reach virtually all potential parents. The school is the logical place for such a program.[16]

A compulsory parent-training course could either be linked to mandatory licensing for parenthood or stand separately. By itself it would be more likely to gain acceptance; as a prerequisite to licensing, however, it would carry more weight in terms of being taken at least as seriously as driver training. Kempe is convinced that if a licensing law for parenthood existed, there would be a dramatic reduction in the number of battered, abused, and unwanted children.[17] Despite the advantages for both children and society in the future, licensing of parents is unlikely to become a reality very soon: "Perhaps in the 21st or 22nd centuries such legislation and licensing programs may end—or diminish—child abuse, battering and neglect. In the meantime . . . ?"[18]

In the meantime, strong intervention strategies such as universal parenting training could be initiated. Hawkins advocates the position that although "the skills a parent needs are complex, [we] already know enough about these skills to begin effective, large-scale instruction in child-rearing."[19] A few courses that include information on child development already exist in schools, primarily at the high school level, but these are usually homemaking courses and thus reach few male students. One reason that few, if any, boys enroll in these courses is that the instruction focuses mainly on the mechanical aspects of child care: e.g., how to feed and change babies. According to Kempe, the schools need to teach students "something about mothering"—about nurturing and what a child needs at different ages and stages and how parents (male and female) should respond to those needs.[20]

The kind of classes needed would not only discuss child rearing but would actually require a substantial amount of practical experience in a day-care center or nursery school affiliated with their high school.[21] This classroom and laboratory work would make up a one-year course in child rearing and would be required of all students. Just as students who take driver training courses are required to learn by driving real cars, students in child rearing would be required to deal with real children and confront the tasks that parents face. Although this program would ensure that young people would be trained for parenthood before marriage, it needs to be supplemented by courses for persons who are already married.

But do high school students want parenting instruction? There is good evidence to suggest that they do. In areas where pilot programs on the prevention of child abuse are being conducted in schools, students have not only expressed an interest in the courses but recognize the need for them.

> Many [students] believe that a curriculum unit on "How to be a parent" should be required for all high school students. . . . Courses on parenthood should be offered to all students and the courses should emphasize how important nurturing—or the lack of it—is to a child's normal growth and development.[22]

Based on an examination of limited evidence, Light argues that "education in child development, an excellent idea in its own right, has not been shown to decisively affect the specific problems of abuse or neglect."[23] A number of other studies, however, indicate that there is a direct association between child abuse and a lack of the knowledge and skills required for parenting.[24] In our survey, an overwhelming proportion of abusing parents said they definitely needed to know more about child development and management; many claimed that if they had known more about how to deal with children, they would not have abused their children.

We do not contend that the lack of skills in child development and management is the sole cause of child abuse. But there is ample evidence to suggest that it is a contributing factor in many cases. This fact alone should be enough to justify parent-training courses that would emphasize child development and management, but because these courses would also be likely to affect the incidence of not only child abuse but a number of other problems related to poor parenting, there seems to be little reason for delay. As Hawkins notes, however:

> A move to institute parent training in our schools will strain the system and generate resistance. Some persons will object to the instructing of adolescents in behavior-modification techniques. They will raise the old cry that we should not teach persons to manipulate their children. But these child-rearing methods are not new. People have always taught and learned complex behaviors through these methods. . . . It is only our ability to analyze, isolate, name and teach the components of the art of teaching that is new.[25]

Obviously, one does not need to be a specialist in behavior modification to understand the principles and techniques of child rearing and management. Many other practical approaches are available to help potential parents manage their children without resorting to an undue amount of physical discipline. For example, we teach token

economy systems and the techniques of Parent Effectiveness Training.

Of course, knowledge of good parenting skills alone
will not keep child abuse from occurring in a family. It
should be clear by now that many other factors contribute
to the problem. For instance, parents may be knowledgeable about parenting skills but not use them; they may have
psychological problems or be under so much environmental stress that emotional forces overwhelm their cognitive
skills. But these factors cannot be used as an excuse for
failing to institute parent training. The findings clearly suggest that the overwhelming majority of abusing parents do
not fail to use their knowledge of parenting skills; they
simply lack that knowledge in the first place.

Some individuals who become parents are so lacking
in basic nurturing qualities that teaching them the skills of
parenting will not be enough to ensure the safe and healthy
development of their children. Neither will sending mother
surrogates into the home or placing the children temporarily outside the home. For these parents, there must be
an alternative. At one time in our history the extended
family provided an alternative. If the biological parents
could not do the job of child rearing, a grandparent, aunt,
or uncle could. Today we must create other alternatives,
which leads us to the idea of "professional parents": persons who are equipped by upbringing and training to give
children the nurturing, care, and nonphysical discipline
they need. These parents would be certified for compe-
tency on the basis of their experience, training, and record.

With a proper change in public attitudes and policy,
biological parents who lack the qualities and skills necessary for child rearing would feel free—and would be encouraged—to contract with professional parents to do the
job for them. Toffler has suggested that the biological parents could fill the role of interested godparents and spend
time with the child as interested outsiders.[26] They would be

permitted to visit, telephone, and spend summer vacations with the child, and they would be assured that the child would grow up to be as successful, effective, and constructive a member of society as they want him to be.

Family Planning

For most present and future parents, training in child development and management would be enough, particularly if supportive services were available in the form of parent aides and homemakers. Thus these parents would not need to contract with professional parents. Knowledge and skills would provide them with the means of doing effective child rearing. But primary prevention of child abuse requires knowledge in yet another area—the area of family planning. According to Elmer and Gil, there seems to be a definite relationship between the number of children in the family and child abuse.[27] Light holds that "family size data suggest that widespread family planning education might be more effective in preventing child maltreatment" than courses in child development and management.[28] Both types of education are needed. But to make family planning widespread, there must be reliance on more than traditional agencies. Just as parent training should be compulsory, there should also be a required high school course in family planning, which would include a close look at the consequences of having an excessive number of children. It is imperative to reach a maximum number of young people before they begin their own families. Although voluntary use of family planning agencies is increasing, such programs cannot reach the large numbers that high schools can. Again, there will be resistance to requiring family planning courses in high schools, but the potential benefits, in terms of a reduction in the amount of child abuse and other social problems related to large families, should be great enough to overcome that resistance.

A third and final course that must be instituted in American high schools to combat the problem, not only of child abuse but of mental and emotional dysfunction, involves the nature of human needs and how to meet them. There is ample evidence concerning what these needs are.[29] Symbiosis, a central concept in child abuse, stems from an individual's failure to meet his own needs, which results in turning to others in an effort to be cared for. If young people learn how to obtain strokes, to find stimulation, and to structure their time without manipulating others, they can avoid symbiotic as well as other relationships that result in either emotional problems or social dysfunction. And if they learn how to meet the human need for responsibility, affection, and control and mastery, they will be more likely to avoid the pitfalls of delinquency, crime, alcoholism, and other social problems. The Cooperative Commission on the Study of Alcoholism reported in 1967 on the need to improve the public's general understanding of human emotions and interpersonal relations—not only as a means of combatting alcoholism but of reducing other psychological and social problems as well.[30]

We have found that most people are ignorant of the nature of human needs, not to mention how to meet them. It is much easier to teach persons about needs and how to satisfy them *before* they inflict violence on a child or encounter other problems than after they have done so. Ideally, this learning would begin in elementary school, but the course on human needs should be compulsory beginning in junior high school.

We do not mean to imply that cognitive understanding alone will protect a person from all psychological and social problems. Obviously, he must act on his understanding. But it is also obvious that without understanding, there is little hope of acting in a way that will bring satisfaction to oneself and others.

There are signs that school systems now recognize the need to teach more than traditional academic subjects and basic vocational skills. The most common reason that people fail to function adequately in their jobs, marriages, and communities is related to their lack of understanding of themselves and others, not to a lack of preparation in traditional school subjects. Family life courses are now offered in some schools; courses in values clarification and "Patterns of Healthful Living" are being offered in others. But what is also needed to address not only the problem of child abuse but other psychological and social problems as well is the kind of instruction that will provide students with a clear understanding of human needs and how to meet them. Again, courses on human needs must be mandatory to reach the widest number of young people possible.

Compulsory courses in high schools, licensing for parenthood, and the national health screening program are all examples of broad-scale methods of primary prevention. Each has a broad-based approach—the broadest being the national health screening program. They are nonspecific approaches in the sense that no specific high-risk groups would be singled out. They are also nonspecific in that they would be beneficial in more than one way: i.e., they would not only prevent child abuse but other problems arising from poor parenting as well. Massive numbers of people would be contacted on the theory that this is the best way to reach those who would commit abuse if the intervention program did not exist. But because these nonspecific programs would be costly and controversial, they may stand little chance of becoming public policy. They raise all kinds of questions about parental rights and elicit widespread and vocal opposition, despite the dividends in social and personal well-being that may accrue. But other nonspecific programs that have been suggested for the prevention of child abuse are even more all-encompassing than those we have mentioned. For example, Gil believes that

> primary prevention of child abuse, on all levels, would require ... a reconceptualization of childhood, of children's rights, and of child rearing. It would necessitate rejecting the use of force as a means for achieving societal ends, especially in dealing with children. It would require the elimination of poverty and of alienating conditions of production, major sources of stress and frustration which tend to trigger abusive acts toward children in adult-child interaction. And, finally, it would necessitate the elimination of psychological illness.[31]

SPECIFIC STRATEGIES

An alternative (or complement) to the nonspecific approach to primary prevention is the specific approach, which would require identification of specific high-risk groups or conditions. Using the public health triad, intervention would occur at the level of high-risk parents, high-risk children, high-risk environments, or a combination of the three.

High-risk Parents

Because the profile of the abusing parent is fairly well established, steps can be taken ahead of time to assist potential abusers. One step would be to develop a questionnaire that could be administered to new parents and parents-to-be to assess their potential for abuse. A predictive questionnaire that focuses on feelings of isolation, reaction to criticism, feelings toward spouse, parental treatment, expectations of children, attitudes toward punishment and feelings of nervousness, distress, and potential loss of control has been described by Schneider, Helfer, and Pollock.[32] These attitude areas closely parallel the problem areas that we explore when working with abusing parents: symbiotic relationships with spouse and family of origin, isolation, talking and sharing with mate, impatience and temper, and child development and management (see Chapters 5 and 6).

Use of any predictive instrument requires establishing careful policies, procedures and safeguards. Every parent and parent-to-be would be given a full explanation as to the purpose of the questionnaire and the steps taken to preserve confidentiality of information. A parent could refuse, of course, to take the questionnaire. The idea would be not to label parents who fall in a high-risk category, but to offer them support and guide them to helpful services. We recognize that establishing ways to do this will require careful study and attention. What is being suggested here is that the predictive questionnaire would be of much value provided policies and procedures are worked out so that no abuse of the instrument could occur.

Spouses who scored high in the various attitude or problem areas on the questionnaire would receive several forms of support, including counseling (group therapy, if necessary), the services of a parent aide or homemaker who would spend 10 to 15 hours a week with the family after the baby comes home, and courses in parent training and in human needs. The course in parent training would be more than didactic; it would involve parents in on-going nursery programs so that they could see firsthand how children should be cared for and played with.

The courses would be offered by the city or county health departments at sites that are convenient for parents —either at the hospital or in neighborhood health centers. Parents would be urged to attend them by their physician, the hospital authorities, and the public health nurse. It would be the public health nurse's responsibility to act as a health advocate and visit periodically with the family. In difficult cases, group therapy should be offered. The family would also receive printed information about community resources that could help them in time of need: crisis centers, baby nurseries, emergency shelters, and manpower service centers to help solve employment problems. In addition, the parents would have the office and home telephone numbers of their parent aide, homemaker, and public health nurse, and would be encouraged to use them in times of crisis.

Although hospitals would be a central source for identifying high-risk parents, physicians in private offices could be equally helpful because they see more cases of child abuse than anyone else. But in most areas of the country they report it less.[33] There are various reasons why physicians often fail to report cases of child abuse.[34] As for carrying out primary prevention strategies, no one knows how many cases of abuse physicians may be preventing through early intervention, but it is agreed that much more needs to be done. What can physicians do? They can observe the early interaction between mother and child and pick up cues on the potential for abuse. A complete list of these cues has been widely circulated among professionals. For instance, the high-risk mother often views her infant as ugly or unattractive, is unconcerned about supporting the baby's head, handles the baby roughly, does not coo or talk to it, believes that the baby does not love her and makes adult judgments about her and her abilities, and cannot see any physical or psychological attribute in the infant that she values in herself.[35]

Even during pregnancy, the high-risk mother provides clues that the physician can use as a basis for intervention and assistance: e.g., she expresses doubt about her ability to cope, is overly concerned about fetal deformities, suffers from psychosomatic problems, complains about her husband's lack of support, and so forth.[36] In short, the high-risk mother says in one way or another that she wants someone to take care of her and that, in a reversed symbiosis, she may expect her baby to meet her needs.

Once a physician has identified a high-risk mother, he should have community resources to which to refer her: for example, courses on human needs and child development and management and the services of a parent aide or homemaker. If he detects severe problems between the spouses, they should be referred for group therapy.

There is, however, much that the physician can do on his own.[37] Before the baby is born, he can make sure that the high-risk parent gets in classes on the care and behavior of babies. He can prepare parents for the fact that some babies keep crying even when the parent has done everything to soothe them. He can do "discipline counseling" with the parents, emphasizing that spanking is inappropriate treatment of babies. He can hold family planning discussions with high-risk parents to discourage them from having additional children. He can encourage early placement of the child in day-care centers so that high-risk parents will not be over-stressed. He can promote the mother's early return to work, since the high-risk parent is often happier on a job than at home where she feels incompetent in caring for her child.

Although physicians are a vital part of the team for prevention as well as treatment of child abuse, we also emphasize the role of the public health nurse. As we noted earlier, she should act as a health advocate for children, visit with families periodically, and supervise parent aides or homemakers who work with them. Like the physician, she too can do much to identify potentially abusive mothers during pregnancy.

The public health nurse is the ideal person to take a leading role in primary prevention of child abuse. She is the one member of the public health profession who already works in this field and has the respect of other health professionals and the community. Furthermore, as the least threatening professional she "can gain entrance to homes where no one else is accepted. . . . She is also the most available professional and in small communities she may be the only resource."[38]

As we suggested earlier, the public health nurse, in her role as health visitor or advocate, would be able to observe not only the signs of potential abuse but also the forewarnings of many other problems. "In the long run it is possible that a well-organized preventive movement of this kind could do more to alleviate social and individual problems than any other effort one might conceive."[39]

The contacts the public health nurse has with pregnant women in their homes and in obstetrical clinics provides her with an opportunity to help physicians screen mothers before their babies arrive. The following factors are linked with high-risk mothers: (1) the mother denies her pregnancy by avoiding prenatal care until late in the third trimester, or goes into labor insisting that she was unaware of her pregnancy; (2) seeks an abortion or has unsuccessfully attempted one; (3) agrees to give up the baby for adoption but changes her mind after it is born; (4) does not exhibit nesting behavior or neglects to prepare her home for the baby; (5) is addicted to alcohol or other drugs and is unable to take care of herself or the baby; (6) has recently been abandoned by the baby's father or rejected by her family; (7) has already injured another child or has temporarily lost custody of another child because of neglect; and (8) the father has a criminal record of assault or has been psychiatrically diagnosed as a sociopath.[40]

Later, when we discuss "claiming" behavior in the section on high-risk children, it will be obvious that the public health nurse and physician can also do much in the way of primary prevention once the baby is born. By observing how the mother responds to her new baby while it is still in the hospital, the nurse and physician can detect the following signals that suggest high-risk: (1) the mother does not exhibit "claiming" behavior: e.g., she is not interested in naming the baby or in feeding and holding him; (2) she indicates her rejection of the child by remarking on how ugly, defective, or disappointing he is; (3) she is repelled by the child's odor, drooling, regurgitation, or stools; (4) she exhibits extreme postpartum depression that may be related to feeling overwhelmed by a new baby she does not want, for example, rather than to a rapid drop in estrogen levels; (5) she visits her premature baby less and less often after she has been discharged from the hospital; and (6) she is unable to control her impulses, e.g., she spanks or becomes enraged at her newborn infant.[41]

In the weeks and months after the baby is born, the public health nurse and the physician should observe whether the mother increasingly enjoys her infant and the tasks she does for and with him, develops a greater understanding of his emotional states and learns to comfort him more appropriately, and recognizes his need for new stimuli and senses his fatigue more readily.[42]

High-risk Children

Just as strategies can be designed for intervention on the parent (host) level, primary prevention can also be based on intervention with the child at risk (agent). As we mentioned earlier, premature, illegitimate, difficult, congenitally malformed, and mentally retarded children seem especially prone to abuse. Although we will discuss specific intervention programs for premature, illegitimate, and difficult children, similar approaches can be used with malformed and retarded children.

Premature or Low Birth-Weight Babies. The fact that a disproportionate number of premature or low birth-weight babies are found among abused children has been investigated by a number of researchers.[43] For example, one explanation is that prematurity predisposes a baby to anoxia, which in turn causes irritability and fussiness. Another explanation is that babies who weigh less than five and one-half pounds at birth may have subtle dysfunctions of the central nervous system which result in restlessness and distractibility. In his study of 674 cases of abuse, Lenoski found that 22 per cent involved children who had been premature babies. This compared with 10 per cent of 500 control cases. Thirty per cent of those in the abused group had been delivered by Caesarian section (compared with 3.2 per cent in the control group) and 9 per cent had complicated deliveries (compared with 4.2 per cent in the control group).

Low birth-weight babies also are unlikely to be picked up as often as normal-weight infants, and this factor possibly has an unfavorable influence on the neonate's development, resulting in unresponsive behavior. Another theory is that because premature infants are separated from their parents for the first several weeks of life, the establishment of the child-caretaker bond is delayed, which in turn adversely affects the interaction between baby and mother— especially the mother's response to the infant. One strategy for determining whether delayed bonding affects the mother's claiming behavior and responses toward her child is to record the times she visits her baby in the hospital and inquires about him. One study concluded that mothers who infrequently visited or called the hospital neglected or abused their child later.[44]

To prevent disorders of mothering that may result from separating a mother from her premature baby, hospitals must arrange for early contact between mother and child and encourage frequent visiting. The mother should be allowed inside the nursery to handle and feed the baby as soon as possible. Better still, Care-By-Parent Units such as those established in Kentucky hospitals should be available so that mothers of premature babies can become accustomed to and take complete responsibility for their infants before leaving the hospital. If a high-risk mother lives with her baby and cares for it for a week or two before taking the infant home, she has the opportunity to develop claiming behavior and learn how to handle the baby. In Kentucky, mothers of premature first-borns spend time in a Care-By-Parent Unit before taking their babies home.[45]

Because separation of the premature or low birth-weight infant from its parents can result in unresponsive and difficult behavior, such a baby can be at especially high risk if his parents are under stress or seek nurturing themselves. The same can be said of irritable and fussy babies who may have suffered from anoxia or subtle brain damage.

The local health department should assign a public health nurse to visit families of low birth-weight babies. How frequent the visits should be would depend on how well the baby and its parents get along and how successful the Care-By-Parent program has been. All parents of premature babies should receive printed material which points out that babies who were underweight at birth may be difficult and that parents should not hesitate to seek help when they need it. The material should also include information on how to obtain the services of a parent aide or homemaker. In addition, every community should have a crisis nursery or emergency shelter where a mother under stress can take her baby to get some relief from constant caretaking. There should also be a "park-a-tot" facility where the mother can leave her baby for shorter periods.

Illegitimate Babies. A number of investigators have identified illegitimate and unwanted children as high risks for abuse.[46] If a mother is ashamed of her baby or does not want him, she is likely to reject him. Furthermore, the baby's behavior may contribute to her rejecting or abusive behavior. Illegitimate and unwanted babies are especially prone to be irritable and colicky. Some investigators suggest that the mother's emotional state during pregnancy influences the unborn child. For instance, Landis and Bolles suggested that if an expectant mother is under stress, her baby may be colicky and irritable.[47] One source of stress for a pregnant woman is concern that she is not married or does not want the child. Furthermore, because a colicky or irritable baby is difficult to care for, he simply compounds his mother's tendency toward rejecting. Even if the mother does want the baby, his difficult behavior can make her feel inadequate and resentful. And if her stress continues or if she looks to the baby for love, abusive behavior may be triggered. The unwed mother sometimes seeks a symbiotic relationship with her child, not for the child's well-being but for her own. If she feels rejected by the child's father, she may view the child as her last chance to obtain the love and nurturing she never received from her own parents or from boyfriends. When the child fails to provide this love and nurturing, abuse may occur.

Hospitals must facilitate observation of interactions between mothers and newborn infants. The nurse on the ward is an invaluable source of information concerning the child's responsiveness to its parents and how often the parents visit.[48] Rooming-in arrangements such as the Care-By-Parent Unit should be instituted so that a mother has early contact with her baby and can be responsible for feeding and holding him. If a mother is clearly rejecting, she should receive counseling before taking the baby home. She should also be encouraged to attend courses on human needs and child development and management. When the mother and baby go home, a parent aide or homemaker should be assigned to the case, reporting to a public health nurse on developments. The mother should also be referred for group therapy if necessary.

Difficult and "Mismatched" Children. According to Kagan, "the difficult child does not establish regular feeding or sleep patterns, reacts intensely to imposition or frustration, and withdraws passively from strange events or people. He seems to require a long time to adjust to anything new and is difficult to rear."[49] This kind of child is hard to manage and evokes frustration and resentment in his parents. Jenkins, acknowledging the role of temperament in a child's behavior, describes as difficult the "irritable youngster, the constantly crying baby, the hyperactive child, and the child who fails to maintain toilet habits."[50] Some of the reasons for a child's difficult behavior have already been discussed; other causes are unknown. It is known, however, that each neonate has a unique congenital and temperamental makeup, which in part is related to his prenatal and perinatal experiences. Thus parent-child relationships are a two-way exchange.

In any event, the match between baby and parent is important. A difficult child can be a problem to almost any parent, but this type of child is at even greater risk if his mother or father, because of his or her temperament and characteristics, expects or demands docile, compliant behavior from the child. Martin and Beezley found that even if the child is not especially difficult or does not have an unpredictable temperament, there still may be a

> disparity between characteristics of the infant and the parent's capability and capacity to parent that type of child. The characteristics of the infant and child need not be abnormalities, but rather idiosyncratic traits within a spectrum of normalcy. . . . . Assessing variations in infants' behavior repertoires may prove extremely helpful in preventing abuse by identifying those parent-child matches which need intervention.[51]

Again, hospital policies that facilitate close observation of interactions between parents and their newborn child must be instituted. A living-in arrangement not only provides hospital staff with the best opportunities for these observations but offers mothers and fathers a chance to get acquainted with their infants in a protected environment.

The difficult baby can be detected early, based on the way he reacts when his parents handle and feed him. The mismatched parent can also be detected in this way.

If the parents of a difficult baby do not have the profiles of potential abusers, then the intervention plan would consist of periodic visits by the public health nurse. However, before the parents leave the hospital with the baby, they should be given counseling sessions to prepare them for dealing with a difficult child. They should also be taught parenting skills while the mother and baby are still in the live-in unit. The parents should also understand that if some crisis arises at home, they can call the public health nurse or use the crisis nursery in the community. They should also be aware that there is a respite center or emergency shelter, which will enable them to get away from the baby for a few days, as well as a park-a-tot facility for shorter breathers.

If the baby is not difficult but is mismatched with his mother or father, the intervention strategy would consist of having the parents attend the courses on child development and management and on human needs. In these courses the parents would learn how to maintain realistic expectations of the child and to meet their own needs. They would also learn what a child needs at various stages of development; how they should respond to him, although their own temperaments may call for a different response; and how they can manage the child without undue use of physical discipline. The public health nurse would assess how well the parents and child get along at home and would decide how often the family should be visited. She would also assess whether the parents would benefit from group therapy. Printed information about resources that are available in time of crisis would also be given to the parents.

The Vulnerable Child Committee (VCC) of Brockton, Massachusetts, which has developed a system of identifying high-risk children in the area, provides proof that hospitals and agencies can move toward prevention of abuse, given the necessary commitment and coordination.

> The general goals of the VCC are to establish early identification of children vulnerable to abuse and neglect, to provide their families with preventive resources to help them maintain adequate care for the physical and psychological development of their children, and to offer public education and consultation to the professional and lay community in relation to child abuse and neglect.[52]

The VCC and six cooperating hospitals use the following guidelines to identify vulnerable children: Has the child been injured three times within one year? Do his parents refuse to follow medical advice? Do the parents demonstrate inappropriate concern or a lack of concern? Is the child's mother or the family situation inadequate? Does either parent abuse alcohol or other drugs? Is there a lack of parental supervision in the home?

The VCC has set up a cross-indexing system to alert cooperating hospitals and social agencies to the vulnerable children it encounters. The following excerpt is an example of early identification and alerting:

> A 3-year-old boy was brought to a hospital by police ambulance. Reportedly, the child had fallen from his second floor window during his naptime. There was no injury. The parents' explanations of the accident were contradictory and suspicious. The mother, a very anxious woman, told the staff that she was "abused by her parents as a child"; then she became tearfully upset and said she could not cope with the pressures of her life. The case was indexed for the purpose of bringing social services to the family, and alerting participating hospitals to the possibility of future injuries.[53]

Although some of the VCC's interventions are on a secondary rather than primary level—that is, some children have already been injured by the time they are identified—

the VCC represents one of the few known programs that uses a coordinated system designed to head off child abuse.

High-risk Environments

Unemployment. The environmental condition that is cited most often as placing a family at risk in terms of child abuse is unemployment. The stress created by idleness and the lack of a certain source of income predisposes a family to abuse. Our groups of abusing parents contain mothers as well as fathers who have inflicted violence on a child during periods of unemployment. An especially explosive situation is created when the daily child-care duties are turned over to a father who is accustomed to being the breadwinner in the family. Mothers who are in the habit of working and keeping busy outside the house also suffer from frustration and feelings of failure when they are unemployed. Other environmental factors, such as crowded conditions in the home, a large family, and lack of education have been cited as contributing to the potential for child abuse. Light analyzed the effects of unemployment, overcrowding, family size, and lack of education on 1,380 abusing families and reported the following findings:

1. Abusing families in which the father is unemployed are much more likely to live in an apartment and are less likely to share their quarters with other persons or families than are comparable nonabusing families.

2. Abusing families in which the father has been employed for the previous 12 months are more likely to live in an apartment than are comparable nonabusing families.

3. Abusing families in which the father is unemployed tend to have many more children than do comparable nonabusing families.

4. In abusing families where the father is unemployed, a very young child is likely to be abused. If the

father is employed, the target of the abuse is likely to be an older child.[54]

One intervention strategy for guarding against child abuse among the unemployed would require the administration of predictive questionnaires (based on profiles of persons who abuse) to individuals who register for jobs. Although the central site of registration is the state employment agency, some of the unemployed look elsewhere for jobs. Thus the unemployment insurance office would serve as a supplementary site for administering the questionnaire. Only unemployed persons who have more than three children would be asked to fill out the questionnaire, and they would then be given a card indicating that they had done so. Those with high abuse-potential scores would be visited at home by a public health nurse, who would observe interaction between the spouses and between the spouses and the children. She would pay special attention to large families living in apartments and to families with parents who lack high school educations. She would also ask the questions listed on page 233 to gain additional insight into a family's potential for abuse. Based on the nurse's findings during the initial visit, a schedule of home visits would be set up at fairly short intervals for families with the highest potential for abuse and at longer intervals for those with less potential. High-risk parents would not only receive counseling from the public health nurse but would have the services of a parent aide or homemaker. They would also receive printed material about how to obtain financial and other assistance in times of crisis. Most useful to them in a crisis, however, would be the telephone numbers of the public health nurse or parent aide.

Although these specific strategies are directed toward defusing the potential for abuse among the unemployed, efforts to guarantee jobs for everyone who is able and willing to work are extremely important. Employment should be considered the right of every citizen, not a privilege. During the deep recession of 1974–75, the 94th Congress began to consider employment as a right. Although legislation to this effect would not ensure that there would be no idle adults at home with children, it would reduce the unemployment rate, which would not only enhance national efforts against child abuse, but reduce the stress caused by other social and psychological problems.

Change. Another condition that preliminary evidence suggests may be associated with the occurrence of abuse is the amount of change a family has been subjected to over the previous 12 to 24 months. In Chapter 1 we noted that one distinguishing feature of the abusing family is the experience of too much change too fast: that is, so many changes occur in a given period that the family members are unable to adjust. Table 1–2 (see page 29) shows the sharp difference in life change scores between abusing and nonabusing parents.

Change may be excessive in terms of either amount or severity. But abusing families seem to live in a perpetual state of crisis: i.e., they have exceeded their capacity to cope with stress and handle frustration without losing control.

Remedying this situation is not easy. Much of the stress these families experience is probably self-induced and stems from seeking symbiotic relationships; thus the parent is likely to experience less life crisis only if he changes to the point where he no longer looks for ways to be taken care of. However, it is important to keep in mind that there is a societal feature to life crisis and excessive change. Toffler provided a blueprint of excessive change in *Future Shock.* [55] The society he envisions for the future is one in which people as well as things are disposable and transitory. Abusing families already lack a sense of roots and relatedness; they move frequently and remain isolated. When excessive mobility is coupled with this alienation from others and the complex problems of urban living, it can be a predisposing factor to violence.[56] If society adds a disposable and transitory feature, the problem is compounded.

Thus, to a large extent, the problem of child abuse will have to be solved on a societal scale. A sense of community must be restored to neighborhoods. People need to know who their neighbors are, and neighbors need to stay in one place long enough to develop roots and become acquainted with each other. In other words, people must have decent housing and jobs, lives they can be proud of, and a legacy they will want to pass on to their children. Intervention strategies that will bring about a less abusive society— and fewer abusing families—will require changes not only in public policies but in public and private values.

In the meantime, families that are experiencing moderate or major life crises must be identified. One approach might be for the public health nurse to administer the Social Readjustment Rating Scale during home visits with high-risk parents (parents who are unemployed, parents with abuse profiles, and parents of premature, illegitimate, and difficult children). This scale would identify the amount of change the parents have been forced to adjust to in the previous one to two years. Those with high scores on the scale would receive special attention and more frequent visits. Because individuals who experience life crises often know little about how to meet their own emotional needs, those with high scores on the scale would be urged to attend the course on human needs and make use of community resources that would provide relief from their children. The aim would be to soften the effects of excessive change and teach the parents how to reduce the amount of change in the future.

Identifying families in crisis would offer potential benefits in areas other than child abuse. As mentioned in Chapter 1, life crises are associated with the onset of illness, accident, injury, and psychological problems. The more severe the life crisis, the more serious the illness, accident, or injury. If families in crisis can be detected in advance, steps can be taken to reduce the effects of excessive change in their lives. We believe that illness, accident, or injury can be averted in a number of cases. This intervention strategy, like nonspecific primary prevention programs, would produce dividends in several areas of social and personal well-being.

Other Strategies

Intermediate Forms of Intervention

In addition to the nonspecific and specific approaches to primary prevention, there is an intermediate form of intervention which is nonspecific in the sense that it is not aimed at a high-risk group, but is specific in that it addresses child abuse. An example of intermediate intervention is the pilot program (one of four in the United States funded by the Department of Health, Education and Welfare) that was launched in the Houston area high schools in 1974. The program focuses on students, teachers, and school administrators. A small group of students was chosen to make a film and develop a guide for other students on the causes of child abuse and the characteristics of parents who abuse. Pitfalls such as social isolation were pointed out so that students could avoid them and thus keep from becoming potentially abusing parents themselves.

The program, called "Lift A Finger," was so appealing to the students that it was extended across the state after the first year with prospects of becoming national in scope.[57] The part of the program designed for teachers and administrators consisted of in-service training, a manual about early detection of child abuse, and information about the importance of reporting suspected cases without delay.

Although it will be difficult to evaluate the effects of the "Lift A Finger" program on the incidence of child abuse, similar programs should be encouraged so that large numbers of young people will be reached before they become parents.

"Project Protection" in Montgomery County, Maryland, is another program designed to educate high school students about child abuse and its underlying causes. This program also includes curriculum units on "the importance of nurturing and the 'nurturing imprint' in infancy and will give increased attention to acquainting future parents with the normal developmental stages of early childhood."[58]

In Evanston, Illinois, a parent-training program for high school students was designed for use in churches and social service agencies as well as schools. One idea behind the program is that the demise of the extended family means that parents and children are less likely to have role models to follow and to receive guidance and emotional support. "You didn't have to be as complete a parent in years past because there were always people around to help you cope. Today, many couples are on their own. . . ."[59]

This is particularly true for a number of unmarried adolescent females from lower socioeconomic groups who become pregnant. They, especially, need child-rearing instruction and family-planning information. A program established at Johns Hopkins University has singled out a group of unwed prospective mothers and offers them education in childrearing and nutrition and information about the community services that are available to them.[60] These young women also have the option of electing an abortion.

Public Education

Public education programs on child abuse are another example of efforts with a potential payoff in terms of primary prevention. So far, most of these programs have focused on early detection and on increasing the reporting of suspected cases. (After a statewide public information campaign on child abuse was launched in Texas, reports on suspected cases increased from an average of 2.9 per day to 4.7 in Harris County, the state's most heavily-populated county).

As the public becomes better acquainted with the problem, television and other communications media should address the question of how a person can avoid becoming a child abuser and how a community can build a network of resources to bail people out in times of stress and crisis. Although information alone will not guarantee that a person will not abuse a child, it will go a long way toward reducing the likelihood of abuse—provided the information is received in time for a person to make use of it. To make use of public information, most of which comes from the media, a person must not be confronted with a message that is too strong to take. The media have made the public increasingly aware of child abuse, but in an effort to attract attention, some television programs and newspaper articles emphasize the most gory, gruesome, and atypical cases. M. Fritz, a spokesman for Parents Anonymous, describes this tendency as follows:

> Dead babies sell newspapers. . . . [The media] are so hell bent on exploiting [us] to the extent that they can, the anxiety level around the problem of abuse is so damned high that most people can't deal with it all. And if they do they get so upset that they just can't think rationally. We need to get out of that dead-baby bag so that people can deal with the problem in a rational way instead of with this intense anxiety-fear reaction.[61]

Rather than blowing up pictures of badly battered babies, the communications media should tell people something about how to meet their own psychological needs, get along better with their mates, manage their children without undue physical discipline, relax in times of stress, and make use of community resources to prevent or soften a crisis.

It is only through public education on a broad scale that intervention can be made at the cultural level—the vector level in the public health triad. Cultural scripts in which children are regarded as property and parents have the right to treat children as they see fit must be changed. So must cultural scripts which insist that all babies are cuddly and loving (the "Gerber baby" myth) and all mothers smile sweetly at all times (the "Madonna mother" myth). Parents must be free to recognize their own shortcomings and to seek help with their children before it is too late. Unprepared and ill-equipped parents should not feel guilty about acknowledging that they cannot care for their child properly and need the community's support.

Cultural scripts on the issue of discipline will be the most difficult to overcome. Should all physical discipline be banned, or at least discouraged and placed in the realm of socially unacceptable behavior? Although controversy still rages about the role of corporal punishment in child abuse, there is little doubt that in many families, physical discipline does contribute to the problem. The media will be a decisive factor in the changes that occur in public attitudes toward physical discipline and its possible relationship to child abuse. As attitudes change, so will cultural scripts on the issue.

MANPOWER AND RESOURCES FOR PRIMARY PREVENTION PROGRAMS

In proposing intervention strategies in this chapter, we have referred to a number of different workers and community resources—parent aides, homemakers, public health nurses, crisis nurseries, emergency shelters, park-a-tot centers, and group therapy. Where will the funds come from to support the necessary manpower and resources? We agree with Kempe's view:

> If we wait for the money, we will wait forever. I am satisfied that the resources of this country have never been gathered together in any reasonable way to excite people to do a proper job. I mean the old and the very young.[62]

The social service field has largely ignored the significant help that volunteers could give. As Routh points out:

> Many services can be provided through the use of volunteers. There are not enough professionally trained individuals in the helping and caring professions to do the job at hand. It behooves local community-oriented agencies to realize that many services not presently being provided to clients can be made available through volunteer help.[63]

There are enormous untapped supplies of volunteers in this country who could provide primary prevention services in the specific area of child abuse. Kempe has used volunteers to keep abuse from recurring, and dozens of other voluntary groups across the country are working on the problem, primarily from the standpoint of secondary prevention (see Chapter 7). What it takes to recruit volunteers and put programs into effect is commitment—and a willingness on the part of professionals to admit that laymen can be effective. "We haven't been willing as social workers, as physicians," Kempe says, "to hand over our sacred skills and our stethoscopes to lay people because we are afraid that somehow or other it is going to devalue our money, our skill."[64]

Psychiatrists Pollock and Steele have observed that "sensitive, devoted persons without specific professional training can be extremely valuable, adjunctive 'lay therapists.' "[65] The skill required to go into the home and deal

with high-risk parents and children is the ability to nurture.
This ability cannot be learned in professional training. A
person acquires it by having nurturing parents and by nurturing children of his own.

Every city contains many people who have the ability
to nurture (who have the mothering imprint) and would
serve as volunteers—if asked. In the program we have proposed, the local health department would be responsible for
carrying out the intervention strategies. In other words, the
health department would have to find and use volunteers
in large numbers. Some health departments already use
volunteers, but not for prevention of child abuse—an area
in which the record of public health is dismal. If a health
department does not know how to find or use volunteers,
it can ask juvenile probation departments, mental health
agencies, hospitals, and so forth. In Houston, the Voluntary Action Center, a national organization, supplies volunteers to all these organizations.

Our local child welfare unit, which is responsible for
dealing with child abuse, uses a limited number of volunteers to provide transportation and other services. It also
works with the Houston section of the National Council of
Jewish Women on a family outreach program. Women who
volunteer for this program undergo 10 weeks of training so
they can provide counseling services to parents. The program also offers community education on child abuse as
well as information and referral services. Family outreach
is part of a national project of the Jewish women's organization, which has been extremely successful in cities such as
Dallas, where the caseload rose from six to 600 in one
year.[66]

Our proposals for the extensive use of volunteers on
the abuse problem would free social workers employed by
child protective agencies to provide group therapy for
abusing families. Based on our experience and evaluation,
there is a great need for group therapy, and child welfare

workers are best equipped to be given training for providing it. By training child welfare workers in group therapy, we have been able to expand the number of groups and thus reach abusing parents who otherwise would not obtain help. Again, volunteers are the key to making possible additional therapy groups as well as a number of other services.

How many volunteers would be needed for the programs we have outlined? It would depend on the program and the number of people to be served. If a health visitors program became national policy and the home of every newborn were visited, a regular corps of professional health visitors would have to be established with federal funds, although volunteers could probably do this job too. In Aberdeen, Scotland, there are about 3,000 deliveries a year and 65 health visitors;[67] in Houston, which averages about 32,500 live births each year, more than 650 health visitors would be needed. Although Aberdeen's health visitors are highly trained, Kempe believes that a good neighbor could handle the job. Volunteers could be recruited to do the important job of helping families identified by health visitors as high-risks. They could serve as parent aides, mother surrogates, and, with minimum training, homemakers.

For risk-specific primary prevention programs, the largest number of personnel needed would be parent aides, mother surrogates, and homemakers. Although health departments would have to hire public health nurses to supervise the volunteers, the number of nurses required would be far less than the number of health visitors needed for a national screening program. To a large extent, volunteers could also staff community resources such as crisis nurseries, respite centers, and park-a-tot facilities, many of which could be sponsored by churches. "In this country, churches are standing absolutely empty except for three or four hours a week. They could all be used as day care centers as some of them are. They could be used as crisis nurseries. The manpower really is here."[68] Through such agencies as the Family Service Association, homemakers are already available in many cities. These women are trained to go into a home and help manage the household and children in times of stress and crisis. The family pays for this service on a sliding-fee basis. If a community lacks or has an insufficient number of homemakers, volunteers can be trained to do the job—provided, again, there is commitment.

Where will all the volunteers come from? As Kempe notes: "We haven't begun to really get at people who are able to give time. . . . They have time and they have love. All you need are those two items."[69] When the Volunteer Action Center opened its doors in Houston in 1975, more than 500 volunteers were interviewed and referred for service during the first two months. Many retired people are eager to be asked to do a job. So are many young people. Kempe uses grandparents as volunteers. "We are putting babies that need fostering into homes for the aged, where four or five elderly ladies take four-hour shifts nursing babies and give more mothering than most babies can stand as a matter of fact. The only problem we've had is that some babies don't get enough sleep."[70] Volunteers, then, are both available and an answer to providing the necessary programs at a relatively low cost. Those who question whether there are enough funds to establish the kind of primary prevention programs we propose are simply looking for a way to avoid taking action to combat the problem. Volunteers are already active in secondary prevention, and there is no reason they cannot be used in primary prevention.

> So far in Lansing [Michigan] we have parent aides, we have Parents Anonymous, we have philiotherapy that is just starting, we have a lot of family planning—and we haven't spent any money yet, because we don't have any.[71]

Again, the idea of using volunteers in the area of child abuse is not new. Volunteers not only act on an individual basis as parent aides and the like, they also have formed a variety of organizations without waiting for outside leadership. For example, we have already described CALM (Child Abuse Listening Mediation), which provides a telephone service for distressed parents in Santa Barbara, California. A hot-line service may also be indicated for the primary prevention programs we have discussed. Although most high-risk families would be able to call a parent aide or public nurse, those who had not been contacted should have a public hot-line service and volunteer groups to turn to in time of need. As we pointed out in Chapter 7, volunteer groups that are similar to CALM have been established across the country. And on a broader scale, there is the National Committee for Prevention of Child Abuse, headquartered in Chicago.

Because of this record with voluntary efforts, we believe that it will be far less difficult to find manpower and resources than it will be to get institutions to change their policies so that high-risk parents and children can be identified. Administering predictive questionnaires to parents of new babies will require the cooperation of hospitals. The detection of difficult babies will require the participation of hospital staff. Observations of the interactions between parents and babies would mean that rooming-in arrangements for mothers would have to be instituted in hospitals. Screening the unemployed would require the cooperation of state employment agencies. In other words, all these programs would require major changes in institutional policies and procedures.

Is it worth all this? It is if the rights of children are recognized as legitimate: the right to a safe home, the right to healthy parenting. If Americans have a genuine commitment to their young, the obstacles can be overcome and the necessary manpower and resources will be found. If we

have the necessary commitment, institutions will cooper-
ate. Health departments will provide leadership; courses in
human needs and parenting will be instituted. There may
even be national health screening someday, which will
mean leadership on a national level. But these changes will
occur only if our commitment to the young is genuine.

NOTES

1. "Child abuse her concern," *Dallas Morning News,* June 20, 1975, p. 1C.
2. *Crisis in child mental health: Challenge for the 1970s, report of the Joint Commission on Mental Health of Children* (New York: Harper & Row, 1970), pp. 3–4.
3. See D. Bakan, *Slaughter of the innocents* (San Francisco: Jossey-Bass, 1971), p. 119.
4. C. H. Kempe, "Paediatric implications of the battered baby syndrome," *Archives of Disease in Childhood,* 46 (February 1971), p. 36.
5. C. H. Kempe, testimony presented before U.S. Senate Subcommittee on Children and Youth of the Committee on Labor and Public Welfare, Washington, D.C., March 1973.
6. R. J. Light, "Abused and neglected children in America: A study of alternative policies," *Harvard Educational Review,* 43 (November 1973), p. 559.
7. R. E. Helfer, *A self-instructional program on child abuse and neglect* (Committee on Infant and Preschool Child, American Academy of Pediatrics, and National Center for Prevention and Treatment of Child Abuse and Neglect, Denver, Colo., 1974), p. 1–13.
8. C. H. Kempe, "A practical approach to the protection of the abused child and rehabilitation of the abusing parent," *Pediatrics,* 51 (April 1973), p. 805.

9. See W. S. Craig, *Child and adolescent life in health and disease* (Edinburgh, Scotland: E & S Livingstone, 1946).

10. C. H. Kempe, "A practical approach to the protection of the abused child," p. 805.

11. B. Justice, R. Justice, and I. A. Kraft, "Early warning signs of violence: Is a triad enough?" *American Journal of Psychiatry*, 131 (April 1974), pp. 457–459.

12. B. Justice (ed.), *Your child's behavior* (Project for the Early Prevention of Violence, Houston: School of Public Health, University of Texas, 1973).

13. As quoted in R. P. Hawkins, "It's time we taught the young," *Psychology Today* (November 1972), p. 40.

14. E. Lord and D. Weisfeld, "The abused child," in A. R. Roberts (ed.), *Childhood deprivation* (Springfield, Ill.: Charles C Thomas, 1974), p. 80.

15. A. Toffler, *Future shock* (New York: Random House, 1970), p. 216.

16. Hawkins, op. cit., p. 216.

17. Kempe, "A practical approach to the protection of the abused child," p. 805.

18. Lord and Weisfeld, op. cit., p. 80. See also, Hawkins, op. cit., p. 40.

19. Hawkins, op. cit., p. 40.

20. Kempe, "A practical approach to the protection of the abused child," p. 808.

21. Hawkins, op. cit., p. 31.

22. D. D. Broadhurst, "Project protection," *Children Today*, 4 (May–June 1975), p. 25.

23. Light, op. cit., p. 595.

24. See, for example, M. H. Lystad, "Violence at home," *American Journal of Orthopsychiatry*, 45 (April 1975), p. 338; J. J. Spinetta and D. Rigler, "The child-abusing parent: A psychological review," *Psychological Bulletin*, 77 (April 1972), p. 299.

25. Hawkins, op. cit., p. 40.

26. Toffler, op. cit., p. 217.

27. D. G. Gil, *Violence against children* (Cambridge, Mass.: Harvard University Press, 1970), p. 146; and E. Elmer, "Child abuse: A symptom of family crisis," in E. Pavenstedt and V. W. Bernard (eds.), *Crisis of family disorganization: Programs to soften their impact on children* (New York: Behavioral Publications, 1971), pp. 54–55.

28. Light, op. cit., p. 595.

29. See, for example, A. Maslow, *Motivation and personality* (New York: Harper & Row, 1970), pp. 35–58; E. Berne, *Games people play: The psychology of human relationships* (New York: Grove Press, 1964), pp.

13–65; W. Glasser, *The identity society* (New York: Harper and Row, 1972), pp. 1–101; V. Frankl, "Beyond self-actualization and self-expression," *Journal of Existential Psychiatry*, 1 (Spring 1960), pp. 5–20; and R. W. White, "Motivation reconsidered: The concept of competence," *Psychological Review*, 66 (September 1959), pp. 297–333.

30.   T. F. A. Plaut, *Alcohol problems: A report to the nation by the Cooperative Commission on the Study of Alcoholism* (New York: Oxford University Press, 1967), p. 122. See also, R. H. Ojemann, *Four basic aspects of preventive psychiatry* (Iowa City: State University of Iowa Press, 1957).

31.   D. G. Gil, "Unraveling child abuse," *American Journal of Orthopsychiatry*, 45 (April 1975), pp. 354–355.

32.   C. Schneider, R. E. Helfer, and C. Pollock, "The predictive questionnaire: A preliminary report," in C. H. Kempe and R. E. Helfer (eds.), *Helping the battered child and his family* (Philadelphia, Pa.: Lippincott, 1972), pp. 271–282.

33.   The Connecticut Welfare Department found that physicians ranked last (5 per cent) in number of suspected cases of abuse they reported in fiscal year 1974. Police ranked first with 23.3 per cent; schools, 20.5 per cent; hospitals, 20.3 per cent; social workers, 16.7 per cent; others, 8.9 per cent; and Care-Line, 5.3 per cent. S. Sgroi, "Sexual molestation of children: The last frontier in child abuse," *Children Today*, 4 (May–June 1975), p. 19. A spot survey conducted in Houston also showed that physicians ranked last in terms of reports of cases of suspected child abuse. Neighbors and relatives were first, hospitals second, and teachers third.

34.   See R. E. Helfer, "Why most physicians don't get involved in child abuse cases and what to do about it," *Children Today*, 4 (May–June 1975), pp. 28–32.

35.   See M. Morris, "Psychological miscarriage: An end to mother love," *Trans-Action*, 3 (January–February 1966), p. 11.

36.   F. I. Bishop, "Children at risk," *Medical Journal of Australia*, 1 (March 1971), p. 627.

37.   See B. D. Schmitt and C. H. Kempe, "The pediatrician's role in child abuse and neglect, *Current Problems in Pediatrics*, 5 (March 1975), pp. 35–45.

38.   Ibid, p. 43.

39.   C. H. Kempe and J. Hopkins, "The public health nurse's role in the prevention of child abuse and neglect," *Public Health Currents*, 15 (March–April–May 1975), p. 1.

40.   Ibid., p. 2.

41. Ibid.
42. Ibid.
43. E. Elmer, *Children in jeopardy* (Pittsburgh: University of Pittsburgh Press, 1967), p. 49; M. Klein and L. Stern, "Low birth weight and the battered child syndrome," *American Journal of Diseases of Children,* 122 (July 1971), pp. 15–18; E. F. Lenoski, "Translating injury data into preventive and health care service—child abuse." Unpublished paper, Division of Emergency Pediatrics, University of Southern California Medical Center, Los Angeles, 1973; H. P. Martin and P. Beezley, "Prevention and the consequences of child abuse," *Journal of Operational Psychiatry,* 6 (Fall–Winter, 1974), p. 73; P. H. Mussen, J. J. Conger, and J. Kagan, *Child development and personality* (New York: Harper & Row, 1974); and Elmer, "Child abuse: A symptom of family crisis," p. 55.

44. A. A. Fanaroff, J. Kennell, and M. Klaus, "Follow-up of low birth weight infants—the predictive value of maternal visiting patterns," *Pediatrics,* 49 (February 1972), pp. 280–290.

45. Helfer, op. cit., Unit 3.

46. See, for example, B. F. Steele, "Parental abuse of infants and small children," in J. E. Anthony and T. Benedek (eds.), *Parenthood: Its psychology and psychopathology* (Boston: Little, Brown, 1970), pp. 449–477; and Bishop, op. cit.; and B. D. Schmitt and C. H. Kempe, "The pediatrician's role in child abuse and neglect."

47. C. Landis and J. M. Bolles, *Textbook of abnormal psychology* (New York: Macmillan 1947).

48. E. N. Joyners, Panel Discussion on "A practical approach to the protection of the abused child and rehabilitation of the abusing parent," *Pediatrics,* 51 (April 1973), p. 810.

49. J. Kagan *Change and continuity in infancy* (New York: Wiley, 1971), p. 183.

50. R. L. Jenkins, et al., "Interrupting the family cycle of violence," *Journal of Iowa Medical Society,* 60 (February 1970), p. 85.

51. Martin and Beezley, op. cit., p. 74.

52. H. D. Lovens, and J. Rako, "A community approach to prevention of child abuse," *Child Welfare,* 54 (February 1975), p. 85.

53. Ibid., p. 86.

54. Light, op. cit., p. 587.

55. Toffler, op. cit.

56. B. Justice, *Violence in the city* (Fort Worth: Texas Christian University Press, 1969), pp. 88–92.

57. See *Lift a finger: The teacher's role in combating child abuse* (Houston, Tex.: Education Professions Development Consortium C, 1975).

58. Broadhurst, op. cit., p. 25.
59. "Child abuse and neglect reach epidemic levels," *Houston Post,* July 2, 1975, p. 4AA.
60. W. Sage, "Violence in the children's room," *Human Behavior,* 4 (July 1975), p. 47.
61. Ibid., p. 43.
62. Kempe, "A practical approach to the protection of the abused child," p. 810.
63. T. Routh, *The volunteer and community agencies* (Springfield, Ill.: Charles C Thomas, 1972), p. 3.
64. Kempe, "A practical approach to the protection of the abused child," p. 810.
65. C. Pollock and B. Steele, "A therapeutic approach to the parents," in C. H. Kempe and R. E. Helfer (eds.), *Helping the battered child and his family* (Philadelphia, Pa.: Lippincott, 1972), p. 3.
66. "Program for child abuse prevention begun jointly by two major agencies," *Community Topics,* 2 (May–June 1975), p. 1.
67. See Kempe, "A practical approach to the protection of the abused child," p. 805.
68. Kempe, "A practical approach to the protection of the abused child," p. 810.
69. Ibid.
70. Ibid.
71. Helfer, op. cit., Unit 4.

BIBLIOGRAPHY

Anonymous. "Toward the differentiation of a self in one's own family." In Framo, J. L. (Ed.), *Family interaction.* New York: Springer, 1972.

Arvanian, A. L. "Treatment of abusive parents." In Ebeling, N. B., and Hill, D. A. (Eds.), *Child abuse: Intervention and treatment.* Acton, Mass.: Publishing Sciences Group, 1975.

Bakan, D. *Slaughter of the innocents.* San Francisco: Jossey-Bass, 1971.

Barnes, G., et al. "Team treatment for abusive families." *Social Casework,* 1974, **55,** 604.

Bennie, E., and Sclare, A. "The battered child syndrome." *American Journal of Psychiatry,* 1969, **125,** 975–979.

Berne, E. *Games people play: The psychology of human relationships.* New York: Grove Press, 1964.

Berne, E. *Principles of group treatment.* New York: Oxford University Press, 1966.

Berne, E. *What do you say after you say hello?* New York: Grove Press, 1972.

Bishop, R. I. "Children at risk." *Medical Journal of Australia,* 1971, **1,** 623–628.

Blumberg, M. L. "Psychopathology of the abusing parent." *American Journal of Psychotherapy,* 1974, **28,** 21–30.

Blumberg, M. L. "When parents hit out." *Twentieth Century,* Winter 1964, **173,** 39–44.

Bowen, M. "Family therapy and family group therapy." In Kaplan, H. I., and Sadock, B. J. (Eds.), *Comprehensive group psychotherapy.* Baltimore: William & Wilkins, 1971.

Bowen, M. "The use of family theory in clinical practice." *Comprehensive Psychiatry,* 1966, **7**, 345–374.

Caplan, G. *Principles of preventive psychiatry.* New York: Basic Books, 1964.

Caplan, G., and Grunebaum, H. "Perspectives on primary prevention: A review." In Gottesfeld, H. (Ed.), *The critical issues of community mental health.* New York: Behavioral Publications, 1972.

Carkhuff, R. G., and Berenson, B. G. *Beyond counseling and therapy.* New York: Holt, Rinehart & Winston, 1967.

"Child abuse and neglect reach epidemic levels: Maze of programs may be promoting the crisis, not attacking it." *Houston Post,* July 2, 1975, p. 4AA.

"Child abuse her concern." *Dallas Morning News,* June 20, 1975, p. 1C.

Child abuse listening mediation. Santa Barbara, Calif.: Author, 1974.

"Child abuse statistics." Harris County Child Welfare Unit, Houston, Tex., 1974.

Children in danger. Austin, Tex.: State Department of Public Welfare, 1974.

Cohn, A. H., Ridge, S. S., and Collignon, F. C. "Evaluating innovative treatment programs in child abuse and neglect." *Children Today,* 1975, **4**(2), 10–12.

Craig, W. S. *Child and adolescent life in health and disease.* Edinburgh, Scotland: E & S Livingstone, 1946.

Crisis in child mental health: Challenge for the 1970s. (Report of the Joint Commission on Mental Health of Children.) New York: Harper & Row, 1970.

Crossman, P. "Permission and protection." *Transactional Analysis Bulletin,* 1968, **5**(19), 154.

David, C. A. "The use of the confrontation technique in the battered child syndrome." *American Journal of Psychotherapy,* 1974, **28**, 543–552.

Davidson, S. "At last! Help for the abusive parent." *Women's Day,* March 1973, p. 40.

Davoren, E. "The role of the social worker." In Helfer, R. E., and Kempe, C. H. (Eds.), *The battered child.* Chicago: University of Chicago Press, 1974.

Davoren, E. "Working with abusive parents—a social worker's view." *Children Today,* 1975, **4**(3), 40.

Delnero, H., Hopkins, J., and Drews, K. "The medical center child abuse team." In Kempe, C. H., and Helfer, R. E. (Eds.), *Helping the battered child and his family.* Philadelphia: Lippincott, 1972.

Delsordo, J. D. "A protective casework for abused children." *Children,* 1963, **10,** 213–218.

Dollard, J., et al. *Frustration and aggression.* New Haven, Conn.: Yale University Press, 1939.

Drews, K. "The child and his school." In Kempe, C. H., and Helfer, R. E. (Eds.), *Helping the battered child and his family.* Philadelphia: Lippincott, 1972.

Ebeling, N. B., and Hill, D. A. (Eds.). *Child abuse: Intervention and treatment.* Acton, Mass.: Publishing Science Group, 1975.

Ellis, A. *Humanistic psychology.* New York: Julian Press, 1973.

Elmer, E. "Child abuse: A symptom of family crisis." In Pavenstedt, E., and Bernard, V. W. (Eds.), *Crisis of family disorganization: Programs to soften their impact on children.* New York: Behavioral Publications, 1971.

Elmer, E. *Children in jeopardy.* Pittsburgh: University of Pittsburgh Press, 1967.

Elmer, E. "Hazards in determining child abuse." *Child Welfare,* 1966, **45** (1), 28–33.

Elmer, E. "Identification of abused children." *Children,* 1963, **10,** 180–184.

Erskine, R. G. "The ABC's of effective therapy," *Transactional Analysis Journal,* 1975, **5**(2), 163–165.

Families anonymous. Film produced by The National Center for the Prevention and Treatment of Child Abuse and Neglect, Denver, Colo.

Fanaroff, A. A., Kennell, J., and Klaus, M. "Follow-up of low birth weight infants—the predictive value of maternal visiting patterns." *Pediatrics,* 1972, **49,** 280–290.

Feinstein, H., et al. "Group therapy for mothers with infanticidal impulses." *American Journal of Psychiatry,* 1964, **120,** 882–886.

Felder, S. "A lawyer's view of child abuse." *Public Welfare,* 1971, **29,** 181–188.

Ferro, F. "Combatting child abuse and neglect." *Children Today,* 1975, **4**(3).

Flynn, W. R. "Frontier justice: A contribution to the theory of child battery." *American Journal of Psychiatry,* 1970, **127,** 375–379.

Fontana, V. J. *Somewhere a child is crying.* New York: Macmillan, 1973.

Fontana, V. J. "The neglect and abuse of children." *New York State Journal of Medicine,* 1964, **64,** 215–218.

Frankl, V. "Beyond self-actualization and self-expression." *Journal of Existential Psychiatry,* 1960, 1(1), 5–20.

Friedman, S. B. "The need for intensive follow-up of abused children." In Kempe, C. H., and Helfer, R. E. (Eds.), *Helping the battered child.* Philadelphia: Lippincott, 1972.

Galdston, R. "Observations on children who have been physically abused and their parents." *American Journal of Psychiatry,* 1965, **122,** 440–443.

Galdston, R. "Preventing the abuse of little children: The Parents' Center project for the study and prevention of child abuse." *American Journal of Orthopsychiatry,* 1975, **45,** 372–381.

Gelles, R. J. "Child abuse as psychopathology: A sociological critique and reformulation." *American Journal of Orthopsychiatry,* 1973, **43,** 611–621.

Gelles, R. J. "The social construction of child abuse." *American Journal of Orthopsychiatry,* 1975, **45,** 365.

George, J. E. "Spare the rod: A survey of the battered child syndrome." *Forensic Science,* 1973, **2,** 129–167.

Gibbon, E. *The decline and fall of the Roman Empire.* New York: Collier, 1899.

Gil, D. G. "Incidence of child abuse and demographic characteristics of persons involved." In Helfer, R. E., and Kempe, C. H. (Eds.), *The battered child.* Chicago: University of Chicago Press, 1968.

Gil, D. G. "Unraveling child abuse." *American Journal of Orthopsychiatry,* 1975, **45,** 352–355.

Gil, D. G. *Violence against children.* Cambridge, Mass.: Harvard University Press, 1970.

Glasser, W. *The identity society.* New York: Harper & Row, 1972.

Gordon, T. *Parent effectiveness training.* New York: Wyden, 1970.

Guidelines for schools, teachers, nurses, counselors, and administrators. Denver, Colo.: American Humane Association, 1971.

Haimowitz, N. R., and Haimowitz, M. L. "Introduction to transactional analysis." In Haimowitz, M. L., and Haimowitz, N. R. (Eds.), *Human development.* New York: Thomas Y. Crowell, 1973.

Haley, J. "Why a mental health clinic should avoid family therapy." *Journal of Marriage and Family Counseling,* 1975, **1,** 3–12.

Harrington, J. "Violence: A clinical viewpoint." *British Medical Journal,* 1972, **1,** 228–231.

Hass, G. "Child abuse, the community, and the neighborhood health center." In Ebeling, N. B., and Hill, D. A. (Eds.), *Child abuse: Intervention and treatment.* Acton, Mass.: Publishing Science Group, 1975.

Hawkins, R. P. "It's time we taught the young." *Psychology Today,* November 1972, 40.

Helfer, R. E. *A self-instructional program on child abuse and neglect.* Committee on Infant and Preschool Child, American Academy of Pediatrics, Chicago, Ill., and National Center for the Prevention and Treatment of Child Abuse and Neglect, Denver, Colo., 1974.

Helfer, R. E. "Why most physicians don't get involved in child abuse cases and what to do about it." *Children Today,* 1975, **4**(3), 28–32.

Holmes, S. A., et al. "Working with the parent in child abuse cases." *Social Casework,* 1975, **56**, 3–12.

Holmes, T. H., and Rahe, R. H. "The social readjustment rating scale." *Journal of Psychosomatic Research,* 1967, **11**, 213–218.

Holter, J., and Friedman, S. "Principles of management in child abuse cases." *American Journal of Orthopsychiatry,* 1968, **38**, 133–134.

Hopkins, J. "The nurse and the abused child." *Nursing Clinics of North America,* 1970, **5**, 596.

Houston Report on Children. Houston, Tex.: Child Care Council, February 1, 1975.

Hughes, R. C. "A clinic's parent-performance training program for child abusers." *Hospital and Community Psychiatry,* 1974, **25**, 779–782.

"Identifying the battered or molested child." In *Handbook for school staff members.* Palo Alto, Calif.: Palo Alto School District, January 1972.

Isaacs, S. "Neglect, cruelty and battering." *British Medical Journal,* 1972, **3**, 224–226.

Jenkins, R. L., et al. "Interrupting the family cycle of violence." *Journal of Iowa Medical Society,* 1970, **60**(2), 85–89.

Joyners, E. N. Panel Discussion on "A practical approach to the protection of the abused child and rehabilitation of the abusing parent." *Pediatrics,* 1973, **51**, 810.

Justice, B. "Group therapy for abusing parents." Paper presented before the Mini-Conference on Child Abuse and Neglect, Texas United Community Service, Houston, April 11, 1975.

Justice, B. *Violence in the city.* Fort Worth: Texas Christian University Press, 1969.

Justice, B. (Ed.). *Your child's behavior.* Project for the Early Prevention of Violence, School of Public Health, University of Texas, Houston, 1973.

Justice, B., and Duncan, D. F. "Life crisis as a precursor to child abuse." *Public Health Reports,* 1976, **91**, 110–115.

Justice, B., and Duncan, D. F. "Physical abuse of children as a public health problem." *Public Health Reviews,* 1975, **4**, 183–200.

Justice, B., and Justice, R. "A psychosocial model of child abuse: Intervention strategies and group techniques." Paper presented before the Clinical and Research Training Seminar, Texas Research Institute of Mental Sciences, Houston, February 15, 1974.

Justice, B., and Justice R. " 'Siamese-twinning' in scripts of child batterers." Paper presented before the International Transactional Analysis Association Summer Conference, San Francisco, August 1973.

Justice, R., and Justice, B. "TA work with child abuse." *Transactional Analysis Journal*, 1975, **5**(1), 38–41.

Justice, B., Justice, R., and Kraft, I. A. "Early warning signs of violence: Is a triad enough?" *American Journal of Psychiatry*, 1974, **131**, 457–459.

Kagan, J. *Change and continuity in infancy.* New York: Wiley, 1971.

Keller, O. J. "Hypothesis for violent crime." *American Journal of Correction*, 1975, **37**(2), 7.

Kempe, C. H. "A practical approach to the protection of the abused child and rehabilitation of the abusing parent." *Pediatrics*, 1973, **51**, 791–809.

Kempe, C. H. "Paediatric implications of the battered baby syndrome." *Archives of Disease in Childhood*, 1971, **46**(28), 28–37.

Kempe, C. H. Testimony before U.S. Senate Subcommittee on Children and Youth, Committee on Labor and Public Welfare, Washington, D.C., March 1973.

Kempe, C. H. "The battered child and the hospital." *Hospital Practice*, 1969, **4**, 44–57.

Kempe, C. H., and Helfer, R. E. (Eds.). *Helping the battered child and his family.* Philadelphia: Lippincott, 1972.

Kempe, C. H., and Helfer, R. E. "Innovative therapeutic approaches." In Kempe and Helfer (Eds.), *Helping the battered child and his family.* Philadelphia: Lippincott, 1972.

Kempe, C. H., and Hopkins, J. (Eds.). "The public health nurse's role in the prevention of child abuse and neglect." *Public Health Currents*, 1975, **15**(2), 1–4.

Kempe, C. H., et al. "The battered-child syndrome." *Journal of the American Medical Association*, 1962, **181**, 105–112.

Kiresuk, T. J., and Sherman, R. E. "Goal attainment scaling: A general method for evaluating comprehensive community mental health programs." *Community Mental Health Journal*, 1968, **4**, 443–453.

Klein, M., and Stern, L. "Low birth weight and the battered child syndrome." *American Journal of Diseases of Children*, 1971, **122**(1), 15–18.

Landis, C., and Bolles, J. M. *Textbook of abnormal psychology.* New York: Macmillan, 1947.

Lascari, A. "The abused child." *Journal of the Iowa Medical Society*, 1972, **62**, 229–232.

Laury, G. V. "The battered child syndrome: Parental motivation, clinical aspects." *Bulletin of the New York Academy of Medicine*, 1970, **46**, 678–681.

Lazarus, A. A. (Ed.). *Clinical behavior therapy.* New York: Brunner/Mazel, 1972.

Lenoski, E. F. "Translating injury data into preventive services—physical child abuse." Unpublished paper, Division of Emergency Medicine, University of Southern California Medical Center, Los Angeles, 1973.

Lift a finger: The teacher's role in combating child abuse. Houston, Tex.: Education Professions Development Consortium C, 1975.

Light, R. J. "Abused and neglected children in America: A study of alternative policies." *Harvard Educational Review*, 1973, **43**, 559–588.

Lord, E., and Weisfeld, D. "The abused child." In Roberts, A. R. (Ed.), *Childhood deprivation.* Springfield, Ill.: Charles C Thomas, 1974.

Lovens, H. D., and Rako, J. "A community approach to the prevention of child abuse." *Child Welfare*, 1975, **54**(2), 85–86.

Lynch, A. "Child abuse in the school-age population." *Journal of School Health*, 1975, **35**(3), 141–148.

Lystad, M. H. "Violence at home: A review of the literature." *American Journal of Orthopsychiatry*, 1975, **45**, 328–345.

Martin, H. P. "The child and his development." In Kempe, C. H., and Helfer, R. E. (Eds.), *Helping the battered child and his family.* Philadelphia: Lippincott, 1972.

Martin, H. P., and Beezley, P. "Prevention and the consequences of child abuse." *Journal of Operational Psychiatry*, 1974, **6**(1), 72–73.

Maslow, A. *Motivation and personality.* New York: Harper & Row, 1970.

McFerran, J. "Parents' group in protective services." *Children*, 1958, **5**, 223–228.

McKenna, J. "Stroking profile: Application to script analysis." *Transactional Analysis Journal*, 1974, **4**(4), 20–24.

McLuhan, M. *Understanding media.* New York: McGraw-Hill, 1965.

Melnick, B., and Hurley, J. R. "Distinctive personality attributes of child abusing mothers." *Journal of Consulting and Clinical Psychology*, 1969, **33**, 746–749.

Merrill, E. J. "Physical abuse of children: An agency study." In DeFrancis, V. (Ed.), *Protecting the battered child.* Denver, Colo.: American Humane Association, 1962.

Morris, M. G. "Psychological miscarriage: An end to mother love." *Trans-Action*, 1966, **3**(2), 8–13.

Morris, M., and Gould, R. W. "Role reversal: A necessary concept in dealing with the battered child syndrome." In *The neglected-battered child syndrome.* New York: Child Welfare League of America, 1963.

"Mothers who need help with their mother." *Houston Post,* January 21, 1974, p. 5B.

Murdock, C. G. "The abused child in the school system." *American Journal of Public Health,* 1970, **60,** 105–109.

Mussen, P. H., Conger, J. J., and Kagan, J. *Child development and personality.* New York: Harper & Row, 1974.

Nomura, F. M. "The battered child 'syndrome.' " *Hawaii Medical Journal,* 1966, **25,** 390.

Ojemann, R. H. *Four basic aspects of preventive psychiatry.* Iowa City: State University of Iowa Press, 1957.

Patterson, G. R., and Gullion, M. E. *Living with children: New methods for parents and teachers.* Champaign, Ill.: Research Press, 1969.

Paulsen, M. B. "The law and abused children." In Helfer, R. E., and Kempe, C. H. (Eds.), *The battered child.* Chicago: University of Chicago Press, 1968.

Paulson, M. J., and Blake, P. R. "The abused, battered and maltreated child: A review." *Trauma,* 1967, **9**(1), 136.

Paulson, M. J., and Blake, P. R. "The physically abused child: A focus on prevention." *Child Welfare,* 1969, **48**(2), 95.

Paulson, M. J., et al. "Parents of the battered child: A multidisciplinary group therapy approach to life-threatening behavior." *Life-Threatening Behavior,* 1974, **4**(1), 18–31.

Perls, F. *Gestalt therapy verbatim.* Lafayette, Calif.: Real People Press, 1969.

Pike, E. "C.A.L.M.—a timely experiment in the prevention of child abuse." *Journal of Clinical Child Psychology,* 1973, **11**(3), 44.

Plaut, T. F. A. *Alcohol problems: A report to the nation by the Cooperative Commission on the Study of Alcoholism.* New York: Oxford University Press, 1967.

Pollock, C., and Steele, B. "A therapeutic approach to the parents." In Kempe, C. H., and Helfer, R. E. (Eds.), *Helping the battered child and his family.* Philadelphia: Lippincott, 1972.

Procedures and concepts manual. Redondo Beach, Calif.: Parents Anonymous, 1973.

"Program for child abuse prevention begun jointly by two major agencies." *Community Topics,* 1975, **2**(7), 1.

Radbill, S. X. "A history of child abuse and infanticide." In Helfer, R. E., and Kempe, C. H. (Eds.), *The battered child.* Chicago: University of Chicago Press, 1968.

Rahe, R. H., et al. "Social stress and illness onset." *Journal of Psychosomatic Research*, 1964, **8**(1), 35–44.

Reed, J. "Working with abusive parents—a parent's view—an interview with Jolly K." *Children Today*, 1975, **4**(3), 9.

Resnick, P. "Child murder by parents: A psychiatric review of filicide." *American Journal of Psychiatry*, 1969, **126**, 325–334.

Routh, T. *The volunteer and community agencies.* Springfield, Ill.: Charles C Thomas, 1972.

Ryan, J. H. "Child abuse among blacks." *Sepia*, November 1973, pp. 27–30.

Sage, W. "Violence in the children's room." *Human Behavior*, 1975, **4**(7), 42–47.

Sanders, R. W. "Resistance to dealing with parents of battered children." *Pediatrics*, 1972, **50**, 853–857.

Savino, A. B., and Sanders, R. W. "Working with abusive parents: Group therapy and home visits." *American Journal of Nursing*, 1973, **73**, 482–484.

Schiff, A. W., and Schiff, J. "Passivity." *Transactional Analysis Journal*, 1971, **1**, 1.

Schmitt, B. D., and Kempe, C. H. "The pediatrician's role in child abuse and neglect." *Current Problems in Pediatrics*, 1975, **5**(5), 43.

Schneider, C., Helfer, R. E., and Pollock, C. "The predictive questionnaire: A preliminary report." In Kempe, C. H., and Helfer, R. E. (Eds.), *Helping the battered child and his family.* Philadelphia: Lippincott, 1972.

Selye, H. *The stress of life.* New York: McGraw-Hill, 1956.

Sgroi, S. M. "Sexual molestation of children." *Children Today*, 1975, **4**(3), 19.

Silver, L. B. "Child abuse syndrome: A review." *Pediatrics*, 1968, **96**, 803–820.

Smith, C. A. "The battered child." *New England Journal of Medicine*, 1973, **289**, 322–323.

Smith, J. M., and Smith, D. E. P. *Child management: A program for parents.* Ann Arbor, Mich.: Ann Arbor Publishers, 1966.

Smith, R. "Now experts are trying to draw out these battering parents." *Today's Health*, 1973, **51**, 59–64.

Solomon, T. "History and demography of child abuse." *Pediatrics*, 1973, **51**, 775.

Spinetta, J. J., and Rigler, D. "The child-abusing parent: A psychological review." *Psychological Bulletin*, 1972, **77**, 296–304.

Steele, B. F. "Parental abuse of infants and small children." In Anthony, J. E., and Benedek, T. (Eds.), *Parenthood: Its psychology and psychopathology.* Boston: Little, Brown, 1970.

Steele, B. F. "Working with abusive parents: A psychiatrist's view." *Children Today*, 1975, **4**(3), 3–5.

Steele, B. F., and Pollock, C. "A psychiatric study of parents who abuse infants and small children." In Helfer, R. E., and Kempe, C. H. (Eds.), *The battered child.* Chicago: University of Chicago Press, 1968.

Steiner, C. *Games alcoholics play.* New York: Grove Press, 1971.

Steinmetz, S., and Straus, M. "Some myths about violence in the family." Paper presented before the American Sociological Association, Denver, Colo., 1971.

Sydnor, O. L., Parkell, N., and Hancock, C. D. *Controlling behavior.* Monroe, La.: Children Unlimited, undated.

Ten Have, R. "A preventive approach to problems of child abuse and neglect." *Michigan Medicine*, 1965, **64**, 645–649.

Texas family code. Austin: State Department of Public Welfare, 1973.

Texas penal code. St. Paul, Minn.: West Publishing, 1974.

Thomson, E. M., et al. *Child abuse: A community challenge.* East Aurora, N.Y.: Henry Stewart, 1971.

Thursz, D. "Epilogue." In Roberts, A. R. (Ed.), *Childhood deprivation.* Springfield, Ill.: Charles C Thomas, 1974.

Time, March 17, 1975, p. 88.

Toffler, A. *Future shock.* New York: Random House, 1970.

Tracy, J. J., and Clark, E. H. "Treatment for child abusers." *Social Work*, 1974, **19**, 339–342.

Trouen-Trend, J. B. G., and Leonard, M. "Prevention of child abuse: Current progress in Connecticut." *Connecticut Medicine*, 1972, **36**, 135–137.

"Violent Parents." *Lancet*, 1971, **2**, 1017–1018.

Whitaker, C. "Family therapy." Family Therapy Workshop, Southeast Institute Second Annual Spring Conference, Raleigh, N.C., March 21, 1975.

White, R. W. "Motivation reconsidered: The concept of competence." *Psychological Review*, 1959, **66**, 297–333.

Wolff, H. G., Wolf, S. G., Jr., and Hare, C. C. *Life stress and bodily disease.* Baltimore: Williams & Wilkins, 1950.

Wolpe, J. *The practice of behavior therapy.* New York: Pergamon Press, 1969.

Woolley, P. V., and Evans, W. A. "Significance of skeletal lesions in infants resembling those of traumatic origin." *Journal of the American Medical Association*, 1955, **158**, 539–543.

Zalba, S. "Battered children." *Trans-Action*, 1971, **8**(9), 58–61.

INDEX